Tourism Destination Management

Tourism Destination Management

Wendy Perez

STATES
ACADEMIC PRESS
www.statesacademicpress.com

Published by States Academic Press,
109 South 5th Street,
Brooklyn, NY 11249, USA

ISBN: 978-1-63989-528-1

Cataloging-in-Publication Data

Tourism destination management / Wendy Perez.
    p. cm.
Includes bibliographical references and index.
ISBN 978-1-63989-528-1
1. Tourism--Management. 2. Tourism--Planning. I. Perez, Wendy.
G155.A1 T68 2022
338.479 1--dc23

For information on all States Academic Press publications
visit our website at www.statesacademicpress.com

Contents

Preface

The economic, cultural or social phenomena which necessitate people to move to countries or places which are outside their usual environment for various personal or professional objectives is known as tourism. Such people are called tourists or visitors. Any place which is visited by tourists due to the cultural values, natural beauty, leisure and amusement, and historical significance associated with it is referred to as a tourism destination. Tourism destination management refers to all those strategies and programs which promote and spread the uniqueness that are linked to any particular destination. Its key objective is to increase the inbound flow of tourists and enhance the tourism in a particular region. This book is a valuable compilation of topics, ranging from the basic to the most complex theories and principles in the field of tourism destination management. It elucidates new techniques and their applications in a multidisciplinary approach. This book is a complete source of knowledge on the present status of this important field.

To facilitate a deeper understanding of the contents of this book a short introduction of every chapter is written below:

Chapter 1- The service sector industry which is linked to attracting, accommodating and entertaining tourists is known as tourism industry. Some of the major elements of tourism are transport, place significance, natural attractions, infrastructure and facilities. This chapter has been carefully written to provide an introduction to these elements of tourism and tourism industry.

Chapter 2- The movement of people from one geographical location to another is termed as traveling. It can be accomplished through various means such as automobile, boat, bus, foot, ship and airplane. The diverse aspects of traveling such as travel behavior and travel technology have been thoroughly discussed in this chapter.

Chapter 3- The process which involves synchronized actions in order to control the different aspects of a particular tourism industry is termed as destination management. Some of its major aspects are destination life cycle, destination visioning and destination marketing. This chapter has been written to provide an easy understanding of these varied aspects of destination management.

Chapter 4- All the diverse elements related to the management of a hotel fall under hotel management. Lodging comprises renting a place for a short term stay. A few different types of lodging are homestay, bed and breakfast, guest house and boarding house. This chapter discusses in detail these types of lodging as well as the different elements of hotel management.

Chapter 5- Technology is being increasingly used for various purposes within the tourism industry. A few of these are global distribution system, mobile ticketing, online hotel reservations, passenger service system and passenger information system. The topics elaborated in this chapter will help in gaining a better perspective about these applications of technology in tourism.

I owe the completion of this book to the never-ending support of my family, who supported me throughout the project.

Wendy Perez

Introduction to the Tourism Industry

The service sector industry which is linked to attracting, accommodating and entertaining tourists is known as tourism industry. Some of the major elements of tourism are transport, place significance, natural attractions, infrastructure and facilities. This chapter has been carefully written to provide an introduction to these elements of tourism and tourism industry.

The word "Tourism" is an assemblage of two words i.e. "Tour" and "Ism". The word tour means movement of individuals from one place to another for different activities like leisure, recreation, educational orientation and participation in any event etc. The word ism means to know any ongoing activity, phenomenon, concept or theory etc. thus, Tourism means to know about tour and travel activities and various requirements & formalities associated with them.

Tourism activity

The word "Tourism" was originated from Greek word "Tornus" in 16th century, which means an ancient tool in the shape of circle or wheel. The word turned into "Tourist" and then "Tourism". UNWTO (United Nations World Tourism Organisation) and different researchers have defined tourism as follows:

- Tourism definition according to UNWTO "Tourism comprises the activities of persons traveling to and staying in places outside their usual environment for not more than one consecutive year for leisure, business and other purposes".

- "The sum of the phenomena and relationships arising from the interaction of tourists, business suppliers, host governments and host communities in the process of attracting and hosting these tourists and other visitors".

- Tourism definition according to Northern Arizona University, Parks & Recreation Mgmt.

"Tourism is a collection of activities, services and industries that delivers a travel experience, including transportation, accommodations, eating and drinking establishments, retail shops, entertainment businesses, activity facilities and other hospitality services provided for individuals or groups traveling away from home".

- "The temporary movement of people to destinations outside their normal places of work and residence, the activities undertaken during their stay in those destinations, and the facilities created to cater to their needs".

Distinctiveness of Tourist

The word "Tourist" has been originated from Greek word "Tornus", which means an ancient tool in the shape of wheel or circle. The word tornus changed into tourist and subsequently into tourism. If we revolve a wheel, it regains the similar position, from where it started. Similar is the case of a circle, the starting point is accessed after drawing of full circle.

Tornus: An ancient Greek tool of shape of a wheel.

A tourist is a person, who travels to destinations outside his/her usual place of residence or work spot and stays there for 24 hours or more for leisure, recreation or business.

A tourist is distinct from traveller, visitor, transient and excursionist. Primary concerns for a tourist include safety, health hazards and the crime rate, especially theft at the destination etc.

Personal Safety

- Tourist must avoid places of high crime rates, places where wars are taking place and terrorist hit places.

- Tourists must also notice places of emergency exits in order to react to situations of fire of terrorist attack etc.

Money and Valuables

- Tourist must buy traveller's cheques to minimise the possibility of losing the cash.

- Tourist must not keep the traveller's cheques, credit cards and cash in same place.

- Tourist must put valuables at safe place in hotel.

- Tourist must carry their travel documents with them.

- Tourist must have photocopies of one's travel documents in order to avoid hustle when the originals are lost.

- Tourist must have emergency contact numbers.

Health

- Tourist must check places for various precautions like epidemic hit places etc.

- Tourist must find out the sanitation condition of the country to be visited, in order to find out whether there is requirement of sanitary actions.

- Tourist must bring one's personal first aid kit.

- Tourists eat carefully in order to avoid minor and major health issues.

Types of Tourists

Various types of tourist are as follows:

- International tourist: People, who visit other countries than their native country for fun and enjoyment etc.

- Domestic tourist: Tourism activity in which people of native country visit different places within the same country.

- Regional tourist: Tourism activity in which people visit places located within a region (Intra-regional) or between regions (Inter-regional) in native country.

The tourists can further be categorised on different basis like distance, direction, number etc. as follows:

- On the basis of distance:
  - Long haul tourist (Beyond 3000 Kms).
  - Short haul tourist (Within 3000 Kms).

- On the basis of direction of travel:
  - Inbound tourist.
  - Outbound tourist.
- On the basis of travel pattern:
  - FIT (Free Independent Tour/tourist).
  - GIT (Group Inclusive Tour/tourist).
- On the basis of number:
  - Mass tourist.
  - Selective tourist.
- On the basis of budget:
  - Elite tourist.
  - Budget tourist.

Traveller, Visitor, Transient and Excursionist

1. Traveller: Traveller may be elaborated as a person who is taking a trip within or outside his/her own country of residence, irrespective of the purpose of travel, means of transport used and budget of visit. One who travels, especially to distant lands is called a traveller.

2. Visitor: Visitor is a person, who visits different places for meeting friends, relatives, surveys, work and business purpose etc. There are mainly two types of visitors as follows:

- International visitor: International visitor is a person who travels to a country other than that in which he/she has his/her usual residence but outside his/her usual environment for a period not exceeding twelve months and whose main purpose of visit is other than the exercise of remunerative activity.

- Domestic visitor: Domestic visitor is a person staying in a country, who travels to a place within the country and outside his/her usual environment for a period not surpassing twelve months and whose purpose of visit is other than the execution of remunerative activity.

3. Transient: Transient are those who do not leave the transit area of the airport or the port in certain countries and he/she may involve a stay of one day or more. They are included in the visitor statistics as they make their halt for few hours only.

4. Excursionist: Excursionist are those persons, who travel for pleasure for a period less than 24 hours. They visit the places for fun, recreation and refresh themselves and return to their usual place of residence within 24 hours without making any night stay.

Table: Difference among tourist, traveller, visitor, transient and excursionist.

Tourist	Traveller	Visitor	Transient	Excursionist
Tourist is a person, who visit places other than his usual place of residence for more than 24 hours and less than year for recreation, fun and enjoyment etc.	Any person who is taking a trip within or outside his/her own country of residence irrespective of the purpose of travel, means of transportation used. One who travels, especially to distant lands for variety of purposes.	Visitor is a person, who visit, different places for meeting friends, relatives, surveys, work and business purpose etc.	Who do not leave the transit area of the airport or the port in certain countries, transit may involve a stay of one day or more. In this case they should be included in the visitor statistics as they make their halt for few hours only.	Visitors who do not spend at least one night in the country visited although they might visit the country during one day or more and return to their ship or train to sleep.
Tourist travels to experience different cultural aspects, cuisines and have fun etc.	Traveller covers significant distance on routine basis or at certain period of time for different activities.	A visitor travels to meet friends, patients & relatives etc.	It involves small halt.	They are day travellers only and do not spend any night, there.
A tourist utilises tourist visa.	No tourist visa.	No tourist visa.	Use transient visa.	No tourist visa.
Tourist do not visit places for remuneration.	May travel for remuneration.	May travel for remuneration.	May travel for remuneration.	May travel for remuneration for his overall visit.

Hospitality and Hotels

A hotel customer is called a guest because the hotel offers homely and professional service and establishes an immediate relationship with the guest. Thereafter, it ensures satisfaction by providing nothing less than 'A Home Away From Home'. It is like projecting, 'what is an economic relationship as a personal relationship'. Unlike other business 'a guest hotel transaction even when complete in all respect is futile, if the guest is not satisfied'. The idea behind referring to hotel customer as guest is, offering homely as well as professional service in order to keep happy and satisfied and make his experience as memorable as possible. As compared to other industries, hotel industry, which is a service industry, requires greater personal touch and courtesy. A hotel guest is a customer and unlike a family or social guest, he pays for his stay, food and beverage consumption at the hotel.

Origin and Evolution of Hospitality Industry

The hospitality industry is a part of a larger enterprise known as travel and tourism industry. The travel and tourism industry is a vast group of business with one goal in common: providing necessary or desired services to travellers. Ever since man started to travel in search of food, work, better prospects or leisure, there has been a demand for overnight stay. Lodging houses were built to provide accommodation along the trade and caravan route. Missionaries and religious travellers were accommodated by local people in their houses. From modest origins, hospitality and tourism rose to become two of the largest worldwide industries. Warriors or traders were the early travellers but they did not have hotels to accommodate them. The warriors used tents but the merchants sought to trade tools, clothing and livestock and traded merchandise for lodging. The inns offered little more than a cot or a bench in the corner of a room or a stable. Most of them were private residences that offered temporary residence or lodging to strangers. Guests stayed in large communal rooms where sanitation and privacy were non-existent. After the establishment of money in 6th century BC, Inn keeping was one of the first commercial enterprises and hospitality was one of the first services for which money was exchanged.

But the demand for shelter kept on increasing with the development of highways and technological advancements in modes of travelling. As a result, inns gave way to hotels. Hospitability is a massive industry providing home facilities away from home to millions of tourists. These tourists can be segmented into business and leisure tourists. All have different needs and expectations. However, the hospitality industry is so versatile that it is catering to the needs of all of them. Advances in transportation enabled more people to travel greater distances at less cost spreading tourism across the globe.

In medieval, Europe monasteries rationally offered hospitality to the travellers. The main aim in offering hospitality was for pilgrims as monasteries were found at the site of holy place in early stage. In early Europe inns, they were especially designed as profit making business and it was the first commercial venture in hotel keeping. Hotel keeping has also influenced mode of transport, with advent of railways came station hotels, and with aircraft came airport hotels, with motorways and extensive road travel like motels, boatels and ship bought floating hotels into existence. Inn keeping is believed to be started in 1200 AD. During industrial revolution during 1750-1820, the English Inns were considered finest in the world. Hotel de Henry was one of the 1st European hotels built in 1788 with capacity of 60 rooms. Growth of hotel inns continues with the concept of family hotels i.e. run by the families called Mom & Pop in England.

The industrial revolution, which started in the 1760s, facilitated the construction of hotels everywhere, in mainland Europe, in England and in America. In colonial America, inns were modeled after European inns. Beds and rooms had to be shared with strangers. Throughout 1800s, American innkeepers improved their services and continued to build larger properties. Most of these were located in seaport town since sea transport was very widely used mode or travel and transport then. The Termand house was 1st class hotel made in Boston in 1829 and it provided private guest room, door with lock and free soap bellboy service. It is called Adam and Eve of modern hotel industry.

Hotels were established in city centers in New York first and in Copenhagen. At the beginning of the 1800s, the Royal Hotel was built in London. Holiday resorts began to flourish along the French and Italian Rivieras. In Japan, Ryokan guest houses sprang up. In India, the government-run Dak bungalows provided reliable accommodation for travellers. The first American hotel 'the City Hotel' opened in 1794 in the New York City. It was one of the largest buildings in the city and was built exclusively for hotel purpose. It had 73 guest rooms. 'Adelphi Hotel' in New York was the first highrise structure in the city. In 1822, in Venice, a certain Giuseppe Dal Niel transformed an old palace into a hotel and gave it his name 'Le Danieli'. As trains began to replace horsedrawn transport, highway inns for stage coaches started to decline. During this period, the Shepheard Hotel in Cairo was founded, the result of a complete transformation of an ancient city-centre harem. L' Hotel des Bergues was built in the spring of 1834 AD on the shore of the Lake of Geneva. One of its founders, Guillaume Henri Dufour became a famous Swiss general. In 1840, l' Hotel des Trois Couronnes was established in Vevey in Switzerland and the Baur au Lac in Zurich, fully refurbished since 1995. In New York, the New York Hotel was the first to be equipped with private bathrooms. The 'Bayerischer Hof' was built in Munich in 1841 AD, followed in 1852 AD by the 'Vier Jahreszeiten'. These two famous establishments were completely renovated after the Second World War.

The inauguration of the Grand Hotel in Paris took place on 5 May 1862 in the presence of the Empress Eugenie. The orchestra, directed by Jacques Offenbach, played the Traviata. This building was designed by the architect Alfred Armand, in order to show the elite of travellers from all over the world the progress made under the Second Empire by science, arts and industry. In Athens in 1874, Stathis Lampsas, a chef by profession, realised his dream by building l Hotel Grande Bretagne. Athens was suffering at that time from a shortage of water. It is said that the personnel bought water from carriers in the street to bring to the 80 bedrooms and the two bathrooms. Of course, the establishment has undergone several renovations since that time. The first school for hoteliers was founded in Lausanne, Switzerland in 1890 by J. Tschumi, Director of the Beau Rivage in Lausanne, and A.R. Armleder, the 'father' of the Richemond in Geneve. In Monte Carlo, l' Hotel Hermitage opened its doors in 1896, offering its guests the refined and luxurious atmosphere enjoyed by the rich at the close of the nineteenth century. Shortly afterwards, the Victoria Hotel in Kansas City offered bathrooms with every room. The Netherland Hotel in New York City then became the first to provide all its guests with their own telephone.

The early years of the twentieth century were rich in new hotels which rapidly became prestigious. Edouard Niiermans, the 'architect of palaces', transformed the Villa 'Eugenie', the summer residence of the Emperor Napoleon III and his wife Eugenie de Montijo, in 1900. Mr. Ellsworth M Statler started new chain and made his first hotel 'Buffalo Statler' on 18 Jan 1908. He gave a slogan 'room and a bath for a dollar and a half'. In 1905, he built 'Hotel du Palais' in Biarritz. In 1913 his 'Negresco' was opened in Nice, in the presence of seven kings. In 1950, new concepts such as motels, boatels, floatels, rotesl and loatels were developed after the Second World War and many trained staff joined the army hence standard of service lowered, however occupancy was improved. In 1952, Kemmons Wilson formed Holiday Inn and first Holiday Inn was made in 1952 at Memphis-Tennesse. In 1960, many individual owners merged themselves with large chain such as Sheraton, Hilton, Hyatt and Holiday Inn for franchising by paying a fee and using the name, reservation system, national and international advertisement and operational manuals. In 1970, the hotel industry experienced the construction boom. International business rapidly developed and with this a lot of business executives travelled out and modern hotels were developing as per the needs and wants of tourists and business class guests.

The major boom in the hotel industry began in 1980, marked by more inventive marketing and the development of hotels increasingly adapted to a particular type of clientele. This trend brought the demand for the construction of hotels near airports, hotels for conferences, health hotels, ski holiday hotels, holiday villages and marina hotels. The first Property Management Systems (Fidelio, Hogatex, etc.) appeared in the hospitality market. In the eighties, too, the Far East began to prepare itself to welcome both business people and the tourists who were beginning to discover the countries of the rising sun, such as China, South Korea, Thailand and Japan. The international chains (American for the most part) prepared expansion plans for Europe, the Middle and Far East which were mainly aimed at congress participants and business people. The early nineties were characterized by a recession in the hotel business, indubitably caused by reductions in multinationals' travel budgets and the growing crisis in the Gulf. The Gulf War helped to create great insecurity for both individuals and business. The year 1991 is considered to be the black year of the hotel trade. It forced hoteliers to become more creative in finding ways of attracting guests (special programmes, offers for 'frequent travelers', high performance reservation systems) and thus emerge from the crisis with the minimum damage.

Great Landmarks in the Hotel Industry	
1650	Pascal opened a cafe in Paris and Coffee House in London.
1794	City Hotel (73 rooms) at l5 Broadway, New York. First building specially made for a hotel.
1829	Tremont House. Adam and Eve of modern hotel industry was opened in Boston (170 rooms).
1889	Cesar Ritz introduced luxury hotels such as Savoy, Carlton and Hsrde Park hotels in England.
1890- 1899	Fredrick Gordon and Sir Blundel Maple launched Gordon Hotels and Fredrick Hotels Ltd.
Late19th Century	Famous Waldorf Astoria in New York.
18.1.1908	Buffalo Statler by Ellsworth statler in the US considered to be the birth of commercial hotels.
1927	Stevens Hotel in Chicago, later renamed as Hilton Hotel (3000 rooms).
1930	Depression in world economy Decline in hotel industry.
1950	The new concepts (a) Motels and (b) International chain operations.
2017	Emphasis on more information and technology embedded hospitality operations.

Types of Accommodation Units

The term "tourist accommodation" invariably turns our attention to hotel. But tourist accommodation does not revolve around hotels only. The available types of accommodation can be classified as:

Hotels

Hotel is a place which supplies board and lodging. It is "a large city house of distinction"; "a place for the entertainment of travellers" and "a public building". Hotels provide accommodation, meals and refreshments for at periods of time for those who stay on the premises and pay for the services provided. Hotels can be classified on the basis of following facilities and services:

- Room charges or price: Budget, luxury, etc.
- Range of facilities: Five stars, no star, etc.
- Location: Resort, motel etc.
- Length of stay: Transit, residential, etc.
- Ownership and management: Chain, individual, etc.

Types of Hotels

- International Hotel or Star Hotel: These hotels are modern western style luxury hotels classified based on an internationally accepted system of classification grading and located in almost all metropolitan and other large cities as well as at principal tourist destinations. Usually, they are located at a prime location in the city. There categories range from 7 to 1 Star grade depending upon the facilities and services provided by these hotels. In addition to accommodation various other facilities are provided to make the stay more comfortable. These facilities include – information counters, banquet halls, conference facilities, a number of shops, travel agency, desk business centre facilities, money changing and safe deposit facilities, theme restaurants, beverages, swimming pool, gymnasium, health clubs and other entertainment programmes in the form of games, music and dance, etc.

- Non-Star or Commercial Hotels: These hotels mainly depend upon individual travellers, middle budget tourists and many of the guests are repeat guests. These hotels are located near the business or commercial centres and have easy access to transportation. They provide accommodation, parking space for guests and their visitors, restaurants and sometimes business centre facilities as well. Size of such a hotel varies from small to medium.

- Residential Hotels: These hotels are known as apartment house or apartment hotels with the availability of conventional hotel services. These hotels are largely located in big cities and mostly operate under the European Plans.

- Floating Hotels: These hotels are located on the surface of the water. It may be on seawater or river water or even on a lake. These hotels provide all the facilities and services of a hotel and are very popular with the tourists. In many cases, across the world old ships have been converted into these types of hotels and have become popular among the tourists.

- Capsule Hotels: Capsule hotel is the latest innovation in the budget hotel market. The first of its kind was opened in Osaka, Japan in the year 1979. The capsule is a box made of glass reinforced plastic or cement, open either at one side or one end in which they provide some functions of a traditional hotel such as a bed, a clock, radio, colour TV, flexible lighting, a box for valuables and a miniature table for writing.

- Transit Transient Hotels: The locations of this type of hotel are in close proximity of the airports, catering to guests who stay for a limited period of time from few hours to a few days.

- Heritage Hotels: Old properties of the royal and aristocratic families are renovated and the old aura is recreated for the tourists to stay in heritage surroundings. The heritage properties are an attraction in themselves.

Motels

The motel provides parking space to the travelers travelling by automobiles and the rooms opens to the parking lot.

Resorts

A resort hotel is one which is visited by holiday makers or tourists for relaxation, recreation and/or for entertainment. Resort hotels cater to tourists and are located near place of some scenic beauty, i.e., the sea, mountains or in 'off the beaten track destination. The primary reason for visiting a resort is rest and relaxation and these hotels are built with the objective of indoor recreation activities giving visitors special welcome and atmosphere of informality. The services and amenities offered by resorts include swimming pool, tennis court, skiing, boating, surfing and many others. The clientele of resort hotels is mostly persons with considerable income looking for relaxation and recreation.

Timeshare Apartments/Condominiums

The concept of timeshare is popular as it gives vacation ownership or holiday ownership and offers the purchaser the right to enjoy, for a set period or interval, each year, vacation time in an apartment or other type of lodging that is a part of a tourist complex, equipped with a variety of services and facilities. The period of time sold is usually based on modules of a week, fortnight or a month.

Elements of Tourism

Tourism consists of certain basic and fundamental features without which development cannot be witnessed in the sector. These essential elements include but not limited to transport accommodation, infrastructure, facilities and auxiliary or support services. A tourist needs a mode of transport to reach the destination, whether by road, rail or air and even sea; needs accommodation for comfortable stay and derives satisfaction by the attractions at the destination place. Apart from which a tourist also expects the support services like banks, travel agents, local guides, healthcare, and insurance service in case of need (in today's airports, one can find on-the-spot insurance service to passengers). At the same time the place of interest differs from person-to-person depending on his/her tastes and values. Some may prefer place of historical interest with tall palaces and forts while some others may enjoy sheer beauty of nature such as forests, waterfalls, mountains, rivers, and still some others may prefer a religious location with temples, churches, etc. The essential elements of tourism are listed below:

1. Transport: There is no travel and tourism without the development of modes of transport. Historically, man used to move with the help of animals like horses, camels and donkeys. Post World War I, the revolutionary invention of motorcar has made private transport and travel easy. Some developments taken place in transport are listed below:

- Rail Transport: Rail system was first introduced in England and later in Europe, has given the first technical based travelling to humans. By 1841, the organised rail travel was in place. In USA, the organised rail travel was introduced in the early 1870. It was estimated that in the year 1881, the railways carried an estimated 600 million passengers over the routes operated by more than 100 companies. In India also, the introduction of rail travel was done at the same time—in the late 19th century and today Railways, boasts as one of the largest public sector undertaking in the world, next only to Russia, carrying millions of passengers across the breadth and width of the country.

- Sea Transport: Shipping has made significant contribution to travel, especially in Europe; the steam ship was used to transport passengers and cargo across the continents. Even today sea transport is largely used to ship the cargo and passengers in various countries. With the advancement of technology, sea transport is converted into pleasure travel with the introduction of luxury and cruise shipping.

- Motor Car: Ford motors pioneered the introduction of Motor Car, which has created the privacy to travel and thereby giving the traveller freedom of choice that lead to private tourism. The development of roads and related technology have underwent sea change and today many countries boasts of quality highways with modern cars facilitating travel. It is the motorcar or the automobile in its various shapes and sizes and budgets that has given the much-needed fillip to the modern tourism concept of leisure and travel.

- Air Transport: Tourism got its gift from the technological inventions in the form of Airplane. The invention and subsequent evolution of this flying machine has redefined the travel and tourism. Today airlines of different countries carry millions of passengers on domestic and international travel. Under the guidelines of travelling, the Operators of Air Transport Systems operate with strict code of conduct. Air travel, which was the privilege of the rich and wealthy has slowly started to reach the masses of other classes with the rapid industrialization and improved standards of living. With increased disposable incomes, people from all classes of society started to resort to air travel.

2. Place Significance: People visit different places of worship (Mecca-Medina, Vatican City, Tirupathi), natural beauty (Niagara Falls, African Safaris, Himalayas), places of entertainment (Las Vegas, Casinos in Italy, Singapore), man-made wonders (Eiffel Tower in Paris, Taj Mahal in Agra India, Great Wall of China), and business interest (Beijing, New York, London). Hence, tourism is geographic oriented and cannot be separated from the place of origin.

3. Natural Attractions: For a place to be a tourist destination, it is important to be naturally aesthetic. The rivers, waterfalls, mountains, forests, deserts, lakes, etc., make a place an attractive tourist destination. For example, the forests of Africa, Niagra waterfalls, Sahara Desert, and Himalayas are some of the examples of natural wonders and attract millions of tourists from all over the world.

4. History and Cultural Significance: Destinations with rich historical and cultural heritage show significant influence on the tourism sector. The choice of a place invariably related to the historical background, like the Pyramids of Egypt, ancient forts and palaces of Jaipur, etc., are some famous historical destinations around the world.

5. Infrastructure: One essential element of tourism is the development of infrastructure. The destination should be well connected with rail, road and air for the place to gain importance in the minds of tourists.

6. Facilities: Provision of add-on facilities is a significant contributor for the development of tourism. The place of destination should be artificially developed to the maximum possible extent to expand the visibility and add value to the tourist. However, care should be taken not to disturb the originality of the place. Facilities include, boating in a lake, swimming and surfing on the beaches, trekking, etc.

7. Accommodation: Any place requires adequate and sufficient accommodation or rest places for tourists. Inadequate and insufficient accommodation cause inconvenience to the tourist and may result in adverse publicity leading to poor response from the present and potential customers. Hotels, resorts, lodges, motels, rest houses, campsites and cottages are to be built for attracting all classes of tourists. The other significant feature of accommodation is the provision of food. As any tourist destination attracts diverse customers with different food tastes and preferences, it is essential to bring uniformity in the offerings to satisfy diverse interests of the tourist. It can be

observed that Singapore and Malaysia attract millions of tourists because of their suitable accommodation and food facilities for different categories of tourists from all over the world.

8. Consumed at Destination: Tourism activity begins in a place of origin and is consumed at destination places. People who visit a certain place have to enjoy the pleasure or experience at the destination. It is psychological feeling and contentment. Although a tourist decides the place to visit from his/her homeland, he/she experiences the pleasure after reaching the place only.

9. Distinct Identity: As the place becomes a tourist destination, it becomes unique and is totally transformed place compared to others areas.

10. Involves Development: Tourism develops the place of repute with various facilities as needed by the tourists. It is not just the place alone that shall witness the development but also the entire area that is surrounding and important, as a support to tourism. Hence the development of tourism industry in Maldives has given great fillip to the infrastructure of the State in the form of Airports, Roads and other services like hotels, resorts, restaurants, hostels, hospitals, etc.

11. Creates Diversified Culture: Tourism presents distinct ways that people view, understand and relate to the world. It creates a unique culture of "unity in diversity" at each and every destination a tourist visits. It is a phenomenon noticed all over the world. For example, Singapore accommodates tourists from across the world and at the same time supports all the cultures that are brought into the country by different tourists from different cultural backgrounds.

Creation of courteous and friendly atmosphere at the destination place enhances the goodwill of the place and promotes future tourism. The atmosphere is not only dependent on the facilitations of tourism but also on the natives of the destination along with the administration like public sanitation, police, and communication systems that are in place at the destination that propels the friendly atmosphere. 'Welcome a visitor' and 'send back a friend' is the framework on which many countries operate their tourism. Locals should be trained as to how they can be friendly with the foreign visitors and local administration should take all care in supporting those tourists who cannot speak local language by appointing suitable tourist guides to escort the foreign nationals.

Types of Transport

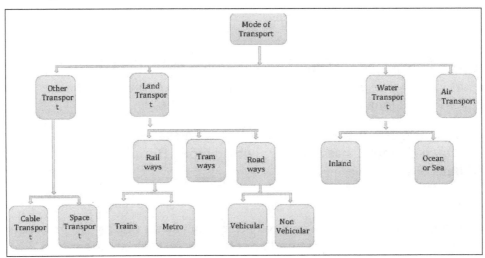

The different modes of transport are land, water, and air transport, which includes rail, road and rope transport. There are various other modes such as cable transport. Sometimes Human-powered transport and animal-powered transport are regarded as separate mode of transport, Each transport is fundamentally different in term of technological solution, infrastructure, vehicles, operations and environment. All means of transportation which utilize the same environment comes under same transport mode.

Land Transport

Land transport is also referred to as ground transport. The movement of goods, people, and animals is from one place to another on land by means of rail or road.

Roadways

The transportation of goods and personnel from one location to another on roads is referred as Road transport. Road is a route between two destinations, either paved or unpaved that enable transportation by way of vehicular or non-vehicular transport. It is the best suitable mode of transportation of delivery of goods between urban areas and small villages. In the pursuit of leisure and tourism novelty activities road transport has becomes inseparable, as it offers excited and thrilling experiences. It is among the basic infrastructure that links people of remote villages to the mainstream life. Road transport is the only option to reach remote places for enjoying rural tourism, ecotourism, adventure tourism, wildlife tourism etc. Road transportation makes it easy to see and appreciate local culture and places. It presents more flexibility than to other modes of transportation. Road Transport is the essential modes of transport. The history of Road Transport goes back to ancient civilizations; slowly it becomes more popular and general means of transport for people. Road Transport further subdivided into:

1. Vehicular Transport: A vehicle usually with wheels and an engine runs especially on roads and used for transporting goods and people on land. For example: Car, Bus, Auto-rickshaw, Hand Carts, Bullock Carts, etc).

- Car: It is one of the most popular types of transport that are used by most people for short and long journeys daily.

- Bicycles: It is the cheapest and environmentally friendly method of transport for travelling around in nature without damaging it.

- Buses: It is ideal for those who take short journeys from one part of an area or town to another. As it is available in almost every villages, cities, and towns. It is preferred mode of transport for city tour. However, it is a cheap method of transport, it offers a range of travel cards, passes and long term tickets for tourists.

2. Non-vehicular Transport: It means mode of transport for transporting goods and people on land that use human or animals as a bearer. For example: Human, Animals like Horse, Camel, Elephant, and Bulls etc).

- Human:
  ○ Palanquin: A palanquin is a covered litter typically for one or two passenger. Palanquin is carried mostly by an even number of bearers on their shoulders.

- ◦ Porter: A porter is also known as bearer. He is a person who carries goods or people for others. The porters are paid to bear heavy burdens at altitude in mountaineering expeditions. Porters are frequently called Sherpas in the mountain region of Himalayas.

- ◦ Pulled Ricksha: A pulled rickshaw is also a mode of human-powered transport. In a pulled rickshaw a runner or carrier draws a two-wheeled cart seated by one or two people.

- Animal:

  - ◦ Tanga: A Tanga or tonga is a light carriage drawn by one or two horses. Tanga are popular mode of transportation among tourists because it is fun to ride in and are usually cheaper to hire in tourist destination. Tanga were still in practice in some parts of South Asia.

  - ◦ Cart: A cart is a vehicle pulled by one or a pair of draught animals using two wheels for transport of goods and people. For transporting, typically two or more horses, oxen, donkeys, camels, or even smaller animals such as large dogs, were used exclusively for transporting humans.

Advantages of Road Transport

- Flexibility of Service: Road transport provides more flexible service than other modes of transport. It can change or adjust routes and timings according to requirements without much inconvenience.

- Service at Door: The road transport provides door to door service. The transportation starts from residence so it reduces loading and unloading expenses.

- Service in Rural Areas: It is most suitable for people in rural areas as they have less or no option of rail, water or air transport. It is also convenient and comfortable mode for travel of people and carrying goods. Road transportation builds the link between large towns and small villages.

- Suitable for Short Distance: Passenger board directly to a road vehicle and ply directly to their place of destination. It is more economic and quicker for tourist to travel over short distances.

- Feeder to other Modes of Transport: Road transport acts as a feeder to the other transport. It helps people by connection them to other mode of transport like railways, ships and airways. The movement of tourist begins and ends at their home place by making use of roads.

- Ownership: People can have their own motor vehicles and initiate their travel or movement without causing any delay in their tour.

Disadvantages of Road Transport

- Nature Dependent: Road transport is more dependent of nature than other as during rainy or cold season. During these roads become less fit and safe for use due to water flooding and fog.

- Accidents and Breakdowns: The vehicles are less prepared for incidents like accidents and breakdowns in any moment in ways of tour. Road transport is less safe and fit.

- Unsuitable for Long Distance: Road transport is less suitable for movement of goods and people over long distances. It is costly and more time consuming for long travel as compared to rail or air transport.

- Less Organised: The road transport is less organised compare to other transport. Road transportation mostly irregular and undependable and the rates charged are also uneven and unequal.

Tramways

Tramway is one of the cheapest, quickest, safest and suitable modes of Land Transport in large cities. A tram is also known as tramcar; streetcar, or trolley car in different part of world. It is a rail vehicle, typically with two or three bogies which runs on laid tracks along public urban streets.

Railways

Rail transport also referred as train transport. It is a means of transport on which vehicles run on tracks and has fixed routes and schedules. The services of rail transport are more organized, uniform and regular as compared to road transport. It is very cost effective modes of transportation for commuting goods and passengers over long and short distances. It is the fastest and dependable as it is the least affected by usual weather turbulences modes of land transport in terms of safety. Railway is one of the most powerful motives for mass travel in this century. It is most suitable for long distance travel. It offers tourist a fascinating experience and an insight into the country and its people as it passes through green vegetation of villages and towns. It plays a key role in accelerating development in commercial and industrial sectors of various countries in remote areas. Railway has brought the greatest revolution in modern mechanical transport.

- Train: A train consists of a series of connected vehicles that runs along a fixed rail track to transport goods or passengers. Trains are generally classified by the average speed. trains are classified according to speed as superfast, mail and express, followed by passenger, Mainline Electric Multiple Unit (MEMU) and Double Multiple Unit (DMU).

- Monorails: A train running on a single rail bogie typically elevated. It is developed to meet growing medium-demand traffic in urban transit.

- Rapid Transit: Rapid transit known by various name like metro, subway, tube, or underground. It is a type of high-capacity public transport to cater the increasing demand of urban areas. Metro systems are electric railways that function on grade separated in tunnels or on elevated railways in an exclusive right-of-way.

Advantages of Rail Transport

- Safety: Rail transport is safer than other transport in case of any accident. The injuries and deaths related to other transport are much lower.

- Speed: It is one of the fastest mode of transport, with advent of bullet train. The improved train speeds and reduced length of their routes, the average time needed to transport people has become quite competitive.

- Comfort: Rail transport offer passengers more comfort. It also provides freedom of movement inside the trains' bogie than road and air transport.

- Environmental Protection: Rail transport consumes lesser energy than other modes of transport. Trains are most energy-efficient means of transportation. It emits less pollution than other transport.

- Capacity: The carrying capacity of trains can be increased or decreased in certain limit and are capable of carrying higher number of than other means of transportation.

Disadvantages of Rail Transport

- Inappropriate for Short Distance: This mode of transport is unsuitable and uneconomical for short distance.

- Lesser Service in Rural areas: Rail transport is less economical in rural areas. The railway service is not operated in large rural areas due to high cost. These rural or remote area are connected through feeder services of road transport and it causes much inconvenience to tourist and people living in the area.

- Lack of Flexibility: The routes and timings is non-adjustable according to the individual requirements. In case of any emergency or requirement passenger have to wait for scheduled timing of train.

Water Transport

It means transportation of people or goods by water over large distances through boat or other waterborne vessel. It is the oldest and the cheapest mode of transport. From Ancient times Greeks and Romans navigated in the vessels to establish and maintain their trade and colonies. It operates on a natural track and does not require construction and maintenance of its track. Water transport has played an important role in bringing world closer for travel and foreign trade. The water transport operates with ports in the coastal area of a country and through the lakes and rivers within the country. Water transport consists of: (i) Inland water transport (ii) Ocean-transport.

1. Inland waterways: Inland waterways may be subdivided into:

- River Transport: Rivers are the nature's water highways. It is suitable for small boats, steamers as well as big barrages. It was highly developed in the pre-railway days. It plays significant role prior to the development of modern land transport. It is mostly used in the areas where rivers are dominant.

- Canal Transport: Canals are the normally built for the purpose of navigation and irrigation or both. Canals are artificial waterways, and require huge investment construction and maintenance of its track.

- Boats: Travelling by rivers is usually by ferry, ship or boats. Ferries are often used for crossings of river. Boats more convenient option as compared to a plane or train in crossing rivers, usually available in river basin.

2. Ocean Waterways: Ocean transport is indispensable for deep sea traveler and foreign trade. It operates on a natural track of the sea so it does not require any investment in term of the construction and maintenance of its track. It is the cheapest mode of transport and brought the different places of the world closer into one global tourism market. Ocean Transport may be subdivided into:

- Coastal Transport: Coastal transport is a cheaper, flexible and economical form of water transport for the movement of bulky and heavy goods. In coastal transport, ships ply between the different ports of a country. It is plays an important role in carrying goods and passengers within the country.

- Overseas Transport: In Overseas transport, ships or cruise moves between different places of countries parted by sea or ocean and are used to carry passengers and goods. It is travels on fixed routes that connect almost all the countries. The overseas transport may be divided into:

  - Liners: A liner is a passenger or cargo vessel, which have fixed routes with fixed places, prescribed schedule or timetable and charges. It provide a uniform and regular services to tourists whether they are filled or not. Liners are usually, a collection of vessels of one owner.

  - Tramps: Tramps have no fixed routes, no set rules or rate schedule. Usually, they do not sail until they filled. They are not as fast in speed as liners but ready to sail anywhere and at any time.

  - Tankers: Tankers are ships which are specially designed to carry liquids like oil and petrol.

Advantages of Water Transport

- Cheap: The ships or boats ply on water so transport channel is quite cheap as it requires less amount of maintenance and running cost as compared rail and road Transport.

- Convenient for heavy Goods: It is convenient for Heavy goods and large number of tourist, as they can be transported easily at little cost between or within country.

- Valuable in time of Natural Calamities: In time of natural calamities like flood, when other transport like rail and road are disrupted. Water transport is invaluable in this time.

Disadvantages of Water Transport

- Speed: It is slower means of transport than air and rail. But it saves time in rivers and canals areas by connecting both sides. It depends on rain; failure of monsoon makes navigation difficult due to fall in the water level of rivers.

- Risky: This mode of transport is more risky than other means. The danger of sinking ships or boats is always there and no one to rescue in case of river and sea.

Air Transport

Air travel is a status symbol for many people as compared to other modes of transport. It has made significant changes in tourist's minds concerning time taking and distance travel. Air travel ensures comfort, safety and speedy travel at the domestic and international places. Passenger enjoys several in-flight services such as food, wine, and music. Over the years to ensure comfortable travel, aircrafts have been modified to improve passenger services, amenities and safety. It connectivity is extended to the places where other mode transport is normally not possible. With the extensive expansion of airline network it plays a significant role in the growth of domestic and international tourism. Over half (52%) of all inbound travellers throughout world travel to their destination country via air. The important elements of tourist travel by air are experience that they get by security of aircraft, comfort, and service.

- Airplanes: Airplanes use a propeller to ignite power to the aircraft, and the fixed wings act as a stabilizer for aircraft for keeping it in the air. A long runway is prerequisite for the vehicles to become airborne. The maximum number of tourists travelling aboard chooses to travel by airplane due to less time consumption and luxurious facilities in the passenger planes.

- Helicopters: Helicopters are powered using horizontal rotors having two or more blades. The blades rotate around the top and lift the body of the helicopter along. It can only carry four to six people. Nowadays, helicopters are used to travel in mountain region or flying to top of mountain or hills.

- Rockets: Rockets are propelled via the chemical reaction of a fluid that is ejected at from the vehicle. The high velocities force from the explosion out of the tail of the rocket push the vehicle upward at extremely high speeds. The rocket is fastest mode of transportation that allowed tourist to travel for suborbital and orbital flights beyond the atmosphere. Rockets are future of transport for space travel and tourism.

Advantages of Air Transport

- High Speed: It is one of the fastest means of transport. Tourist or passenger can be transported effortlessly from one place to another within few hours.

- Monetary value: It is quite convenient to travel to different country within few bucks and hours. It transports costly and perishable goods through air transport.

- Free from physical barriers: Aircraft fly over river, mountains and valleys etc., it is free from physical barriers and helps tourist to travel to any place of their choice.

- Valuable in natural calamities: During any natural calamities like earth quake, flood, and famine, it is used for rescue operations of tourist and people trapped there.

Disadvantages of Air Transport

- High Costs: Due to its high operational costs and costly service. Air transport becomes unaffordable to Middle class, poor people and budget tourist.

- More Risks: Air transport is in high prone to accidents due to unavoidable circumstances and nature in mid-air. A sliest mistake made pilot can put passenger's life in dangerous.

Other Transport

- Cable Transport: Cable transports have cables as the basis for transporting people and goods. It may be driven or passive. The people or goods moved by pulling, sailing, sliding, or by drives and the things being moved on cableways. They are mostly used in mountainous areas. The different modes of cable transport are:

  ○ Aerial lifts: Aerial tramway, Gondola lift, Chairlift and Ski lift etc.

  ○ Surface lifts: Cable car, Cable ferry, and Surface lift etc.

  ○ Vertical lifts: Elevator.

Tourism Paradigms

UN has declared 2017 as the international year of sustainable tourism for development that can make tourism on enamouring and endearing phenomenon had its spurt in the 80s and 90s. Yet, it gained profound traction of late and the slants of sustainable development have strengthened the promotion of alternative tourism. The offshoots of alternative tourism such as agro tourism, hydel tourism, ecotourism village tourism, vineyard tourism, health, and wellness tourism etc., received remarkable boost and were considered as the best remedy to the grave modern ailments like high pollution, global warming, depreciation of forest cover, poaching, levelling of farmlands, cultural corrosion, stress and tension, and wastage of natural resources. No other industry of global importance has evolved so profusely as tourism. Each and every component of tourism undergoes metamorphoses on a regular basis in line with the charger in the attitude, behaviour, interests, tastes, and outlook of tourists. Whether travel, accommodation, cargo, designation management or the allied sectors such as banking insurance, entertainment etc. have changed a great deal to cater to the requirements of the present day tourist. One of the most important paradigms is the specialities of the neo tourism offerings. Even subtle, common interests are marketed with a finesse that goes a long way in stimulating the tourists. For instance, tea tourism. The simple tasting of tea in the natural habitats i.e. the tea plantations and estates and tea trails are packaged as spectacular attractions. The features of tourism paradigms are so lengthy which itself indicates the range, efficacy, and outstanding attributes of the same and also the coinage attained.

Conservation Paradigms

Tourists are now coming out in hordes to support noble causes like offering fresh life for once riveting rivers Volunteerism over the most recent concepts of tourism is central to such endeavors. Volunteerism or volunteering tourism is concerned with tourist's interests in involving or indulging in socially culturally or environmentally uplifting activities without receiving any remuneration for those. Such tourists tend to become pro actives participants in the revamping welfare, educative and other welfare initiatives.

The new paradigms of tourism spearheaded by the sustainable development campaigns and the ideals of responsible tourism gives great hopes to conservation of nature and natural resources like water

'River Crossing','River walks',' Eco trails', etc. are exciting activity highlighted in tour programmes which sensitise the tourists towards conservation of environmental resources. In Finland, spectacular tourism haven in Europe the lake wellness project is integrated with tourism Needless to point out; the relationship between tourism and environment is very solid. When natural resources are used for tourism purposes, there are different adverse effects too. At the same time, if resources like forests and water are promoted for tourism with a sustainable objective, the conservation efforts are bolstered up. Nowadays in lot of places voluntourists are joining hands with the host community members in reviving rivers, nourishing lake beds, protecting jungles, and many other conservation ventures.

The tourism importance of natural resources becomes the clarion call for the government and other stakeholder to rejuvenate them. The extend wholesome support to the project. Though environmental activities are objecting to some tourism projects as they are concerned about the futuristic ill effects, the sustainable attributes imbibed in the tourism initiatives make the local communities and environmentalists enthusiastic. Tourism thus can be mooted as a pivotal platform to take the green message to the masses. As tourism gains traction in the destinations, the activities that take life out of nature like illegal sand mining, quarrying and encroachments will eventually worm out. The green protocol emphasized by tourism is turning out to be the backbone of conservation in many vulnerable places. "Go Green" has emerged as the motto of tourism now.

Technology-Driven Paradigms

The pervasive influences of technological developments on tourism have affected a paradigm shift in all its functions. It will not be an exaggeration to point out that tourism operations are growing from strength to strength owing to the adoption of ICT. The Internet has brought information pertaining to destinations at the fingertips of tourist and promoters. It has also enriched tremendously the awareness level of tourists. They have an array of options to choose from airlines to hotels, every key information lucidly provided through various tourism websites and portals enables the tourists to make decisions that satisfy their desires. The Global Distribution Network (GDN) has transformed the processes involved in tourism including ticket booking and cancellation. The terminals display various sectors, price range, seating arrangement, customised options offers and discounts and alternative choices. Global Positioning System (GPS) and Geographical Information System (GIS) has made traveling to the nook and corner of the world a very smooth exercise. Further, GIS portrays the extent of ecological hazards in the destination where by the planners can take appropriate action in regulating and controlling tourism. Coaches and cars are more GPS enabled to serve the tourists which aid tourists a great deal in reaching even remote tourist spots. It also helps tourists who are keen on self-driving to reach tourism centres.

The advent of online travel portals (OTPs) took the industry to greater heights. Customization become never like before. Efficiency is also fabulous. Tourists are able to choose from the immense options presented to them on a platter by the OTP. Tailor-made packages gradually distinguished itself as the order of the day. Furthermore, the travel and hospitality rating sites like TripAdvisor and Expedia are serving the tourists mainly to determine the best-operating properties and to opt the service(s) of their preferences. Soft wares like IDS enable the customers to have a view of the hotel rooms and take appropriate decisions. The room size, furniture and other amenities can be gauged by the customers. They can also fulfill the choices concerned with beach facing resort rooms, swimming pool, golf courses and all the indoor and outdoor aspects.

Virtual Tourism has a significant role to play other them being a vital marketing tool. It is actually doing a yeoman service to tourists who are physically challenged and incapacitated to visit the destinations. Senior citizen and economically backward section of the society are also benefitted by way of virtual tourism. Various tourism sites such as Great Barrier Reef, Australia have extended the facility of virtual tourism. This facility provided virtual tours to an interested lot in the comforts of their homes and views all the charms of the destination, understand its uniqueness, and get enchanted by artifacts and tourism products. The images mostly are of high quality and projected through 3D in many cases.

Transport technology has undergone a paradigm change. Multiaxle tourist coaches are ruling the roads. They provide excellent comfort and safety to tourists. Royal Caribbean, Queen Victoria and Star Cruise Company offer luxurious cruises that invigorate the tourists. Aviation too has created a sparking image by dishing out quality first class, business class and executive class services for passengers in the most modern carrier. Inflight service employs multimedia tools to entertain the passengers. F&B services have been enhanced in almost all the international carriers.

Hospitality Paradigms

The accommodation sector is witnessing mind-boggling transformation that leverages tourism industry to a very great extent. The paradigm extraordinaire in this sector is that the offerings of hospitality itself have become tourism attractions. There are several examples to substantiate this Ecotels the eco-friendly hotels is a classic case in point Ecotels are drawing tourists in hordes. Ecotels actually glorifies the conservation paradigm by incepting the equipment and gadgets scientifically engineered to conserve water, avoidance of chemicals, prevention of power wastage and the like. Further, houseboats are becoming centres of conferences and the avenues for staging cultural expressions. Houseboats are also venues for screening the performing art forms. These facilities give fillip to MICE tourism and also entertain the tourists. Conducting the conferences in an ambiance in sync with nature and utmost mobile is quite exciting for tourists.

Tourism Projects like tree huts, homestays, agroenterprises, etc. not only offer the finest hospitality but also thrills the tourists abundantly. Boutique hotels are luxury personified. It is being promoted as hotels with a 'Point of View'. The classic features of boutique hotels are scintillating. Heritage hotels are still dazzling. More heritage properties like forts, palaces, traditional buildings, heritage structures, havelis, etc. are being transformed into hotels. This way the heritage properties are prevented from destruction. Hill resorts and beach resorts are here to stay; but eco resorts are very innovative.

Experiential Paradigms

One of the foremost paradigm to be highlighted as regards tourism are the experiential paradigm. Tourism in the present day is not merely an industry for sightseeing and tourists no longer want to be mute spectators at the detonation. The participative character of tourism is gaining momentum at a swift pace. Tourists want to experience the offerings of the tourism centres. They get excited in involving themselves in bullock cart riding, flying kites, safaris (desert elephant, camel, etc.), rowing, playing, traditional games, wearing masks weaving, indulging in local food and drink, pottery, trying their hands in handicraft making, etc. Alternative tourism forms namely farm tourism, gastronomic tourism, rural tourism and ecotourism provide ample avenues in this regard. A stay in a rustic village in an idyllic ambiance away from the hustle and bustle of city life is certainly deemed as dream visitation.

Tourism Projects and its Components

Innovation and Creativity

Tourism is undergoing a transition in consonance with the progressive projects and its enlivening components. Every destination wants to compete with its counterparts by establishing unique projects. Many newer and refreshing tourism projects have been unveiled recently like IMAX Theatres, Amphitheatres, Golf Courses, Underwater Aquarium, 5D Theaters, Theme parks, Shopping Malls, Go Karting centres, Snow Domes, Family Entertainment Centres, Oceanarium, Food courts, Spas, Health & Wellness Resorts, Sculpture Gardens, Eco resorts, View Towers, etc. That apart there are various faculties incepted in tourism products and destinations. The historical monuments have been made more interesting by introducing the sound and light shows. Similarly, the eco-destination has set-up interpretation centres that have hugely impacted eco-tourists. Excellent equipments are now given to adventure tourists for Snorkelling, Scuba-diving and other land, air and water-based activities. Moreover, shopping festivals and film festivals are primarily targeting the tourists.

Marketing and Branding Paradigms

This aspect is very significant in the present scenario of stiff competition in the field of tourism. Moreover, the challenge of offseason can pull back tourist' influx. Monsoon tourism as an ideal trend has put tourism in top gear by offsetting the challenges posed by lean season during the rainy period. The events organised during rainy season are being acknowledged as the offseason strategies in the realm of tourism marketing. Customer Relationship Management (CRM) and services marketing has advanced a great deal. Tourism promoters are coming up with excellent marking strategies for customer acquisition and customer retention. The offers, incentives, and privileges extended to frequent customer are fuelling the CRM initiatives.

Destination branding is now witnessing marvelous changes. The positioning and packages strategies have scaled new peaks. Dedicated advertising agencies are increasingly engaged in devising the marketing campaign. Good and effective public relation (PR) is creating a favorable image for world class tourism destinations. Promotional slogan signifies the tourism brand. For example, the 100% New Zealand campaign has become very popular. Destinations are highlighting their Unique Selling Proposition (USPs) as the hallmarks for wooing tourists. Events are also extensively used to woo the tourists. Some examples in their regard are International Yoga Festival, Olympics, and Rio Carnival. As part of branding obtaining various accreditations and recognition of tourism products and organisations is an ongoing exercise.

Safety and Security Paradigms

The repercussions of tourism are criticised strongly by some sections that comprise social and environmental activities, orthodox governments, crime prevention bureaus, historians, cultural, enthusiasts, etc. Tourism developers at various levels have set-up high standards for s maintaining safety maintaining safety and security in the places of tourist interest. CCTV cameras are installed in sensitive and dangerous locations. Tourism police is being deployed at various destinations to ensure the safety of tourists and also to guide them properly on the dos and don'ts. In beach destinations trained lifeguards are stationed to take care of tourists indulging in swimming and also to prevent hawking and theft. Authorised guides are given adequate training not only to disseminate the information pertaining to destinations pertaining to destination but also to give counsel on the interval codes and observations. Ambulances with extensive facilities are operating 24 hours to ensure the safety of tourists. Highways police is on the prowl to prevent atrocities on the major roads. Descriptive signages indicate the routes and distances and also provide information on the aspects to be taken into account by the tourists including the warnings.

Health and wellness centres are under the scanner for exploiting the tourists. The functioning of such centres including the ayurvedic massage centres are streamlined by giving accreditations and licenses only after fulfilling the prescribed criteria. They are constantly under vigil and even the slightest deviation results in withdrawal or suspension of licenses. For courts, restaurants, and cafes are places tourists' evince doubt on the hygienic and quality-related operations. Regular monitoring and evaluation has been initiated by the destination managers to ensure that quality food items are served to tourists in a hygienic environment. Some destinations regulate atrocities on tourists by legislative manures.

Demographic Paradigms

Designation are now thronged by women travellers some sole and some exclusive groups. Backpackers are increasing day by day. Professionals mostly are resorting to weekend travel. Honeymoon tourists are one prominent market segment currently. Long haul travel is now preferred even by families. Senior citizens and accessible tourists are now induced to travel owing to the facilities incepted in the tourist spots.

Political Paradigms

Countries in any particular region are forming alliances as tourist circuits to intensity tourism promotion. This will foster co-operative and complementary marketing strategies. Memorandum of Understanding (MOUs) and Memorandum of Agreements are being signed between countries to promote technology transfer, sharing of know-how expertise, and infrastructure and also facilitate movement of tourists.

The Promising Paradigms

- From E-Tourism there is a slant towards M-Tourism. Mobile technologies and applications are even more simplifying tourism processes, propositions and practices.

- Medicinal tourism is flourishing now as an organised phenomenon. The roles of stakeholders are being defined.

- Responsible tourism (RT) initiatives are receiving special grants and fiscal aids. Tourists are also supporting the RT ventures.

- GPS navigators have revolutionised the travel sector.

- Eye-Travel, devising specially made glasses for more effective enjoyment of tourism resources is getting acceptance.

- Foreign Travel Cards is a preferred way of carrying cyber cash. It is more secure too.

- Travel Insurance is becoming mandatory. Travel involves lot of risks which are uncertain and insurance schemes such as Overseas Travel Insurance (OTI) are beneficial to tourists. Indian Railways too has dished out such an offer for its passages.

- E-Visa (ETA) is a strong measure to reduce barriers in terms of travel formalities.

- Spectacular promotional strategies like road shows and travel marts are receiving worldwide attention.

- Tourism is now taking place in new terrains like Yacht Tourism in Croatia, Coral tourism in Cook Islands, sand dune tourism in Arurta Desert, Australia and timeshare vacations in the Caribbean.

- Recreation Vehicle (RVs) is becoming a standardised tourism practice.

- Corporate Social Responsibility is steadily becoming a philanthropic endeavour to reckon. As part of CSR initiatives tour operators are adopting destinations; multinational companies are sponsoring the upkeep of monuments.

- Governments are laying thrust on up-gradation of airports and introduction of more sectors.

- Pro-poor tourism is employed as vital instrument to increase fiscal benefits to the poor people.

- Community-based Tourism (CBT) is adopted by majority of the premier tourism destinations across the globe.

- Tourism is used extensively an incentive for heritage preservation.

- The role of NGO's and consultants in promoting and regulating travel is quite promising.

Table: Tourism's role in promotion of five key areas – UNWTO.

Sl. No.	Area
1.	Inclusive and sustainable economic growth.
2.	Social inclusiveness, employment and poverty reduction.
3.	Resource efficiency, environmental protection, and climate change.
4.	Cultural values, diversity, and heritage.
5.	Mutual understanding, peace, and security.

- UNWTO has incepted the International Network of Sustained Tourism Observatories (INSTO) to monitor and ensure sustainable practices of the tourism sector. It will focus on evidence-based decision-making and timely measurement and management of resources and activities, each indispensable factors of sustainable tourism development.

- The concept of sustainability is currently inextricably linked to tourism planning.

- There are development and promotion of SMEs in the tourism supply chains.

- Capacity building ventures are increasing. For example capacity development for youth and women in tourism.

- Environmental auditing and EIAs are now mandatory for tourism projects.

- A strong link is developing between cultural heritage and creative tourism. Through creative industries such as architecture, design, arts, technology, and science, cultural heritage is brought back to life. It also contributes to sustainable tourism development.

- Tourism is now strongly supporting human rights and democratic movements.

- Pro-poor tourism enhances quality of living indices.

- Tourism promotes environmentally responsible marketing.

- Green marketing is the in thing. Green Certification is offered. For example- the green palm.

- Scientific knowledge of visitor impacts is given more stress.

- Familiarisation tours (FAM Tours) are extensively extended for tour operators and travel journalists.

- Social Networking Media including Face book, Twitter, Linkedin, Instagram, etc. are making potential tourists more aware of the various feature and practices of tourism destinations.

- What else can excite the new age tourist:

  ○ Falling into the rapids in the Zambezi River.

  ○ Tracking Gorillas in Uganda.

  ○ Chilling in Antarctica.

  ○ Exploring Transnistria-an unknown destination.

- Safe and seamless travel is rated highly, crisis management task-forces are set up in major destination.

- Pink tourism and LGBT Tourism are approved by UNWTO.

- Travel Blogs are gaining prominence. There are scores of followers and many turn out to be prospective tourists.

- Heritage Walks and Self-guided tours are incepted around monuments and historical sites.

World Tourism

Tourism worldwide has undergone a sea change after liberalization and globalization. Tourism has become the prime source of revenue and foreign currency for most of the countries under UN WTO. Some countries have gone further in giving special status like industry, infrastructure, Key Resource Generation Area etc. to promote tourism related activities. Technological innovation in post liberalization era together with competition in market and other socio-political factors has brought about a drastic change in functioning of the travel and tourism industry.

Most international travel was undertaken for the purpose of leisure and recreation (52%), reaching a total of 395 million. This followed by business travel which accounted for some 16% of the total (120 million) and another 24% covered travel for other motives, such as visiting friends and relatives, religious purposes, and health treatments (185 million). Thus it is revealed leisure and recreation remain as the prime motive for holidaying. Further travelers prefers destinations which are safe to visit, easily accessible, hassle free in terms of services, facilities and infrastructure and clean from environmental point of view. Outbreak of epidemics like SARS, Dengue, Chikun Gunya etc on one hand increasing terrorism are two major reasons for tourists becoming very much safety conscious. The United States of America and others European countries holds top six positions in receipts from international tourism. Top European countries are Spain, France, Italy, Germany and the U.K. China the only one Asian country to be placed in top ten countries in receipts from tourism. World's top tourism destinations as per international tourist arrivals and their receipts from tourism are:

2004 Rank	Country	Arrivals (millions)		Percent change 2004/2003	Market share 2004	Earnings $ in billions	
		2003	2004			2003	2004
1.	France	75.0	75.1	0.1%	9.8%	36.6	40.8
2.	Spain	50.9	52.4	3.1	6.9	39.6	45.2
3.	United States	41.2	46.1	11.8	6.0	$64.3	$74.5
4.	China	33.0	41.8	26.7	5.5	17.4	25.7
5.	Italy	39.6	37.1	-6.4	4.9	31.2	35.7
6.	United Kingdom	24.7	27.8	12.3	3.6	22.7	27.3
7.	Mexico	18.7	20.6	10.5	2.7	-	-
8.	Turkey	13.3	16.8	26.2	2.2	13.2	15.9
9.	Germany	18.4	20.1	9.5	2.6	23.1	27.7
10.	Russian Federation	20.4	19.9	−2.7	2.6	-	-
11.	Austria	19.1	19.4	1.5	2.5	14.0	15.4
12.	Canada	17.5	19.2	9.2	2.5	-	-
13.	Malaysia	10.6	15.7	48.5	2.1	-	-
14.	Ukraine	12.5	15.6	24.9	2.0	-	-
15.	Poland	13.7	14.3	4.2	1.9	-	-
16.	Hong Kong (China)	9.7	13.7	41.1	1.8	-	-

17.	Greece	14.0	13.3	−5.0	1.7	-	-
18.	Hungary	—	12.2	—	—	-	-
19.	Thailand	10.1	11.7	16.4	1.5	-	-
20.	Portugal	11.7	11.6	−0.8	1.5	-	-
21.	Netherlands	9.2	9.6	5.1	1.3	-	-
22.	Saudi Arabia	7.3	8.6	17.0	1.1	-	-
23.	Macao (China)	6.3	8.3	31.9	1.1	-	-
24.	Croatia	7.4	7.9	6.8	1.0	-	-
25.	Egypt	5.7	7.8	35.7	1.0	-	-

Global Organizations

International Travel, Tourism and Hospitality organizations play a major role in advancing the development through the interests of the industry. They provide forums for discussions of common issues, lobby for industry causes, especially those which promote the industry's interests, and allow members from different parts of the world to network and learn from one another. Nearly all organizations are involved in doing research, providing marketing services and training schemes that are most cost effective when done jointly under an umbrella organization.

United Nation World Tourism Organization

The World Tourism Organization (UNWTO) is the United Nations agency responsible for the promotion of responsible, sustainable and universally accessible tourism. As the leading international organization in the field of tourism, UNWTO promotes tourism as a driver of economic growth, inclusive development and environmental sustainability and offers leadership and support to the sector in advancing knowledge and tourism policies worldwide. The UNWTO encourages the implementation of the Global Code of Ethics for Tourism, to maximize tourism's socio-economic contribution while minimizing its possible negative impacts, and is committed to promoting tourism as an instrument in achieving the Sustainable Development Goals (SDGs), geared towards reducing poverty and fostering sustainable development worldwide.

Functioning of UNWTO

The Secretariat is led by Secretary-General, who supervises about 110 full-time staff at UNWTO's Madrid Headquarters. The General Assembly is the principal gathering of the World Tourism Organization. It meets every two years to approve the budget and programme of work and to debate topics of vital importance to the tourism sector. The UNWTO has six regional commissions-Africa, the Americas, East Asia and the Pacific, Europe, the Middle East and South Asia. The Executive Council is UNWTO's governing board, responsible for ensuring that the Organization carries out its work and adheres to its budget. As host country of UNWTO´s Headquarters, Spain has a permanent seat on the Executive Council. Specialized committees of UNWTO Members advise on management and programme content. These include: the Programme and Budget Committee, the Committee on Statistics and the Tourism Satellite Account, the Committee on Tourism and Competitiveness, the Committee on Tourism and Sustainability, the World Committee on Tourism Ethics and the Committee for the Review of Applications for Affiliate Membership.

World Travel and Tourism Council

The World Travel & Tourism Council (WTTC) was formed in 1991 by a group of Travel & Tourism CEOs to study the sector's contribution to economies and job creation. WTTC is the only global body that brings together all major players in the Travel & Tourism sector (airlines, hotels, cruise, car rental, travel agencies, tour operators, GDS, and technology), enabling them to speak with One Voice to governments and international bodies. The WTTC uses empirical evidence to promote awareness of Travel & Tourism's economic contribution; to expand markets in harmony with the environment; and to reduce barriers to growth. It is important that WTTC has the broadest geographical representation and includes all aspects of the sector, including organizations that provide vital services to Travel & Tourism. With Chief Executives of over 140 of the world's leading Travel & Tourism companies as its members, the WTTC has a unique mandate and overview on all matters related to Travel & Tourism. The body advocates partnership between the public and private sectors, delivering results that match the needs of economies, local and regional authorities, and local communities, with those of business, based on: Governments recognizing Travel & Tourism as a top priority business balancing economics with people, culture and environment a shared pursuit of long-term growth and prosperity.

Research of WTTC

- Economic Research: It studies and publishes research on the sector's direct, indirect, and induced impact at a national, regional and global level on jobs, GDP, and trade and investment.

- Policy Research: A range of other research projects focused on issues impacting the Travel & Tourism sector, related to the three strategic priorities of Freedom to Travel, Policies for Growth, and Tourism for Tomorrow.

International Air Transport Association (IATA)

The International Air Transport Association (IATA) is the trade association for the world's airlines, representing some 265 airlines or 83% of total air traffic. IATA was founded in Havana, Cuba, on 19 April 1945. It is the prime platform for inter-airline cooperation in promoting safe, reliable, secure and economical air services for the benefit of the world's consumers. The international scheduled air transport industry is more than 100 times larger than it was in 1945. At its founding, IATA had 57 members from 31 nations, mostly in Europe and North America. Today it has some 265 members from 117 nations in every part of the globe. The IATA is the successor to the International Air Traffic Association, founded in The Hague in 1919-the year of the world's first international scheduled services. In April 2017, IATA celebrated 72 years of flying.

- IATA maintains an international perspective and provides a unique global voice on behalf of its members.

- With over 60 offices worldwide, IATA maintains relationships with governments and other industry stakeholders around the world, advocating on behalf of its members on key industry issues.

Vision and Mission of IATA

- Vision: To be the force for value creation and innovation driving a safe, secure and profitable air transport industry that sustainably connects and enriches our world.

- Mission: IATA's mission is to represent, lead, and serve the airline industry.

Representing the Airline Industry

The IATA improves understanding of the air transport industry among decision makers and increases awareness of the benefits that aviation brings to national and global economies. Advocating for the interests of airlines across the globe and stopping unreasonable rules and charges, holding regulators and governments to account, and striving for sensible regulation are four important activities. IATA helps airlines to operate safely, securely, efficiently, and economically under clearly defined rules. Professional support is provided to all industry stakeholders with a wide range of products and expert services.

IATA Members

From 57 founding members in 1945, IATA now represents some 265 airlines in over 117 countries. Carrying 83% of the world's air traffic, IATA members include the world's leading passenger and cargo airlines. IATA membership is open to airlines operating scheduled and non-scheduled air services that maintain an IATA Operational Safety Audit (IOSA) registration.

IATA Airline Membership Benefits

- Increasing Communication:

  ○ Participation in member conferences, committees and groups offers unprecedented access to a variety of airline and industry partners.

  ○ The IATA Annual General Meeting and World Air Transport Summit bring together representatives from leading international airlines.

  ○ IATA helps members gain influence with the travel agent community through the IATA Agency Program.

- Providing Key Commercial Services & Training:

  ○ IATA provides training in major fields such as passenger, cargo and safety.

  ○ IATA programs help to strengthen the capabilities of aviation industry professionals.

  ○ IATA members can receive discounts up to 30% on a number of IATA publications.

International Civil Aviation Organization (ICAO)

The International Civil Aviation Organization (ICAO) is a UN specialized agency, established by States in 1944 to manage the administration and governance of the Convention on International Civil Aviation (Chicago Convention). ICAO works with the Convention's 191 Member States and industry groups to reach consensus on international civil aviation Standards and Recommended Practices (SARPs) and policies in support of a safe, efficient, secure, economically sustainable and environmentally responsible civil aviation sector. These SARPs and policies are used by ICAO Member States to ensure that their local civil aviation operations and regulations conform to global norms, which in turn permits more than 100,000 daily flights in aviation's global network to operate safely and reliably in every region of the world.

In addition to its core work resolving consensus-driven international SARPs and policies among its Member States and industry, and among many other priorities and programmes, ICAO also coordinates assistance and capacity building for States in support of numerous aviation development objectives; produces global plans to coordinate multilateral strategic progress for safety and air navigation; monitors and reports on numerous air transport sector performance metrics; and audits States' civil aviation oversight capabilities in the areas of safety and security.

Vision and Mission of ICAO

- Vision: Achieve the sustainable growth of the global civil aviation system.

- Mission: To serve as the global forum of States for international civil aviation.

ICAO develops policies and Standards, undertakes compliance audits, performs studies and analyses, provides assistance and builds aviation capacity through many other activities and the cooperation of its Member States and stakeholders.

How ICAO Develops Standards?

The establishment and maintenance of international Standards and Recommended Practices (SARPs), as well as Procedures for Air Navigation (PANS), are fundamental tenets of the Convention on International Civil Aviation (Chicago Convention) and a core aspect of ICAO's mission and role. SARPs and PANS are critical to ICAO Member States and other stakeholders, given that they provide the fundamental basis for harmonized global aviation safety and efficiency in the air and on the ground, the worldwide standardization of functional and performance requirements of air navigation facilities and services, and the orderly development of air transport.

The development of SARPs and PANS follows a structured, transparent and multi-staged process – often known as the ICAO "amendment process" or "standards making process" – involving a number of technical and non-technical bodies which are either within the Organization or closely associated with ICAO. Typically, it takes approximately two years for an initial proposal for a new or improved Standard, Recommended Practice or procedure to be formally adopted or approved for inclusion in an Annex or PANS. Occasionally, this timescale can be expanded or compressed depending on the nature and priority of the proposal under consideration.

United Federations of Travel Agents Associations (UFTAA)

In the 1960s at the dawn of mass tourism, a few tourism professionals with great foresight saw the need of a global umbrella organization for the travel agency industry. By merger of Fédération internationale des agencies de voyages (FIAV) and Universal Organization of Travel Agents' Associations (UOTAA), the Universal Federation of Travel Agents 'Associations (UFTAA) was formed on

November 22nd 1966 in Rome. Its first President was an Italian, Giuliano Magnoni, later followed by 24 leading personalities from all parts of the world. The federation was later renamed United Federation of Travel Agents´ Associations, still known under the same well-established acronym UFTAA.

As a globally recognized body UFTAA is the longest established negotiating partner with the leading travel and tourism organizations in the world. Of a special importance is the close co-operation with IATA, representing the interest of individual travel agents and as a partner in the IATA-UFTAA Training Programme. Two other organizations with close relationship are the International Hotel and Restaurant Association (IH&RA) and the International Road Union (IRU). Also in areas which are more distanced from the daily worries of travel agents has UFTAA actively been and still is a spokes-person for the agent´s interest. Particularly worth mentioning are the World Tourism Organization (UNWTO) through its Affiliate Member Programme and at various occasions the World Health Organization (WHO), UNESCO, International Chamber of Commerce (ICC), International Forum of Travel and Tourism Advocates (IFTTA) and many more. The high-level contacts have enable UFTAA to assist national associations in their contacts with authorities and also to help individual agencies.

Through its history UFTAA has been a faithful, active and neutral advocate for all associations and independent travel agencies, irrespective of size and location. In the competitive environment of today a neutral umbrella organization like UFTAA is needed more than ever before to defend and promote the interests of travel agencies in their professional work on behalf and for the travelling consumers. UFTAA gets ready to celebrate its 50 years of successful contribution to the Travel & Tourism Industry. UFTAA offers to its membership the valuable opportunity to be involved with UFTAA's networking global platform in order to support good health of travel and tourism industry. UFTAA encourages associations; organizations; institutions and individual member agencies in Travel, Tourism and Hospitality industry to get connected via UFTAA.

Mission of UFTAA

UFTAA's mission is to be an international forum where matters affecting the world travel industry are addressed, representing and defending the interests of incoming and outgoing tour operators, travel and tourism agencies before the governmental bodies, suppliers and other entities of international scope. It also aims at strengthening its members' image and enhances the world travel and tourism industry and a sustainable tourism.

Functions of UFTAA

To comply with its mission, the Confederation develops the following functions:

- To unite and consolidate the Federations of Travel Agents' National Associations and to globally enhance the interests of their members.

- To represent the travel agents activities before various world-wide bodies, governmental authorities and suppliers.

- To work towards the adoption of measures that will ease travel for the consumer and to offer services to its member federation.

- To offer, as a voluntary mechanism, an arbitration service which assists in solving conflicts resulting from commercial relations for which amicable settlement cannot be reached.

- To organize a world congress of travel agents and other meetings necessary to the exchange and transmission of knowledge.

International and Hotel and Restaurant Association

January 1869, 45 Hotelmen met together in Koblenz at Hotel Trier, Germany and decide to create an Alliance between them under the name of All Hotelmen Alliance (AHA) to defend their interest, and they start to grow and get organized. Hotels were from different standards. April 1921 various Local European, African, Latin, American hotels association met together and decide to merge into a new international Association and it becomes International Hotels Alliance (IHA). November 1947, after the end of the second world war and the creation of the United Nations, Hoteliers from International Hotels Alliance met together with The European Aubergistes association and the Asian Innkeepers Association and decide to merge into a large International Association to defend the Private sector worldwide from Governments, Public sectors, Military etc. and create International Hotels Association (IHA) in London.

The IH&RA is the only international trade association exclusively devoted to promoting and defending the interests of the hotel and restaurant industry worldwide. It is a non-profit organization and is officially recognized by the United Nations. IH&RA monitors and lobbies all international agencies on behalf of the hospitality industry.

Who are its Members?

- International, National and Regional Hotel and/or Restaurant Associations.

- International and National Hotel and/or Restaurant Chains.

- Owners, Developers and Investors.

- Individual Hotels and Restaurants.

- Institutions of the Industry (hotel schools, educational centers, universities).

- Students/Independent Hoteliers and Restaurateurs.

What Does IH&RA do?

- Monitor issues that are raised by major international organizations involved in tourism.

- Represent the collective industry interests before policy makers.

- Lobby for better recognition of the hospitality industry worldwide.

- Lobby against damaging or costly attempts to regulate the industry.

- Create Global Councils around industry issues to debate positions & create solutions.

- Listen to its members to ensure that all issues are addressed.

- Plan a series of informative Council and Board meetings and an annual Congress.

- Provide support where requested to lend weight to local and regional issue.

Advocacy

As the only international trade association devoted to protecting the interests of the global hospitality industry, the International Hotel & Restaurant Association's role is to monitor, research, and where possible, pre-empt the passage of regulation and taxation at the international level when this is deemed to run contrary to industry interests. The representation work involved in doing this is termed "advocacy", i.e. advocating or defending the interests of a specific sector before public (and sometimes private) sector decision-making bodies.

Why to Undertake Advocacy?

The Travel & Tourism explosion of the last three decades has focused government attention on the hospitality sector as never before, bringing in its wake a surge of new regulation and taxation. Although laws are enacted at national level, they frequently have their genesis in international agencies (principally those of the United Nations) which have seen their role and mandate expand exponentially in recent decades. As a result advocacy (or lobbying) to promote and defend the hospitality industry's interests has been repeatedly stressed by Chain and National Association Chief Executives within IH&RA as the activity that constitutes their major expectation of membership. As a membership-driven association and the "voice of the industry", IH&RA must be vigilantly proactive in protecting the global interests of the hospitality industry it represents. To do this, it is essential to monitor research and even more importantly, forecast the issues of concern and importance to its members and the industry at large.

Pacific Asia Travel Association (PATA)

Founded in 1951, the Pacific Asia Travel Association (PATA) is a not-for profit association that is internationally acclaimed for acting as a catalyst for the responsible development of travel and tourism to, from and within the Asia Pacific region. The Association provides aligned advocacy, insightful research and innovative events to its member organizations, comprising 95 governments, state and city tourism bodies, 29 international airlines, airports and cruise lines, 63 educational institutions, and hundreds of travel industry companies in Asia Pacific and beyond. Since 1951 PATA has led from the front as the leading voice and authority on travel and tourism in the Asia Pacific region:

- In partnership with private and public sector members, PATA enhances the sustainable growth, value and quality of travel and tourism to-from-and-within, the region.

- PATA's Strategic Intelligence Centre (SIC) offers unrivalled data and insights including Asia Pacific inbound and outbound statistics, analyses and forecasts as well as in-depth reports on strategic tourism markets.

- PATA's Strategic Intelligence Centre (SIC) offers unrivalled data and insights including Asia Pacific inbound and outbound statistics, analyses and forecasts as well as in-depth reports on strategic tourism markets.

- The PATA Foundation contributes to the sustainable and responsible development of travel and tourism in Asia Pacific through the protection of the environment, the conservation of heritage and support for education.

PATA Chapters

PATA Chapters are established throughout the world to assist in the fulfilment of the objectives of the Association. They are local community organizations of travel industry professionals who join in a co-operative Endeavour – within the framework of PATA – to develop travel and tourism to, from and within the Asia Pacific area. There are 40 PATA Chapters around the world that make valuable contributions to local travel industry communities.

Tourist Attractions in USA

Grand Canyon

This incredible natural attraction is one of the most visited places in the United States. Carved out by the Colorado River, the Grand Canyon cuts deep into the landscape, creating dramatic cliff walls and ledges. Visitors standing on the rim of the canyon can see down to the canyon floor a mile below, and look out over the ridges and cliffs that run as far as the eye can see. The South Rim, about 4.5 hours by car from Las Vegas, is the most visited section of Grand Canyon National Park. This is where you'll find a large visitor center, regular bus service along the Rim in the high season, and a walkway that runs along the canyon with numerous viewing points and platforms. Several wonderful hikes, including the Bright Angel Trail, leave from here. The Skywalk, a glass bridge leading out over the edge of the Grand Canyon is another popular attraction. It is located at Eagle Point, on the West Rim. This area is about a four-hour drive from the South Rim, but usually less than a 2.5-hour drive from Las Vegas. If you are planning a day trip from Las Vegas, this area is a good option. The North Rim, which also has lookout areas, provides a different perspective. This section of the park is less visited and has limited access from November to May due to snow and winter conditions.

Niagara Falls

Situated along the Canada-US border, Niagara Falls is one of the most famous waterfalls in the world. The water from Lake Erie flows into Lake Ontario over these massive waterfalls, known for the great quantity of water that is constantly tumbling over the vertical drop. Niagara Falls is actually a set of three falls: It consists of the largest section, known as Horseshoe Falls, with a drop of 187 feet; a second section on the American side of the river, known as the American Falls, with a drop of 89 feet; and a much thinner section located next to the American Falls, known as Bridal Veil Falls, with a drop of 78 feet. Views are good on both sides of the river, but the Canadian side gives a very different perspective and is worth a visit if you don't mind crossing the border into Canada.

View of American Falls in winter from the Canadian side.

Summer is the most popular time to visit Niagara Falls, when the weather is warm, gardens are in bloom, and wandering around is pleasant. Winter provides a unique opportunity to see the snow-covered shores and ice-covered railings, street signs, and trees. It's truly a winter wonderland. On clear days, the plume of mist rising from Niagara Falls can be seen from as far away as the CN Tower in downtown Toronto, Canada, on the opposite shore of Lake Ontario.

Statue of Liberty

A universal symbol of freedom, the Statue of Liberty is America's most familiar icon and the largest statue in the world. Standing proudly in New York Harbor, visitors can admire the statue from various points around the city, particularly Battery Park, or take a ferry right to the statue. For people who plan to go out to the statue, options include grounds tickets, pedestal tickets, or crown tickets, which allow different levels of access to the site. One of the best options is to take a tour and see both the Statue of Liberty and Ellis Island. A popular tour is the Skip-Line Statue of Liberty & Ellis Island Tour + Pedestal Ticket Upgrade, which will remove all the complexity of visiting this sight.

White House

The White House is the official residence of the President of the United States, and should be on the top of your list of things to see in Washington. This historic structure has been the home of every president except George Washington. Lafayette Park is on the north side of the White House; beyond is a pedestrian-only zone, full of interesting characters, and an excellent spot to get a great photo. It was originally built by James Hoban in 1792 and, after being burned down by British forces in 1814, was rebuilt in 1818. Tours of the White House are free, but reservations must be made a minimum of three weeks in advance. Strict security rules are always in effect.

Walt Disney World Resort

This mega amusement park in Orlando is the top family attraction in America, and has been catering to both young and old for decades. Opened in 1971, Walt Disney World has managed to maintain its relevance and its allure for children and even many adults throughout the years. Walt Disney World Resort encompasses not only the various theme parks, it also includes water parks, Downtown Disney with shopping and theaters, and much more, from fine dining to golf. This is a place where you can spend a day or a week. If you feel the need for a bit of sand and surf, the beaches of Florida's Atlantic coast are only an hour away.

Waikiki

Home to the most popular beach in the Hawaiian Islands and possibly the most famous beach in the Pacific, Waikiki has been a tourist destination for over a century. Today this area is a cross between tropical paradise and modern city. Relaxing on this beautiful stretch of sand with palm trees blowing in the wind will certainly let you know you are in the tropics, but the high-rise buildings and busy street in behind are a reminder that you are not far from civilization. Shopping, dining, surfing, and sunbathing are all part of what makes this small section of Oahu so popular with tourists of all ages from all parts of the world.

Las Vegas Strip

Walking along the Las Vegas Strip, the main street leading through the city past the mega resorts, is like strolling through an amusement park for adults. Recreations of the New York skyline, the Eiffel Tower, the canals of Venice, and many more foreign sites line this famous street. Beginning at one end with the Luxor Hotel, designed in a pyramid shape, a walk down the street will reveal an erupting volcano and dancing fountains, while inside the resorts are all kinds of oddities and entertainment. Many of the best things to see and do in Las Vegas are sights that can be seen for free.

One of the main attractions in Las Vegas is the constant lineup of shows. World-famous singers looking to settle down turn to Las Vegas as a home base, where they perform regularly. Unique performing groups from magic to comedy and acrobatics can also be found here nightly. When you've had enough of the nightlife and city lights, you can still explore the nearby attractions on a day trip from Las Vegas. See nearby Death Valley National Park, Hoover Dam, or Valley of Fire State Park. Explore the desert on hiking trails around Las Vegas, some of which are just minutes from downtown.

Yosemite National Park

One of America's most loved parks, Yosemite National Park is one of the best places to visit in California, particularly for nature lovers. Famous sights, like the incredible granite domes of El Capitan and Half Dome, have to be seen in person to fully appreciate their grandeur. The massive waterfalls that tumble off sheer cliffs from mountain snowfall or sudden summer rainstorms are another of the park's highlights. Yosemite National Park is full of activity-based things to do that include hiking, climbing, walking, and horseback riding. Hiking trails lead to some of the most scenic areas and are a good way to escape the crowds at lookouts.

View of Half Dome from Glacier Point.

For those less inclined to be physically active, the sheer natural beauty of Yosemite can be enjoyed from a picnic table over a leisurely home-packed lunch. You can also see the highlights on a driving tour through the park. Accommodation is limited in the park to several lodges and a number of very nice campgrounds. Outside the gates, more options are available.

Golden Gate Bridge

Arching across San Francisco Bay, joining San Francisco and Marin County, the Golden Gate Bridge has been a California icon since it was built in the 1930s. Contrasting with the blue water, the bridge's orangish-red color is an aesthetic accent that brings a unique quality to the city. It also has a unique presence when it's shrouded in fog with just the peaks of the main towers projecting through the low-lying cloud. The bridge is approximately two miles long and part of Hwy 101 or SR. If the day is clear, one of the best viewing spots is on Conzelman Road, located in Golden Gate National Recreation Area.

Times Square

Bustling Times Square, famous for its flashing billboards, New Year's Eve count down, and constant throngs of people, lies at the heart of Midtown Manhattan. This intersection, in normal times, is really about the energy one feels when standing on the corner as taxi cabs rush by and lights flash overhead, rather than any individual site on the square. While it is an interesting place to visit during the day, it is probably best seen at night to experience the full impact.

Freedom Trail in Boston

Boston's Freedom Trail is a 2.5-mile walking route that leads past some of the city's most important historical attractions. A line of red bricks, inlaid in the sidewalk marks the route, making it an easy way for tourists to find their way around. Information on the trail and the sites can be found at the Visitors Center in the Boston Common, which is a good place to start your tour. Sites along the Freedom Trail include the State House, Old State House, the Old Granary Burying Ground, Old City Hall, Faneuil Hall, Paul Revere House, and many more.

Yellowstone National Park

Yellowstone National Park is home to a huge ancient volcano, which has resulted in a dramatic landscape and awesome natural phenomena. Geysers and hot springs, along with incredible waterfalls along the Yellowstone River are just some of the attractions drawing in huge numbers of tourists each year. The park, the oldest national park in the USA, is also home to all kinds of wildlife, with free-roaming bison, bighorn sheep, antelope, black bears, and grizzly bears. The park is also a wonderful place to camp, with a total of 12 campgrounds containing 2,000 sites.

San Antonio River Walk

San Antonio's River Walk is a beautiful location and a great place to spend some time, whether you are looking for a place to wander, enjoy a meal, or look for souvenirs. Stretching along the San Antonio River in the heart of the city, this pedestrian area is lined with restaurants and outdoor dining areas, with everything from casual to fine cuisine. Small boats meander along the river and scenic arching bridges complete the tranquil scene. Large old trees drape over the river and walkway providing shade. The River Walk also features a variety of entertainment, with occasional live music and seasonal events.

Kennedy Space Center

Shuttle Atlantis at Cape Canaveral, Kennedy Space Center.

For those who have ever dreamed about what it would be like to blast off into space, a trip to the Kennedy Space Center is a must-do. The spacecraft of NASA along with the history of space exploration make for an entertaining and educational experience. This is a popular attraction with all ages and one of the top things to do in Florida. You may think that your visit will be a quick one; see a few spaceships and then head on your way. However, many people are surprised when they become fully engrossed in their visit and end up spending most of the day at the center. Things to see include the rocket garden, the real Space Shuttle Atlantis, the Heroes and Legends exhibit, and the Journey to Mars exposition, along with many others.

St. Louis Arch

This famous "Gateway to the West" in St. Louis is both symbolic and eye-catching. Rising above the city, gleaming in the midday sun and illuminated at night, the arch can be seen from miles away on the otherwise flat surroundings. It was built in the early 1960s and stands in Jefferson National Expansion Memorial Park. Elevators offer transportation to the top of the arch where visitors are treated to great views out over the city and surroundings.

Glacier National Park and the Going-to-the-Sun Road

Montana's Glacier National Park offers some of the most beautiful mountain scenery in the United States. Mountains, lakes, glaciers, valleys, and waterfalls combine to form a spectacular alpine landscape. One of the best ways to truly appreciate the terrain is from the famous Going-to-the-Sun Road. This narrow road, hugging the mountain side as it winds its way up and over the 7,747-foot Logan pass, opened in 1932.

Due to the elevation and climate, the road is only open during the summer months. The sights along this road are superlative, and you'll likely find yourself stopping at handy pull-outs to soak it all up. Glacier National Park also has some unique historic lodges, including the East Lodge, with its huge timbered interior. The park is also a top hiking destination in the state; hiking trails leading to wonderful alpine vistas greet those willing to put in a bit of effort. The park is relatively isolated, so most people plan for a few days for their visit. Accommodation is available in the historic lodges and hotels in West Glacier, and if you feel like camping, 13 campgrounds are available.

Tourist Attractions in Europe

Eiffel Tower, France

The Eiffel Tower is one of France's most famous sights. Sitting in the heart of the Champ de Mars in Paris, the wrought-iron tower was originally built to serve as the entrance to the 1889 World's Fair. Engineer Gustave Eiffel received much criticism for his design, with people calling it a monstrosity and "an impossible task"-at the time of construction, the 324-meter-tall tower (equivalent to an 81-story building) was the tallest structure in the world. The tower's three levels house restaurants and cafés, gift shops, exhibits about the history of the tower, the original restored office of Gustav Eiffel, and several observation decks. The first two levels of the Eiffel Tower can be accessed via a staircase or a lift, but the third level is only accessible to visitors via an elevator. At night, the entire tower is illuminated with golden lights.

Colosseum, Italy

Rome's Flavian Amphitheater, better known as the Colosseum, remains one of the most iconic symbols of Imperial Rome and is one of the most visited tourist sites in Italy. It was built in AD 70-80 using travertine limestone and volcanic rock. At the time of its construction, and for a long time after, it was the world's largest amphitheater and held up to 80,000 spectators. With an outer wall height of 48 meters and a base area of 24,000 square meters, the Colosseum is an imposing structure. At the peak of its glory, it contained a velarium (a retractable awning to protect spectators during bad weather) and a thick wooden floor covered by sand. Under this floor, an underground labyrinth of tunnels held animals and gladiators before the fights. Although most famous as the site for gladiator fights, the Colosseum was also home to many other shows and spectacles, including re-enactments of famous battles and executions. More impressively, it was also the home of mock sea battles, when the arena was filled and drained rapidly with water so vessels could float during the shows. Over the following centuries, the amphitheater served as a fortress, a shrine, and makeshift housing. It was also heavily looted by stone robbers.

Acropolis of Athens, Greece

Watching over Athens from atop a rocky outcrop, the ancient citadel is one of Greece's most famous tourist destinations. The Acropolis' most famous buildings were all constructed in the fifth century BC under the watchful eye of statesman and general Pericles. The heart of the Acropolis is the Parthenon, a temple built to thank the gods for the victory over Persian invaders (though it also served as the city treasury for a time). Other prominent buildings include the gateway Propylaea (which serves as the entrance to Acropolis), the Erechtheion Temple (dedicated to Athena and Poseidon), and the tiny but beautiful Temple of Athena Nike. Many of the buildings in the Acropolis were damaged during the Morean War in 1687. Most of the ancient artifacts found within the temples that survived the damage have been since moved to the Acropolis Museum nearby.

The Acropolis of Athens with the Parthenon Temple on top of the hill at sunset.

Stonehenge, England

The prehistoric monument of Stonehenge is one of the most famous landmarks in the UK. Built between 3000 BC and 2000 BC, Stonehenge sits in an area of England known for its many burial mounds. A massive ring of four-meter-tall sandstones with an inner horseshoe-shaped stone circle, the breathtaking Stonehenge and its surroundings are a UNESCO World Heritage Site. The purpose of Stonehenge remains a mystery. Archaeologists believe it could have been a burial ground dating back to 3000 BC. It could have also served as a Neolithic calendar (as the layout of the stones is set to mark sun movements), a religious place, or a scientific observatory. The stones, which weigh an estimated 25 tons each, were transported at least 19 kilometers to their current location.

Louvre Museum, France

View over the Seine River to the Louvre Museum.

The world's largest art museum, and the most visited, sits right on the bank of the Seine River. The original 13th-century Louvre Palace that once stood here was expanded and rebuilt over the centuries, resulting in the massive almost 73,000-square-meter building you see today. Outside, the museum's glass and metal pyramid has become a modern symbol of the Louvre. It measures 34 meters on each side and 21.6 meters tall and is now used as the main entrance to the museum. Of the Louvre's stunning collection of 380,000 objects, about 35,000 are on permanent display. These include not only paintings but also drawings, sculptures and archaeological items. In addition to Leonardo da Vinci's La *Mona Lisa* and the *Venus of Milo*, the museum is also home to the eight-feet-tall *Winged Victory of Samothrace* sculpture and the magnificent six- by nine-meter *Coronation of Napoleon* painting.

Prague Castle, Czech Republic

Almost two million people visit Prague Castle every year, making it one of the most popular attractions in the Czech Republic. Recognized by the *Guinness Book of Records* as the largest castle complex in the world, Prague Castle is a stunning combination of Gothic and Romanesque architectural styles. While the castle itself dates back to the 9th century, some of the other structures inside the 70,000 square meters of the complex were built centuries later. Some of the most stunning buildings within the Prague Castle complex include St. Vitus Cathedral, St. George's Basilica, and the 16th-century Golden Lane. This lane of small medieval houses once housed the palace guards and goldsmiths, and centuries later, writer Franz Kafka and Nobel prize winner Jaroslav Seifert. The Castle grounds are also home to the office of the President of the Czech Republic and to a secret room that holds the Bohemian Crown Jewels. The National Gallery has a small museum branch within the castle, and there's also a toy museum focused on wooden toys.

Berlin's Brandenburg Gate, Germany

Built by orders of Prussian king Frederick William II in the 18th century, the Brandenburg Gate has become the symbol of Berlin. A massive 26 meters high and over 65 meters long, the gate is crowned by a quadriga or chariot drawn by four horses. The gate owes its name to the town of Brandenburg an der Havel as it sits where the road connecting Berlin and Brandenburg town starts. Over the past two centuries, the gate has had center stage in many of the historical events that shaped Germany. It was used as a Nazi symbol and survived WWII despite heavy damage from explosions and shootings. Years later, the gate became the unofficial border between East and West Berlin until the construction of the Berlin Wall. And when the Wall fell in 1989, 100,000 people gathered at the Gate to celebrate.

Venice Canals, Italy

Italy's magical "floating city" has a wealth of beauty, romance, and history to please every visitor. Over 150 canals run through Venice, connecting 118 tiny islands via some 400 bridges and a number of walkways. The magic of Venice doesn't end in the water. Charming alleyways and passageways, hidden courtyards, and stunning examples of Gothic and Renaissance architecture line the banks of the canals. Much of the beautiful architecture can be better appreciated from the water as you travel under bridges and around corners of the Grand Canal on a gondola sightseeing tour or a *vaporetto*, Venice's water bus. Venice's Grand Canal, the main water-traffic corridor of the city, is flanked by many palazzos and churches, including the 15th-century Venetian Gothic Palazzi Barbaro and the Rococo-style Ca' Rezzonico Palace, with a facade completely covered in white marble.

Gondolas on the Grand Canal in Venice.

The Matterhorn, Switzerland

At 4,478 meters high, the Matterhorn is one of the highest summits in Europe. The stunning mountain sits right over the Swiss town of Zermatt, on the border between Switzerland and Italy. A popular hiking destination in the Alps, the Matterhorn is unique because it's a pyramid-shaped mountain that can be climbed on all four sides. For the non-climbers out there, it's also possible to complete a 10-day trek around the mountain. This is considered one of the most beautiful hikes in the Alps, crossing glacial lakes, Alpine forests, and flowering meadows. The area around the Matterhorn and Zermatt attracts skiers and snowboarders during winter, with the Zermatt and Breuil-Cervinia resort offering ski lifts high up the Theodul Pass. There's also the Matterhorn Museum, chronicling the fascinating history of Alpinism, and a chance for an up-close-and-personal view of the snow-covered peaks via a helicopter tour.

Amsterdam's Canals, The Netherlands

Aptly known as "the Venice of the North," Amsterdam is fueled by the many hundreds of kilometers of grachten (canals) that cut through the city. The city has three main canals-Herengracht, Prinsengracht, and Keizersgracht-and over 1,500 bridges connecting the islands. The Prinsengracht canal is probably the most famous canal in the Netherlands, as a number of notable buildings are situated along its shores. These include Anne Frank's house; Amsterdam's tallest church, Westerkerk; the 17th-century Deutzen Hofje house, and a number of other impressive historical constructions. The Singelgracht canal, though not one of the largest, is well known for bordering the very upscale Jordaan neighborhood, where Rembrandt spent the last few years of his life. Another famous canal, the Brouwersgrach, was once used by ships returning with spices from Asia. Today, it's a favorite canal to park houseboats, and it's flanked by warehouses that have been converted into chic, expensive apartments and lofts.

The Vienna Hofburg, Austria

The House of Habsburg originally had the palace built in the 13th century to house one of the most influential royal families in Europe. Once an imperial palace, home to kings and emperor of the Holy Roman Empire, the Hofburg is now the official residence of Austria's president. The palace was expanded over the centuries with the addition of royal residences, a chapel, the Hofreitschule (Spanish Riding School), the Court Library, and the imperial court theater (which is the National Theater of Austria in Vienna today). The Vienna Hofburg is massive at 240,000 square meters divided into 18 wings-and much of it is open to the public. The sprawling complex also houses 19 courtyards and over 2,500 rooms, many of which are still occupied by the people who work and live here.

Hofburg Imperial Palace at night.

The Alhambra and Generalife Gardens, Spain

The Alhambra in Granada.

The palace and fortress complex Alhambra-which literally translates to "the red one"-was originally built in 889 CE, though it didn't achieve its current look and massive 142,000-square-meter size until the mid-13th century. The fortress was neglected and vandalized over the centuries, and though it was also partially restored, it wasn't always done with great care. Still, the Alhambra stands as one of the most magnificent displays of Muslim art and architecture in Spain. Built using a mix of red clay, layered brick, and stone, the natural earth red color of the Alhambra is its most stunning feature. Inside, intricate stucco work covers the many Moorish palaces, royal baths, and fortified towers. The adjoining Palacio de Generalife, with its terraced Persian gardens is also worth a visit-not only for its magnificent views of the Alhambra but also because the summer palace, with its many colonnades and pavilions, is a beauty in itself.

Mosteiro dos Jerónimos, Portugal

The Jerónimos Monastery

The Jerónimos Monastery is one of Portugal's most recognizable constructions. Built in Lisbon near the Tagus River, the UNESCO World Heritage Site monastery is a beautiful example of Manueline or Portuguese late Gothic style. Manueline architecture is notable for its ornate details, with lots of semicircular arches in doors and windows, and for incorporating maritime elements, such as shells and pearls, into the design. Construction on the monastery began in 1501 and took just over 100 years. The original structure is built of gold-colored limestone, but different kings and architects over the years added their touch via imposing murals, gold-tiled ceilings, and lots of detailed woodwork. The main entrances to the monastery are through the gates of the Church of Santa Maria, including a 32-meter, two-story-high side entrance and the smaller southern doorway, which opens directly to the main altar. The monastery itself has large grounds and gardens, where fountains, 16th-century buildings, and pavilions offer plenty to explore and discover.

Alternative vs. Mass Tourism

The development of mass tourism is parallel to the developments in technology and the changes in economy and society. The factors namely, technology, production and management related changes in the progress may be grouped as Developmental factors which cleared the way for mass tourism. Mass tourism began after the World War II as the result of industrial revolution, the economic development of society, introduction of paid holidays, rising standards of living, a rapid improvement in the means of transportation especially in air travel, and government initiatives in promoting tourism. There were other factors which also caused an increase in tourism. This resulted in the mass tourism phenomenon which can be grouped as Constitutional factors. A highlight of the factors that led to the emergence of mass tourism is given in the diagram.

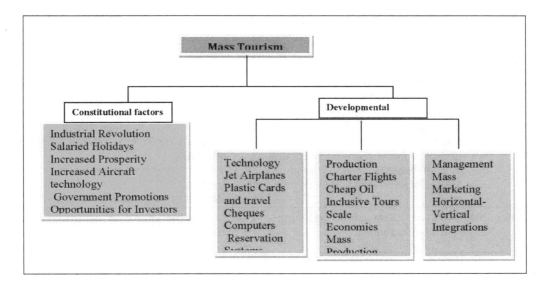

Characteristics of Mass Tourism

Mass tourism, as a form of tourism based on the volume of tourist and their travel behaviour has a number of characteristics:

- Mass tourism is confined to a limited number of tourist sites or attractions.

- It is characterised by concentration of large number of tourist in a site or destination.

- Involves movement of large number of tourists with less surplus income. Hence demand is highly price elastic.

- There arises the need for large number of infrastructure and superstructure for the requirements of mass tourists.

- Mass tourism is highly season oriented business.

- The main focus of mass tourism is to generate business- It is sale oriented, not customer oriented.

- Mass tourism creates intense pressure on the natural as well as cultural environment due to the assemblage of large numbers of tourists in small area which is certainly a major threat to environmental balance.

Impact of Mass Tourism

Like any other business, consumers are the mainstay of tourism also. In the early years of tourism business, the focus was selling as much as possible. In brief, it was a sale oriented approach rather than consumer oriented. There are a number of advantages for an area due to mass tourism. But at the same time, notable challenges are also resulted while promoting mass tourism. The following table gives a list of positive and negative impacts of mass tourism.

	Positive	Negative
Economic Impacts	• Brings money to the local economy. • Creates job for local community. • Supports the industries supplying products to tourism.	• Most of the benefits are kept aside by the industry itself.
Social Impacts	• Young people are likely to stay in own place due to more job opportunities. • Improved infrastructure and communication benefits for local community. • Means for livelihood and empowerment.	• Job security and career growth are limited. • Payment is not very attractive for people to stick on. • Traffic congestion causes inconvenience for natives. • Behaviours of some tourists can offend locals.
Environmental Impacts	Income from tourism can be used for protecting the environment.	• Mass activities in destination may lead to pollution (Environmental, visual, water and air). • Destruction to natural habitat. • Global warming due to the emission of CO_2.

Emergence of Alternative Tourism

It was in early 1980's that the 'Alternative Tourism' as a generic term was widely discussed across the tourism community when the negative impacts of conventional Mass tourism were visible on a larger scale. Hence, alternative tourism can be considered as an early engagement with the idea of Sustainability. The widely discussed negative impacts of conventional mass tourism paved the way for looking for "Alternatives" which in turn lead to new forms of tourism which has less impact on the environmental and socio-cultural dimensions. Reducing or avoiding the impacts was the first concern which can be resolved by better planning and more careful development within the prevailing tourism model. Government and Private sectors played a good role here. Finding the alternatives or creating new forms of tourism which has less negative impacts was the second concern, and NGOs and Small private sectors found to be the key actors here. Rejecting tourism with wider negative effects was the third visible response in developing countries or in rural areas. Sociologists, anthropologists, community developers, NGOs have adopted this anti tourism stance.

Re-modelling the existing tourism frame work was mandatory and working on development of tourism in destinations where more benefit goes to the local community rather than pleasing tourists became evident in many areas. Many tourism development areas undertook better planning within the conventional tourism framework and introduced alternate forms of tourism. Three influential drives which made the emergence of Alternative tourism possible include:

- The recognition of the negative impacts of conventional tourism on environment and society.

- An appearance of new development ideology which was against growth oriented development.

- Humanitarian considerations and recognition of rights of local people to be benefited out of the changes in their region.

The Concept and Definitions of Alternative Tourism

The broadness of alternative tourism is surprisingly high that there is no single or absolute definition, although several good attempts were made and many writers have listed out criteria with which it can be accessed. Alternative tourism is a form of tourism which has evolved in order to reduce the negative impacts of conventional mass tourism at ecologically, socio-culturally sensitive destinations. During the era of adaptation "ecotourism" was originally conceived as an environmentally based form of alternative tourism. Alternative tourism fosters as a more appropriate small-scale, community-controlled option to mass tourism in environmentally or socio-culturally sensitive destinations. The meaning of alternative tourism is better understood with the following definitions:

- Alternative Tourism is a process which promotes a just form of travel between members of different communities. It seeks to achieve mutual understanding, solidarity and equality amongst participants.

- Forms of tourism that is consistent with natural, social, and community values and which allow both hosts and guests to enjoy positive and worthwhile interaction and share experiences.

- Term applied to commercial tourism activity which is generally small scale, and is concerned with minimizing the impacts on, or in some way enhancing, the social, cultural and environmental characteristics of an area. With alternative tourism the emphasis for participants falls upon interpretation and understanding as opposed to merely sightseeing.

- A generic term that encompasses a whole range of tourism strategies (e.g. 'appropriate', 'eco', 'soft', 'responsible', 'people to people', 'controlled', 'small scale', 'cottage', and 'green' tourism) all of which purport to offer a more benign alternative to conventional mass tourism in certain types of destinations.

Defining Alternative tourism contains lot of ambiguity that he adopted six different fields and put forward the guide lines that may be applied to it. They are:

- The Tourist as an Individual: Self Motivated, which may include active tourism (trekking rambling), exploring, voluntary services and other self-sacrificing work.

- The Practitioners: They do not want to be called as clients or consumers and includes drifters, backpackers and long distance travellers.

- The Journey's Destinations: This may be 'virgin' unexplored locations often compliment with local culture and involvement of local community.

- The Type of Accommodation: Should be of supplementary accommodations like small local family hotels, camping, village inns, private rented house, paying guests, dormitories, bread and breakfasts, youth hostels.

- Travel Organizers and Partners: Lower level travel organizations (NGOs, individual travel set ups especially of non-lucrative type.

- The Mode of Insertion in the Local Community: This involves the participation of local community in the development of tourism and improves the guest host relationship. Prominence of local system in overseeing the tourism is given importance.

Nature and Characteristics of Alternative Tourism

Unlike conventional mass tourism, Alternative tourism offers a way to prevent the impacts and reform tourism to more benign forms. Rather than mere enjoyment and economic concern it has started focusing on educative aspects, community based ventures, fostering tourism more driven to responsible tourism and managing the tourist impact to benefit the society and environment they interact with. More or less the forms of alternative tourism are found to be giving relevant importance for enriching relation between the guest and host. It takes into account the dignity and rights of both the parties as well as respect to religious, social and physical environment. This nature of Alternative tourism gives it dominance over the then prevailing Conventional mass tourism. The following are the features or characteristics of alternative tourism:

- Tourism which attempts to minimize its impact upon the environment is ecologically sound and avoids negative impact.

- Active promotion of development which complements the local attributes.

- Aimed at preservation, protection and enhancement of quality of resources at a destination.

- Development of infrastructure, economic growth and improvement of local conditions not exceeding carrying capacity of the natural environment or the limits of social environment.

- Emphasis on not only ecological sustainability but also on cultural sustainability which does not damage the culture of host community through education and organised encounters.

- Respect to religious, cultural, social and physical environment.

- Providing viable option to exploitation and destruction to elements of mass tourism.

- Built on dialogue with local people who ought to be aware of its effects.

- Established on sound environmental principles, sensitive to local culture and religious tradition.

- Means of giving the poor a reasonable and more equal share in gains.

- Tailored to match the capacity of the local area measure on aesthetic and ecological terms.

- Cater to the needs of changing paradigm of interests of tourists.

Mass Tourism vs. Alternative Tourism

From mass tourism to alternative tourism, four major platforms were crossed till new age tourism-Advocacy Platform, Adaptancy platform and Knowledge based platform. The differences in the approach towards tourism during the different periods are given in the table.

Sl. No	Platforms	Approach
1.	Advocacy Platform	• 1950s-1960s. • The golden period of mass tourism. • This period viewed tourism only as an activity which brings economy to the country. • This view has encouraged mass tourism.
2.	Cautionary Platform	• During the 1970s. • The advocacy platform was challenged. • Regarded mass tourism in a critical light and started questioning the validity of benefits.
3.	Adaptancy Platform	• 1980s. • Seeks new strategies for tourism. • Introduced the concept of 'alternative tourism' as an alternative to mass tourism.
4.	Knowledge	• From 1990s onwards.
5.	Based Platform	• Intended to contribute to the holistic treatment of tourism.

Alternative tourism is an alternate to mass tourism. Even if both are different based on common characteristics, comparison is possible. Tourism researchers have given a comprehensive comparison between Alternative Tourism and Mass Tourism.

Characteristics	Mass Tourism	Alternative Tourism
Markets		
Segments	Psychocentric-Mid-centric.	Allocentric-Mid-centric.
Volume & mode	High, Package tour.	Low, Individual arrangements.
Seasonality	Distinct – High & Low season.	No distinct seasonality.
Origin	A few dominant markets.	No dominant market.
Attractions		
Emphasis	Highly commercialized.	Moderately commercialized.
Character	Generic, 'contrived'.	Area specific, 'authentic'.
Orientation	Tourists only or mainly.	Tourists & locals.
Accommodation		
Size	Large-scale.	Small-scale.
Spatial Pattern	Concentrated in 'tourist areas'.	Dispersed throughout area.
Density	High density.	Low density.
Architecture	'International' style; obtrusive, non-sympathetic.	Vernacular style, un- obtrusive, complementary.
Ownership	Non-local, large corporations.	Local, small businesses.
Economic Status		
Role of tourism	Dominates local economy.	Complements existing activity.
Linkages	Mainly external.	Mainly internal.
Leakages	Extensive	Minimal
Multiplier effect	Low	High
Regulation		
Control	Non-local private sector.	Local 'community'.

Amount	Minimal; to facilitate private sector.	Extensive; to minimise local negative impacts.
Ideology	Free market forces.	Public intervention.
Emphasis	Economic growth, profits; sector-specific.	Community stability & well- being; integrated, holistic.
Timeframe	Short-term.	Long-term.

Among the market based characteristics, mass tourism focuses on Psycho centric tourists in large volume who visit destination as part of a package tour. Mass tourism is a highly seasonal affair, usually generates in high volume during peak and mid-season and low during off season. Whereas, Alternative tourism is centred on Allocentric markets, who are independent tourists doing travel arrangements themselves or travel as part of a customised itinerary. There is no seasonal choice for alternative tourists and they do not belong to any specific market segments.

Mass tourism attractions are meant for commercial purpose, intended mainly for tourists and marketed to the generic market. For e.g. Theme parks. Alternative attractions are authentic natural or cultural products or services, which are not meant for tourism. The specialised tourists get a chance to experience it in a responsible way. For e.g. Indigenous culture of an area. The accommodation facilities in mass tourism centres are mass constructions concentrated in the centre of the destination, constructed in international quality and standards owned by international chains or groups. Alternative accommodations are small scale establishments, usually locally owned like home stays spread across the region, which are sustainable in nature. Mass tourism supports the destination in general, but the benefits goes out of the local community as the leakages dominates extensively to external sources. Whereas in Alternative tourism, the external leakage is minimum local community gets the direct benefit out of tourism.

Mass tourism regulations are planned for short term with more emphasis on sector wise business, profit and development. It supports private sectors and hence amount of regulation is minimum. Alternative tourism works with high amount of regulations to control the negative impacts to the community. Alternative tourism is a long term plan with more emphasis on community wellbeing and stability. In brief, Mass Tourism is business oriented and Alternative tourism is based on customer preferences, community wellbeing and sustainable development.

Typology of Alternative Tourism Products

Alternative tourism has been classified on the basis of form of activities or modes of travel and the kind of supportive services they demand. Those which come under activity forms are like eco-tourism, pro-poor tourism, community based tourism, adventure tourism, indigenous tourism, educational tourism etc. And those which belong to support services include for example nature retreats, cottages, hunting lodges, health farms, home stays, farm stays, vacation farms/farm stays etc.

- Eco–Tourism: Eco-Tourism is classified as one of the new form of alternative tourism which was initiated in 1980s and has become the most popular one. As like other forms of alternative tourism it shifts away from the mainstream towards responsible and sustainable forms of tourism. Responsible tourists travel to nature based areas that conserves the environment and improves the well-being of local community.

- Community based tourism: Community based tourism is similar to Eco-tourism in which the active participation of local community is seen more and the profit is shared equally with the local community and are promoted under sustainable tourism concept.

- Pro-poor Tourism: It is an approach that aims to increase opportunities to the poor in terms of economic gain, livelihood benefits or participation in decision making. Pro-poor tourism doesn't focus on a specific product or sector but it includes access of the poor to market, commercial viability, policy framework and implementation in the local context.

- Fair trade tourism: Fair trade tourism is nothing but it seeks tourism policies which create social cultural and economic benefits local people and prevents economic leakage. And it involves open trading operations, ecologically sustainable and respect to human rights.

- Indigenous Tourism: It is a form of tourism that promotes the participation of indigenous people either they are directly involved or having their culture serve as essence of the attraction. It involves local community to control and maintain their resources.

- Adventure Tourism: It is a form of tourism in which adventure is the key aspect which involves physical challenge, education and contact with nature. It can be small or large scale and includes trekking, bird watching, scuba diving, white water rafting etc. It has eco-tourism characteristics and in some cases it is not environmental friendly as well.

- Rural Tourism: Rural tourism is tourism that happens in rural areas and focus on local cultural heritage and services of farmers. Some time it is known in the form of agro tourism as well. It involves farm stay, farm activities, working in the fields, sale of local products etc. Rural tourism is mostly managed by local people.

- Volunteer Tourism: Volunteer Tourism includes a diverse array of experiences and settings that involve tourists who receive no financial compensation for undertaking various social/ environmental works in destination.

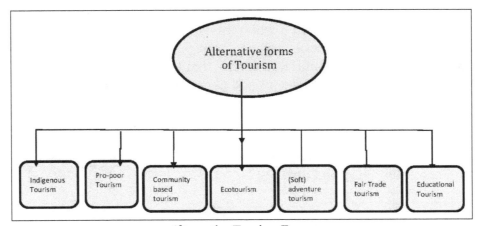

Alternative Tourism Form.

Benefits of Alternative Tourism

There are varieties of reasons like reduction in number of tourists, change in the types of tourists, educating all the parties involved and the impacts resulting from new activities. Alternative tourism in developing counties faces lot of constraints. Even with all these limitations, there is increasing demand for the following reasons:

- Alternative forms of tourism will have negative effects on destination areas and population.

- Alternative tourism helps in cleaning and conserving physical environment.

- Alternative tourism protects the distinctive native culture and the cultural heritage of a region.

- Alternative tourism ensures a fair distribution of benefits and costs.

- Alternative tourism incorporates planning and appropriate management of carrying capacity of ecosystem.

- Alternative tourism monitors areas and manages the impacts of tourism.

- Alternative tourism demonstrates the responsible use of natural and cultural resource.

Travel Documents

A travel document is an identity document issued by a government or international treaty organization to facilitate the movement of individuals or small groups of persons across international boundaries following international agreements. The need of travel documents arise as they usually assure other governments that the bearer may return to the issuing country, and are often issued in booklet form to allow other governments to place visas as well as entry and exit stamps into them. The most common travel document is a passport, which usually gives the bearer more privileges like visa-free access to certain countries. However, the term is sometimes used only for those documents which do not bear proof of nationality such as a refugee travel document is sometimes used only for those documents which do not bear proof of nationality, such as a refugee travel documents.

The Travel documents which are required while travelling for international and domestic travel are few but important .A person cannot travel without possessing them especially in case of international travel .Passengers are required to ensure that they are in possession of all documents necessary for travel, apart from their tickets. Valid photo identification, namely:

- Valid Passport.

- PAN.

- Election Photo Identification Card.

- Valid Driving License.

- Photo identity card issued by the employer, being government and reputed private sector organizations.

- Photo Credit Card.

- Children should carry their school identification cards or any other photo identification proof.

- Valid birth certificates of infants.

- For travel under Concessionary fare types valid relevant IDs.

- In case the Customers do not possess any of the above documents, they should carry a relevant attested document that contains a recent photograph of the travelling Customers.

- For Foreign Nationals, the only valid photo ID for travel is Passport.

Passport

A passport is a document, issued by a national government, which certifies the identity and nationality of its holder for the purpose of international travel. There are different elements of identity in passport .They are name, date of birth, sex, and place of birth. It is an official document issued by a competent public authority or official; usually the sovereign head of the country. Throughout world there are different issuing authorities in different countries. Passport is a privilege issued to citizens of a country, or aliens residing in that country, for a period of time. It is every citizen's birth right. The rights to consular protection arise from international agreements, and the right to return arises from the laws of the issuing country. Indian passports also subject to an Emigration clearance from the office of Protector of Emigrants. This is applicable for some of the countries. Europe, U.S., Canada and some other countries are exempted. But it is required for all countries in the Middle East & some Asian & African countries. For tourist purposes, a waiver is required for each trip.

Visitors Intended Stay Abroad: VISA

A visa is a document showing that a person is authorized to enter the territory for which it was issued subject to permission of an immigration official at the time of the actual entry. As per TIM, a Visa is an entry in a passport or other travel document made by a consular official of a government to indicate that the bearer has been granted authority to enter or re-enter the country concerned.

Types of Passport

- Tourist Passport/Regular Passport: It is the most common form of passport, issued to citizens and other nationals. Occasionally, children are registered within the parents' passport, making it equivalent to a family passport.

- Official Passport/Service Passport: It is issued to government employees for work-related travel, and their accompanying dependants.

- Diplomatic passport: It is issued to diplomats of a country and their accompanying dependents for official international travel and residence. Accredited diplomats of certain grades may be granted diplomatic immunity by a host country, but this is not automatically conferred by holding a diplomatic passport. Any diplomatic privileges apply in the country to which the diplomat is accredited; elsewhere diplomatic passport holders must adhere to the same regulations and travel procedures as are required of other nationals of their country.

- Emergency Passport (also called temporary passport): Emergency passport is issued to persons whose passports were lost or stolen, without time to obtain a replacement. Laissez-passer is also used for this purpose.

Other types of Passport include:

- British Emergency Passport: It is a collective passport which is issued to defined groups for travel together to particular destinations, such as a group of school children on a school trip.

- Family passport: It is issued to an entire family. There is one passport holder, who may travel alone or with other family members included in the passport. A family member who is not the passport holder cannot use the passport for travel without the passport holder. Few countries now issue family passports; for example, all the EU countries and Canada require each child to have his or her own passport.

- Non–Citizen's passport: Non-citizens in Latvia and Estonia are individuals, primarily of Russian or Ukrainian ethnicity, who are not citizens of Latvia or Estonia but whose families have resided in the area since the Soviet era, and thus have the right to a non-citizen passport issued by the Latvian government as well as other specific rights. Approximately two thirds of them are ethnic Russians. Followed by ethnic Belarusians, ethnic Ukrainians, ethnic Poles and ethnic Lithuanians. Non-citizens in the two countries are issued special non-citizen passports as opposed to regular passports issued by the Estonian and Latvian authorities to citizens. This practice has been described as xenophobic.

In America non-citizen U.S. nationals may reside and work in the United States without restrictions, and may apply for citizenship under the same rules as resident aliens. Like resident aliens, they are not presently allowed by any U.S. state to vote in federal or state elections although, as with resident aliens, there is no constitutional prohibition against their doing so.

Other Types of Travel Documents

- Laissez-passer: It is issued by national governments or international organizations such as the U.N.as emergency passports travel on humanitarian grounds, or for official travel.

- Interpol Travel Document: Issued by Interpol to police officers for official travel, allowing them to bypass certain visa restrictions in certain member states when investigating trans-national crime.

- Certificate of identity (also called alien's passport, or informally, a Travel Document): Issued under certain circumstances, such as statelessness, to non-citizen residents. An example is the "Nansen passport" .Sometimes issued as an internal passport to non-residents.

- Refugee travel document: Issued to a refugee by the state in which she or he currently resides allowing them to travel outside that state and to return. It is made necessary because refugees are unlikely to be able to obtain passports from their state of nationality.

- Permits: Many types of travel permit exist around the world. Some, like the U.S. Re-entry Permit, and Japan Re-entry Permit, allow residents of those countries who are unable to obtain a permit to travel outside the country and return. Others, like the Bangladesh Special Passport, the Two-way permit, and the Taibaozheng (Taiwan Compatriot Entry Permit), are used for travel to and from specific countries or locations, for example to travel between mainland China and Macau, or between Taiwan and China.

- Chinese Travel Document: Issued by the People's Republic of China to Chinese citizens in lieu of a passport.

- Hajj Passport: A special passport used only for Hajjand Umbra pilgrimage to Mecca and Medina.

Types of Visa

There are 185 different types of Visa. There are several visas that a foreign national may apply for to be lawfully admitted into country either temporarily or permanently. A few of the commonly utilized visa categories are:

- Temporary Visa: The following Visa comes under temporary Visa:

  - Tourist/Visitor Visas: Available to all visitors coming to any country for business or pleasure.

  - Treaty and Investor Visas: Investors and traders and their employees may receive visas to carry on their businesses.

  - Student Visas: Persons seeking to pursue a full course of study at a school are eligible for a visa for the course of their study plus, in some cases, a period for practical training in their field of study.

- H-1B Specialty Occupation (Professionals) Visas: Professional workers with at least a bachelor's degree (or its equivalent work experience) may be eligible for a non-immigrant visa if their employers can demonstrate that they are to be paid at least the prevailing wage for the position.

- J-1 and Q-1 Exchange Visitor Visas: Persons coming to the country for approved exchange program may be eligible for the J-1 Exchange Visitor's visa. J-1 programs often cover students, short-term scholars, business trainees, teachers, professors and research scholars, specialists, international visitors, government visitors, camp counsellors and au pairs.

- K-1 Fiance (e) Visas: A Fiance (e) of a US citizen is eligible for a non-immigrant visa conditioned on the conclusion of the marriage within 90 days.

- Permanent Residency Visas ("Green Cards"):

  - Family Sponsored Immigration Visas: Individuals in this can petition for spouses, parents, children and siblings. Permanent residents may petition for spouses and children.

  - Employer-Sponsored Immigrant Visas: This is given via employer for employment.

  - EB-1 Foreign Nationals of Extraordinary Ability, Outstanding Professors and Researchers and Multinational Executives and Managers: Individuals in this category can petition for permanent residency without having to go through the time consuming labor certification process.

  - EB-2 Workers with Advanced Degrees or Exceptional Ability in the Sciences, Arts or Business: Visa holders in this category normally must have a job offer and the potential employer must complete the labor certification process. The labor certification involves a testing of the job market to demonstrate that the potential visa holder is not taking a job away from a U.S. worker. In cases where an individual can show that his entry is in the national interest, the job offer and labor certification requirements can be waived.

  - EB-3 Skilled Workers and Professionals: Visa holders in this category normally must have a job offer and the potential employer must complete the labor certification process.

  - EB-4 Special Immigrant Visas for Religious Workers: Ministers of religion are eligible for permanent residency.

Other types include:
- Project Visa
- Gratis Visa
- Journalist Visa
- Business Visa
- Missionary Visa

- Mountaineering Visa

- Medical & Medical Attendant Visa I

- Universal Visa

- Diplomatic/Official/UN Official Visa

- Transit Visa

- Entry Visa

- Tourist Visa

- Employment Visa

- Research Visa

Health Regulations

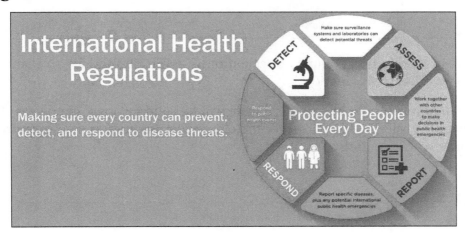

The health regulations form an integral part of travel documentation process. No travel documentation process can be complete without following health regulations. Any person, (excluding infants below six months) arriving by air or sea without a vaccination certificate of yellow fever shall be kept in quarantine isolation for a period up to six days. Some countries require visitors to take some precautionary vaccinations prior to a visit. These are normally for Yellow Fever & Cholera infected zones. Pax must have these vaccinations endorsed in a booklet, format for which is prescribed by the WHO. Persons exempted from production of vaccination certificate. The following types of persons are exempted from production yellow fever vaccination certificate:

- Infants below the age of six months are exempted.

- Any person suffering from some chronic illness and poor resistance is thereby exempted from being vaccinated.

- Crew and passengers of an aircraft transiting through an airport located in yellow fever infected area provided the Health Officer is satisfied that such persons remain within the airport premises during the period of stay.

Yellow Fever

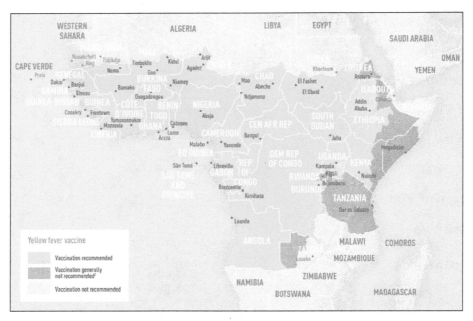

- Validity of Vaccination (Primary Vaccination): Certificate valid for 10 years beginning 10 days after primary vaccination.

- Re-vaccination within validity: Certificate will be valid for another 10 years beginning on the date of re-vaccination. However the old certificate must be shown during the first 10 days after re-vaccination.

Cholera

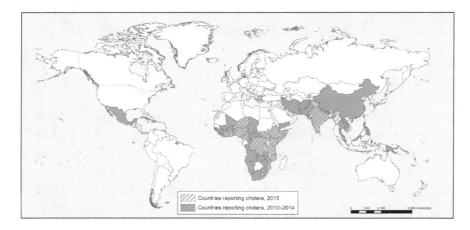

- Validity of Vaccination Primary Vaccination: Certificate valid for 6 months beginning 6 days after primary vaccination.

- Re-vaccination within validity: Certificate will be valid for another 6 months beginning on the date of re-vaccination. However the old certificate must be shown during the first 6 days after re-vaccination.

Currency Regulations

Currency regulations are imposed to check the inflow and outflow of currency from one country to another. There is a limit of currency which an individual as tourist can carry from origin to destination. Currency Regulations are currency regulations for each country. This includes details of Currency Import & Export from one place to another .Import of currency includes how much of currency a passenger can bring into the country. Export of currency include how much Foreign Exchange can a passenger carry out of the country. Foreign currencies include currency notes, traveller's cheques, cheques, drafts etc.

Aviation and Airline

Important air travel terminologies are as follows:

1. Airport Codes: Airport codes are designated by IATA to depict the name of an airline (UA is United Airlines, QF is Qantas, etc).

2. Actual Flying Time: Actual flying time can be described as the actual time that an aircraft is in the air which does not include time on the ground (For instance, waiting in line for take-off).

3. Base Fair: It is the cost of a ticket prior to adding any taxes.

4. ADT: ADT stands for the abbreviated form for Approved departure time.

5. Air Rage: Air rage is term used to depict a situation where passengers become violent towards crew members or passengers.

6. APEX: APEX stands for Advance Purchase Excursion Fare. It generally refers to international fares that have been discounted.

7. Joint Fare: Joint fare is termed used for an agreement among certain airlines to charge particular fares when a passenger uses more than one airline.

8. Air Traffic Control: A game played by airline pilots and air traffic controllers. The game has no

rules, and neither side knows how it is played, but the goal is to prevent flights from arriving in time for passengers to make connecting flights.

9. Aerial: That part of the aircraft most frequently broken off during the walk-around pre-flight inspection that pilots do to see if anything is broken off.

10. Airframe: When the FAA inspector knows that you have only a student license and he sends his kids to bum a ride with you in the plane.

11. Air Mass: Impromptu religious service held on board an aircraft immediately following an announcement by the pilot that he is lost, having an engine problem, or running out of fuel.

12. ACI (Airport Council International): An international association of more than 450 airports.

13. AEA: The Association of European Airlines. An association of the largest European scheduled airlines.

14. EVRA: ICAO code for RIGA International Airport.

15. Catchment Area : The number of people living within an area in which people have approximately two hours of transport by bus, car or train to an airport. The size of the catchment area is of great importance to an airline's choice of routes and thus of airports.

16. Luggage: Personal belongings presented for registration during the flight check-in. During the flight, luggage is kept in special storage area of the airplane and is taken out after the flight. The rules and fares for luggage transportation are set by the airline companies.

17. Luggage Sticker: A sticker attached to the passenger luggage registered for transportation in the airplane.

18. Civil Aviation: Aircrafts, airfields and other objects serving the purpose of transportation by air and specific aviation functions, as well as sport aviation, aviation popularization and other public and private needs.

19. Civil Aviation Agency: A state institution responsible for the coordination and supervision of the National civil aviation safety program. The purpose of the Civil Aviation Agency is to execute the civil aviation and flight safety policies.

20. Civil Aviation Safety: A set of actions involving rules, people and material resources aiming to protect the civil aviation against the illegal interference in its operation.

21. Civil Aviation Safety Program: A set of events necessary for protecting the civil aviation against the illegal interference in its operation.

22. Civil Aviation Aircraft: aircraft registered in the civil aviation aircraft registry, which is not used for military, custom or state border control institutions.

23. Civil Aviation Aircraft Staff: Individuals entrusted by the related aviation institutions to operate the aircraft during the flight.

24. Dispatcher Commands: Instructions from the air traffic control service dispatcher to the pilot in relation to a specific action.

25. Security: Measures taken on entry to the airside area to prevent illegal acts against civil aviation.

26. Security Check: A manual or technical check to detect weapons, objects or substances which must it be assumed can be used in an illegal act against civil aviation.

27. Safety: Measures taken in the airport area to prevent acts that may cause danger or inconvenience to traffic at the airport.

28. Aircraft captain: A pilot responsible for the aircraft operation and safety during the flight.

29. Aircraft Type: Aircrafts with the construction of a same type, including the modifications, except the modifications with the different air dynamic data.

30. Aircraft: A flying machine holding in the air using the interaction with air, if it does not involve the interaction of air with land or water surfaces.

31. Aircraft Parking Lot: A place on the apron for parking the aircraft.

32. Air transportation: Aircraft flight carrying passengers, luggage, cargo and mail on the basis of payments or rental agreement.

33. Air traffic: Movement of aircrafts in the air and on the manoeuvring area of the airfield.

34. Jet Bridge: The Bridge connecting an aircraft to the gate so that passengers can embark and disembark without getting their feet wet.

35. Air route: Controlled air space or part of it is the form of a corridor secured for use of air transportation.

36. IATA: International Air Transport Association. It is a global association of more than 200 airlines.

37. ICA: International Civil Aviation Organisation. It is a UN body for international civil aviation.

38. Departure Sector: An area for passenger entrance in the aircraft usually marked with special numbers or letters.

39. Airport Office: RIX official office, from which flights are handled. Representatives from the press,etc. must report to the Airport Office for photography and access permits.

40. Republic of Latvia Civil Aviation Aircraft: Civil aviation aircraft registered in the Civil Aviation Registry of the Republic of Latvia.

41. Airspace of the Republic of Latvia: Air space above the land of the Republic of Latvia and its internal and Baltic Sea territorial waters.

42. Air Field Restricted: It is that part of the airport building and airfield with restricted access.

43. Airfield Manoeuvring Territory: A part of the air field for aircraft landing, take-off and manoeuvring needs.

44. Air Field Traffic: All traffic on the territory of manoeuvring field as well as flights above the territory around the air field.

45. Air Field Traffic Area: Air space of a certain size above the territory around the air field to ensure the safety of the air field traffic.

46. Air Field: A certain land or water territory as well as building, objects and equipment fully or partially intended for organization of aircraft departures and arrivals (including airplane landing, take-off, manoeuvring, parking, passenger entrance, luggage, cargo and mail loading and unloading, technical maintenance and fuelling).

47. Flight Restricted Area: Restricted air space above the land and internal and Baltic Sea territorial waters for aircraft flights according to the special rules.

48. Airport ID Card: ID card held by airport staff.

49. Illegal Interference in the Civil Aviation Operations: Actions endangering or possessing a possibility of danger to aviation safety (unauthorized entry of a person at the airport restricted areas or aircrafts, possession of dangerous and explosive substances or weapons without permission, use of weapons against the aircraft personnel or passengers, aircraft kidnapping, etc).

50. OneWorld: An alliance of the following airlines: American Airlines, British Airways, Cathay Pacific, Finnair, Iberia, Japan Airlines, Lan Chile, Malev, Qantas and Royal Jordanian.

51. Passenger Transportation: Transportation of passengers between terminal and aircraft.

52. Passenger Area: An area beyond the safety and passport control. Allowed only for passengers and assigned airport personnel.

53. Carrier: Aircraft operator conducting air transportation on the basis of assigned rights.

54. OAG (Official Airline Guide): The function of the airline service at the airport refers to airport non-stop domestic departing flights per week. It is determined in two ways: from OAG for the period when airport surveys were conducted and from the airport airline weekly activity records excluding non-air carrier or commuter and international flights.

Air Tickets

Travel agents are an important contributor to the airline industry. The formal part of their responsibilities includes being authorized to sell and issue airline tickets. Accredited agents accept payments from customers on behalf of the airlines whose tickets are issued. It is essential that customers and airlines can rely on those agents for tickets to be issued according to the required standards, and for payments to reach the airlines in a timely manner.

1. Computerized Reservation System: Initially "Airline Reservations System (ARS)" was introduced so as to improve effectiveness. ARS ultimately evolved into the Computer Reservations System (CRS). A Computer Reservation System is designed for the reservations of a specific airline and interfaces with a Global Distribution System (GDS) which supports travel agencies and other distribution channels in making reservations for most major airlines in a single system.

2. Inventory Management: Inventory management refers to the effective and efficient management of airline's inventory which comprise of all flights with their available seats. An airline's

inventory is usually divided into service classes (e.g. First, Business or Economy class) and up to 26 booking classes, for which different prices and booking conditions apply. Inventory data is imported and maintained through a Schedule Distribution System over standardized interfaces. One of the main functions of the inventory management is the inventory control. Inventory control depicts the number of seats that are available in the various booking classes, by opening and closing individual booking classes for sale. Along with the fares and booking conditions stored in the Fare Quote System the price for each sold seat is determined. Mostly inventory control has a real time interface to an airline's Yield management system to assist a permanent optimization of the offered booking classes in response to changes in demand or pricing strategies of a competitor.

3. Availability Display and Reservation: An airline's inventory can be accessed by the user using an availability display. It comprises of all available flights for a specific city-pair with their available seats in the different booking classes. This display contains flights, which are operated by the airline itself as well as code share flights which are operated in co-operation with another airline. If the city pair is not one on which the airline offers service it may display a connection using its' own flights or display the flights of other airlines. The availability of seats of other airlines is updated through standard industry interfaces. Depending on the type of co-operation, it supports access to the last seat (Last Seat Availability) in real-time. Reservations for individual passengers or groups are stored in a so-called Passenger Name Record (PNR). Among other data, the PNR includes personal information such as name, contact information or Special Services Requests (SSRs) for instance for a vegetarian meal, in addition to the flights (segments) and issued tickets.

Some reservation systems also allow storing customer data in profiles for avoiding data re-entry each time a new reservation is made for a known passenger. Moreover, most systems have interfaces to CRM systems or customer loyalty applications (aka Frequent Traveller Systems). Before a flight departs the so-called Passenger Name List (PNL) is handed over to the Departure Control System that is used to check-in passengers and baggage. Reservation data such as the number of booked passengers and special service requests is also transferred to Flight Operations Systems, Crew Management and Catering Systems. After flight has departed the reservation system is updated with a list of the checked-in passengers (e.g. passengers who had a reservation but did not check in (No Shows) and passengers who checked in, but didn't have a reservation (Go Shows). Lastly, data required for revenue accounting and reporting is handed over to the administrative systems.

Fare Quote and Ticketing

The Fares data store includes fare tariffs, rule sets, routing maps, class of service tables, and some tax information that make the price-"the fare". Rules such as booking conditions (for example minimum stay, advance purchase, etc.) are customized differently between different city pairs or zones, and allocated a class of service corresponding to its suitable inventory bucket. Inventory control can also be influenced manually through the availability feeds, dynamically controlling how many seats are offered for a specific price by opening and closing specific classes. The compiled set of fare conditions is known as a fare basis code. There are two systems set up for the interchange of fares data – ATPCO and SITA. Along with it, there are some system to system direct connects. This system distributes the fare tariffs and rule sets to all GDSs and other subscribers. Every airline employs staff who code air fare rules in line with yield management intent. Revenue managers are also present so as to watch fares as they are filed into the public tariffs and make competitive suggestions. Inventory control is in general manipulated from here, with availability feeds to open and close classes of service. The function of the Ticketing complex is issuing and storing electronic ticket records and the very few paper tickets which are still issued.

Major Systems

The major computer reservation systems are shown in table:

Table: Major Computer Reservation Systems.

Name	Description
Takeflite Solutions	Online Airline Management & Maintenance Software System.
SkyVantage Corporation	SkyVantage Airline Management System. Full suite of reservations and operations software.
AccelAero	A Low Cost Carrier (LCC) oriented Airline Reservation System.
KIU	A computer reservations system (CRS) and global distribution system (GDS).

Airport Guidance and Location

Airport guidance signs show the direction and information for taxing aircraft and airport vehicles for their safe and expedient movement. There are two modules of signage at airports namely:

- Operational Guidance Signs: Operational guidance signs refer to the location signs, direction/runway exit signs. These signs are featured through the color of marking on the operational side of the airport (Runways) such as:

  - Location Signs: Yellow on black background, identifies the runway or taxiway currently on or entering.

  - Direction/Runway Exit Signs: Black on yellow background identifies the intersecting taxiways the aircraft is approaching, with an arrow indicating the direction to turn.

  - Other Signs: Many airports use conventional traffic signs such as stop and yield signs throughout the airport.

- Mandatory Instruction Signs: Mandatory instruction signs give the guidance of using the operational site of airside management. These signs are displayed by pictogram through marking white on red. They show entrances to runways or critical areas. Vehicles and aircraft are required to stop at these signs until the control tower gives clearance to proceed.

  - Runway signs: This signs identify a runway intersection ahead.

  - Frequency change signs: This identifies a stop sign and an instruction to change to another frequency. These signs are used at different areas of ground control.

  - Holding position signs: This sign is marked through a single solid yellow bar across a taxiway indicates a position where ground control may require a stop. Two solid yellow bars and two dashed yellow bars indicate a holding position for a runway intersection ahead. Runway-holding lines must never be crossed without permission. At some airports, a line of red lights across a taxiway is used during low visibility operations to indicate holding positions.

Airline Terminal Management

The airport terminal area, comprised of passenger and cargo terminal buildings, aircraft parking, loading, unloading and service areas such as passenger service facilities, automobile parking, and public transit stations, is a vital component to the airport system. The primary goal of an airport is to provide passengers and cargo access to air transportation, and thus the terminal area achieves the goal of the airport by providing the vital link between the airside of the airport and the landside. The terminal area provides the facilities, procedures, and processes to efficiently move crew, passengers, and cargo onto, and off of, commercial and general aviation aircraft. The term terminal is in fact somewhat of a misnomer. Terminal implies ending. Although aircraft itineraries begin and end at an airport's terminal area, the itineraries of passengers and baggage do not. It is vitally important to understand that the airport terminal is not an end point, but an area of transfer along the way.

Historical Development of Airport Terminals

Just as there were no runways or other airfield facilities during the very earliest days of aviation, there certainly were no terminals, at least the way they are recognized today. The first facilities that could be remotely considered airport terminal areas evolved in the early 1920s with the introduction of airmail service. Airmail operations required small depots in order to load and unload mail, fuel aircraft, and perform any required maintenance. Little in the way of formal passenger or cargo processing was required, and hence, airport terminal facilities were little more than single-room structures with the most basic of infrastructure.

The introduction of commercial passenger air service in the late 1920s resulted in the need to develop certain basic passenger processing policies. The earliest passenger processing strategies evolved from the major intercity transportation mode of the day, the railroads. Tickets and boarding passes were issued for passengers, and similar to policies set for rail transport, cargo rates were also charged, typically by the weight of the cargo being transported. (Sometimes passengers were weighed as well, primarily to ensure that the aircraft did not exceed its maximum take-off weight!) The facilities required for performing basic ticketing and weighing functions, as well as for aircraft boarding and alighting the relatively few passengers and little cargo that used civil air transportation could be, and were often, incorporated into one-room facilities, strikingly similar to the facilities that served the railroads.

Unit Terminal Concepts

These first terminals were the earliest centralized facilities, centralized meaning that all passenger processing facilities at the airport are housed in one building. These first centralized facilities became known as the earliest simple unit terminals, because they contained all required passenger processing facilities for a given air carrier in a single- unit building. In addition to passenger processing facilities, the airport's administrative offices, and even air traffic control facilities, were located within the unit terminal building became known as the combined unit terminal. In larger metropolitan areas, separate buildings were constructed for each airline, each building behaving as its own unit terminal. This terminal area configuration became known as the multiple-unit terminal concept. Even though the multiple-unit terminal area consisted of separate facilities for each airline, it is still considered an individual centralized facility because all passenger and cargo processing required for any given passenger or piece of cargo to board any given flight still exists in one facility. The early centralized terminals, including the simple-unit, combined-unit, and multiple-unit terminals, employed the gate arrival concept. The gate arrival concept is a centralized layout that is aimed at reducing the overall size of terminal areas by bringing automobile parking as close as possible to aircraft parking.

The simple-unit terminal represents the most fundamental type of gate arrival facility, consisting of a single common waiting and ticketing area with exits onto a small aircraft parking apron. Even today, the gate arrival concept is adaptable to airports with low airline activity and is particularly applicable to general aviation operations whether a smaller general aviation terminal is located separately from a larger terminal for commercial air carriers or is the operational centre for an airport used exclusively for general aviation. Where the terminal serves airline operations, close-in parking is usually available for three to six commercial aircraft. Where the simple-unit terminal serves general aviation only, the facility is within convenient walking distance of aircraft parking areas and adjacent to an aircraft service apron. The simple-unit terminal facility normally consists of a single-level structure where access to aircraft is afforded by a walk across the aircraft parking apron.

Linear Terminal Concepts

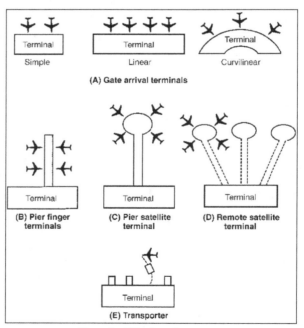

Terminal Design Concepts.

As airports expanded to meet the growing needs of the public, as well as the growing wingspans of aircraft, simple-unit terminals expanded outward in a rectangular or linear manner, with the goal of maintaining short distances between the vehicle curb and aircraft parking that existed with unit terminals. Within linear terminals, ticket counters serving individual airlines were introduced and loading bridges were deployed at aircraft gates to allow passengers to board aircraft without having to be outside on the apron, thereby improving convenience and safety for passengers. In some instances airports were extended in a curvilinear fashion, allowing even more aircraft to park "nose-in" to the terminal building while maintaining short walking distances from the airport entrance to the aircraft gate. In many respects, the linear and curvilinear terminal concepts are mere extensions of the simple-unit terminal concept. More sophisticated linear terminals, particularly those that serve high volumes of passengers, often feature two level structures where enplaning passengers are processed on one level and deplaning passengers on the other level. Passenger walking distances from the "curb to the gate" are typically short, on the order of 100 feet. The linear configuration also lends itself to the development of automobile parking that is close to the terminal building, and provides extended curb frontage for loading and unloading of ground transportation vehicles.

One of the main disadvantages of linear terminals becomes evident as the length of the terminal building increases. Walking distances between facilities, particularly distantly separated gates, become excessive for the passenger whose itinerary requires a change in aircraft at the airport. Prior to airline deregulation the percentage of these transfer passengers was insignificant. After 1978, however, this percentage increased dramatically and the issue of long walking distances between gates became a major issue, particularly at the hub airports.

Pier Finger Terminals

The pier finger terminal concept evolved in the 1950s when gate concourses were added to simple unit terminal buildings. Concourses, known as piers or fingers, offer the opportunity to maximize the number of aircraft parking spaces with fewer infrastructures. Aircraft parking was assigned to both sides of a pier extending from the original unit terminal structure. The pier finger terminal is the first of what are known as decentralized facilities, with some of the required processing performed in common-use main terminal areas, and other processes performed in and around individual concourses.

Many airports today have pier finger terminals in use. Since the earliest pier finger designs, very sophisticated and often convoluted forms of the concept have been developed with the addition of hold rooms at gates, loading bridges, and vertical separation of enplaning and deplaning passengers in the main-unit terminal area. As pier finger terminals expanded, concourse lengths at many terminal buildings became excessive, averaging 400 feet or more from the main terminal to the concourse end. In addition, as terminals expanded by adding additional piers, distances between gates and other facilities became not only excessive in distance, but also confusing in direction. Moreover, often the main-unit terminal facility and corridors connecting the individual fingers were not expanded along with the construction of additional concourses, leading to passenger crowding in these areas. Another of the disadvantages of pier finger terminals is that expansion of terminals by adding or lengthening concourses may significantly reduce the amount of apron space for aircraft parking and movement. Also, the addition of concourses to the terminal tends to put constraints on the mobility of aircraft, particularly those that are parked closer to the main terminal building.

Pier Satellite and Remote Satellite Terminals

Similar to pier finger terminals, pier satellite terminals formed as concourses extended from main-unit terminal buildings with aircraft parked at the end of the concourse around a round atrium or satellite area. Satellite gates are usually served by a common passenger holding area. Satellite terminal concepts, developed in the 1960s and 1970s, took advantage of the ability to create either underground corridors or Automated Passenger Movement Systems (APMs) to connect main terminal buildings with concourses. Such terminals are said to be built on the remote satellite concept. The main advantage of the remote satellite concept is that one or more satellite facilities may be constructed and expanded when necessary while providing sufficient space for aircraft taxi operations between the main terminal building and satellites. In addition, although distances from the main terminal to a satellite may be quite large, APMs or other people-mover systems such as moving walkways or shuttle buses are provided to reduce walking distances.

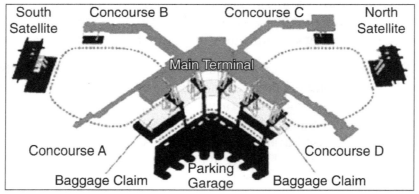

Terminal Configuration at Seattle: Tacoma International Airport, One of the First Airports to Employ APMs to Reach Remote Satellite Terminals.

Another of the advantages of the satellite concept is that it lends itself to a relatively compact central terminal with common areas for processing passengers, because aircraft with large wingspans, which for all intents and purposes dictate the size of terminal gate areas and thus concourses and satellite, are parked at remote satellites rather than at the central facility. As with the pier finger concept, the expansion of pier satellite and remote satellite concept terminals tend to result in terminal facilities that not only have large distances between key points within the terminal, but also often become confusing for passengers in their attempts to find their way to their respective gates, baggage claim areas, or other desired facilities.

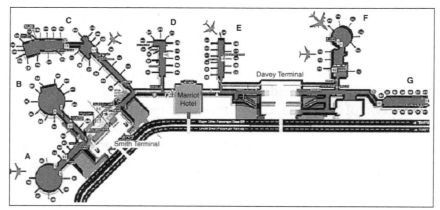

The Old Pier Finger Terminal Complex at Detroit's Metropolitan Airport.

Mobile Lounge or Transporter Concept

In 1962 the opening of Dulles International Airport west of Washington D.C., designed as the first airport specifically for the new jet aircraft of the day, introduced the mobile lounge or transporter concept of airport terminals. Sometimes known also as the remote aircraft parking concept, the Washington Dulles terminal area attempted to maximize the number of aircraft that may be parked and maximize the number of passengers that may be processed, with minimal concourse infrastructure. In this concept, aircraft are parked at remote parking locations away from the main-unit terminal building. To travel between aircraft and the terminal building, passengers would board transporters, known as mobile lounges that would roam the airfield among ground vehicles and taxiing aircraft. With the mobile lounge concept, walking distances were held to a minimum because the main, relatively compact, terminal building contains common passenger processing facilities, with automobile curbs and parking located in close proximity to the terminal building entrances. Theoretically, expansion to accommodate additional aircraft is facilitated by the fact that there is no need to physically expand concourses, piers, or satellites, just merely add additional mobile lounges, if necessary.

Despite its theoretical advantages, the mobile lounge concept did not on the whole win approval from passengers. Mobile lounge boarding areas in the main terminal often became excessively congested as passengers with carry-on baggage would crowd the area, often arriving early so as not to miss their assigned mobile lounge boarding time. Moreover, the relatively small mobile lounges offered far less room for passengers than the aircraft from or to which they are transitioning, especially in comparison to large "wide-body" aircraft introduced in the late 1960s, leaving passengers crowded and often uncomfortable while on the mobile lounge. In addition, mobile lounges require constant maintenance, which over time becomes an excessive cost element of operations. In the mid-1990s Dulles in effect abandoned the mobile lounge concept by constructing satellite or midfield concourses on the airfield. Today, the remaining mobile lounges at Dulles are still in service and act as transporters merely between the main terminal building and the satellite concourses rather than directly to aircraft. Current plans at Dulles call for construction of an underground transporter between the main terminal and the remote concourses and removing the mobile lounges from the terminal area entirely. In the United States, no other airports have relied entirely on the mobile lounge concept for their terminal areas, with the exception of providing shuttle bus services to aircraft that must be parked in remote parking spots because of lack of available gate space at the terminal building or concourses. In other countries, particularly in the Middle East, the mobile lounge concept has been met with higher levels of success.

Hybrid Terminal Geometries

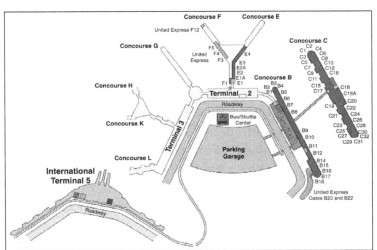

Chicago O'Hare International Airport Combining Unit, Linear,
Pier and Satellite Terminal Concepts.

With the volatile changes in the amount and behaviour of civil aviation activity, with increasing numbers of large aircraft (with high seating capacities and large wingspans), volumes of passengers, and changes in route structures, particularly after airline deregulation, airport management has had to expand and modify terminal areas to accommodate almost constantly changing environments. As a result, many airport terminal geometries expanded in an ad hoc manner, leading to hybrid terminal geometries incorporating features of two or more of the basic configurations.

In addition, for airports that accommodate an airline's hub, airport terminal planning became necessary to accommodate up to 100 or more aircraft at one time and efficiently handle record volumes of passengers, particularly those passengers transferring between aircraft. It's no coincidence that during past years public sentiment for the planning and management of many airport terminals in the United States was declining. Issues including congestion, long walking distances, confusing directions, as well as limited amenities and passenger services became popular issues of criticism. As a result, airport planners began to redevelop terminal area designs, focusing on strategic planning and design of terminals that can accommodate requirements of accessing ground vehicles, passengers, and aircraft, with sufficient flexibility to adapt to ever-changing levels of growth and system behaviour.

Airside–Landside Concept

The most significant terminal area concept to emerge involved a more physical separation between facilities that handle passengers and ground vehicles and those that deal primarily with aircraft handling. The airside-landside concept emerged with the opening of the Tampa International Airport and has proliferated throughout the United States at airports such as Pittsburgh International Airport and Orlando International Airport. The airside-landside concept relies heavily on automated pedestrian movement systems to quickly and efficiently shuttle passengers to and from two separate facilities. In the landside facility, all passenger and baggage processing can be performed without being physically close to an aircraft. In addition, sufficient ancillary facilities, such as concessions, atriums, and the like, are located in landside facilities to provide amenities to facilitate a pleasurable experience for the passenger. Airside facilities, which have been built in various shapes and sizes, from X shapes to long concourses, focus on the efficient servicing of aircraft, including fuelling, loading, and unloading. Separating each of the two processes allows greater flexibility in adapting to changes in either environment, whether it is new aircraft or changes in passenger processing policies.

Off-Airport Terminals

In the 1980s the airside-landside concept formed the basis for a series of experimental concepts known as off-airport terminals. With the notion that certain passenger processes, such as ticketing and baggage check-in, and certainly automobile parking, did not need to be within any proximity of aircraft, such processes weren't necessarily required to be performed on airport property. As a result, facilities located miles away from the airport itself were introduced whereby passengers could park their personal vehicles, check themselves and their baggage in for their flights, and then take a shuttle bus to the airport. With the use of these off-airport terminals, passengers would avoid the often significantly more crowded passenger processing facilities at the main terminal. Also the passenger would not be required to find parking at the often more crowded and expensive parking facilities at the main terminal.

Off-airport terminals serving the San Francisco Bay Area, Los Angeles, and Las Vegas were met with positive response, with increased passenger convenience being the prime characteristic of the systems. Because of increased security measures following the attacks of September 11, 2001, however, off-airport terminals have had to discontinue any passenger or baggage check-in processes, and are now primarily used merely as off-airport parking facilities. However, the off-airport terminal concept set the precedent for implementing the idea of passenger processing at sites away from the main airport terminal, setting the stage for the potential future of airport terminal planning.

Present-Day Airport Terminals

With over 650 million passengers travelling annually, each with different agendas, itineraries, needs, and desires, airport terminals have become complex systems in their own rights, incorporating both necessary passenger and baggage processing services as well as a full spectrum of customer service, retail shopping, food and beverage, and other facilities to make the passengers' transition between the airside and landside components of the airport system as pleasant as possible. It is clear that no single airport terminal configuration is best for all airports. The airfield, schedules of airlines, types of aircraft, volumes of passengers, and local considerations, such as local architecture, aesthetics, and civic pride, dictate different choices from airport to airport and from one time to another. The airport terminal planner has the dubious task of anticipating conditions up to 10 years in the future in an environment that seems to change by the day. To ensure that present-day airport terminal plans will be effective in the future, the airport planner must rely on the fundamental requirements of airport terminals and behaviours of passengers, and also must plan with the idea of flexibility in mind, such as considering facilities that can be expanded modularly or can provide the opportunity for relatively low-cost, simple modifications that future circumstances might demand.

For airport management, airport terminal areas, when properly planned and managed, have provided significant sources of revenue from airline leases to retail concessions. Airport terminals have also become a sense of pride for communities in general, as they are typically the first impression that visitors get of their destination city and the last experience they get before leaving. Several airport terminals today appear more to be shopping malls than passenger processing facilities, and other airport terminals are fully equipped with hotels and conference centres. These facilities have actually encouraged visitors to use the facilities at the airport without ever intending to board an aircraft. The size and shape of airport terminal configurations has both an uncertain yet exciting future. New security regulations imposed by the Transportation Security Administration have established the need to expand airport security facilities, whereas advances in information technologies have suggested the ability to reduce the size of other passenger processing facilities such as staffed ticket counters. No matter how policies, regulations, technologies, and behaviours change, however, the basic function of the airport terminal area, that of efficiently linking passengers and cargo to the airside and landside components of the civil aviation system, should always be understood by airport managers and planners alike.

Components of the Airport Terminal

The airport terminal area is in the unique position of accommodating the needs of both aircraft and the passengers that board them. As such, the component systems of the airport terminal area may be thought of as falling into two primary categories: the apron and gate system, which is planned and managed according to the characteristics of aircraft, and the passenger and baggage handling systems, which are planned and managed to accommodate the needs of passengers and their baggage in their transition to or from the aircraft.

Apron and Gate System

The apron and gates are the locations at which aircraft park to allow the loading and unloading of passengers and cargo, as well as for aircraft servicing and pre-flight preparation prior to entering the airfield and airspace. The size of aircraft, particularly their lengths and wingspans, is perhaps the single greatest determinant of the area required for individual gates and apron parking spaces. In fact, the grand size of airport terminals is a direct result of large numbers of gates designed to accommodate aircraft of wingspans reaching 200 feet in length. The size of any given aircraft parking area is also determined by the orientation in which the aircraft will park, known as the aircraft parking type. Aircraft may be positioned at various angles with respect to the terminal building, may be attached to loading bridges or Jetways, or may be freestanding and adjoined with air stairs for passenger boarding and deplaning. Some aircraft parking types require aircraft to be manoeuvred either in or out of their parking spaces by the use of aircraft tugs, whereas other parking types allow the movement of aircraft in and out under their own power. The five major aircraft parking types are nose-in parking, angled nose-in, angled nose-out, parallel parking, and remote parking.

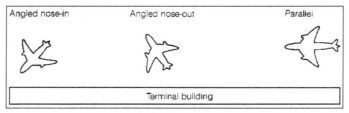

Aircraft Parking Positions.

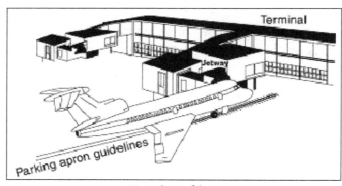

Nose-in Parking.

- Nose-in Parking: Most large jet aircraft at commercial service airports park nose-in to gates at the terminal and connect directly to the terminal building by loading bridges. Aircraft are able to enter nose-in parking spaces under their own power, and tend to be pushed out by an aircraft tug and oriented so that they may move forward on the apron without coming into contact with any other structures. The primary advantage to nose- in parking is that it requires less physical space for aircraft than any other aircraft parking type. The majority of commercial service airports, particularly those with large volumes of jet aircraft operations, have primarily nose-in parking. With nose-in parking, only the front-entry door on the aircraft is used for boarding, because the rear doors are typically too far from the terminal building to extend a loading bridge. This has some, but not an entirely significant, impact on the efficiency of passenger boarding and deplaning.

- Angled Nose-in Parking brings aircraft as close to the terminal building as possible while maintaining enough manoeuvring room so that aircraft may exit the parking space under its own power. Angled Nose-in Parking is typically used by smaller aircraft, such as turboprops or small regional jets. Air stairs are typically used to board and deplane passengers, removing the necessity for loading bridges. Angled nose-in parking requires slightly more parking area over nose-in parking for aircraft of similar size. However, because smaller aircraft tend to use angled nose-in parking, the difference in sizes of the two parking areas is not significantly different.

- Angled Nose-out Parking brings aircraft slightly farther from the terminal building than nose-in and angled nose-in parking, because the blast from jets or large propellers has the potential of causing damage to terminal buildings if too close to the facility. Angled nose-out parking is typically used by larger general aviation aircraft and at facilities with relatively low levels of activity.

- Parallel Parking is said to be the easiest to achieve from an aircraft manoeuvring standpoint, although each space tends to require the largest amount of physical space for a given size of aircraft. In this configuration, both front and aft doors of the aircraft on a given side may be used for passenger boarding by loading bridges. Typically, however, parallel parking is employed only by smaller general aviation aircraft with relatively large amounts of parking space near the terminal building. In addition, cargo aircraft may parallel park at their respective cargo terminals to facilitate the loading and unloading of their respective loads.

- Remote Parking may be employed when there is limited parking area available at the terminal building itself or when aircraft parked may be stationed there overnight or for longer durations. Remote parking areas are typically comprised of a series of rows of parking spaces, sized to accommodate varying sizes of aircraft. Smaller commercial and general aviation aircraft may be boarded and deplaned from the remote parking areas with the use of shuttle buses or vans. Larger commercial aircraft are typically taxied to a close-in parking space prior to passenger loading.

Most airports have more than one aircraft parking type to accommodate the various types of aircraft that serve the different terminal geometries and air carrier or general aviation activities. Furthermore, airports with a high number of based aircraft or air carrier aircraft that remain overnight (RON) at the airport, must take into consideration higher volumes of remote parking that is flexible to accommodate aircraft of various shapes and sizes. Taxilanes are found on airport aprons to direct aircraft taxiing between airfield taxiways and aircraft parking areas on the apron. Taxilanes exist as single-lane taxiways, where there exists sufficient room for one aircraft, and dual-lane taxiways, with sufficient room for two aircraft taxiing in opposite directions to move simultaneously. Dual-lane taxilanes are typically found at the busiest of airports serving larger aircraft.

Aircraft Gate Management

One of the most important and sometimes most challenging aspects of planning and managing the apron concerns the number of aircraft parking areas, or gates, that are required for efficient operations. The number of commercial aircraft gates required at an airport, for example, over any given operating day is dependent on a series of factors, including: the number and type of aircraft scheduled to use a gate, each aircraft's scheduled turnaround time (also known as gate occupancy time), and the type of gate usage agreement that each air carrier has with the airport. The number and type of each aircraft scheduled to use a gate is of course vital to the planning of gate facilities. For each type of aircraft that uses the airport, there should be at least one aircraft parking area that can accommodate the aircraft. For smaller airports that are frequented by larger aircraft on a sporadic basis, a remote parking facility with sufficient space may be appropriate, whereas aircraft that operate more often should be considered for their size when constructing permanent gate facilities. At many airports, gates for larger aircraft are planned for the ends of linear terminals or satellite configurations, where aircraft wingspans are accommodated with minimal sacrifice of space for additional aircraft, and gates for smaller aircraft tend to be located nearer the centre of the terminal.

The turnaround time of each aircraft directly affects the number of aircraft that can use a gate over the course of a day. Turnaround times of aircraft vary widely, based in part on the size of aircraft, the itinerary of the aircraft, the number of passengers, the volume of cargo to be loaded and unloaded, and the schedules of the air carrier. Turnaround times of smaller commercial service aircraft flying relatively short routes, carrying less than 50 passengers, for a regional airline, for example, may be as low as 15 minutes, whereas wide-body aircraft flying on international routes may require 3 or more hours turnaround time. As such, a gate serving small regional air carrier aircraft gates may serve 30 or more aircraft in an operating day, and gates serving international flights may accommodate only two or three aircraft per day. The gate usage agreement that each air carrier has with airport management also plays a significant role in the total number of required gates at the airport terminal. The three most common types of gate usage agreements are exclusive-use, shared-use, and preferential-use agreements.

As the name implies, under an exclusive-use agreement, an air carrier retains sole authority to use a particular gate or set of gates at an airport terminal. This agreement gives the air carrier flexibility when adjusting flight schedules, assuring the carrier that gates will always be available when needed. Operationally, however, this type of agreement leads to inefficiencies in overall gate use, because when the air carrier is not currently using its gates, the gate sits idle, despite the fact that another air carrier may desire a gate parking space at that time. Air carriers signing exclusive-use agreements, usually do so for a premium, and for a relatively long contract period, and thus are identified typically as signatory carriers at the airport. Signatory carriers tend to have the majority of operations at the airport, thus warranting exclusive-use agreements. Under shared-use agreements, air carriers and other aircraft schedule use of gates in coordination with airport management and other air carriers serving the airport. Thus individual gates may be shared by multiple air carriers. Shared-use agreements are usually arranged by air carriers that have relatively few operations scheduled at the airport. For example, international air carriers tend to arrange shared-use agreements with United States airports, because they each have perhaps only a few operations per day at any given airport. For air carriers that have many operations at an airport, shared-use agreements reduce the flexibility in schedule planning. From an airport management perspective, however, shared-use agreements are operationally efficient, maximizing the number of aircraft that may use gates over the course of a schedule day.

Preferential-use agreements are hybrids of the exclusive-use and shared-use agreements. Under a preferential-use agreement, one air carrier has preferential use of the gate. However, should that air carrier not be using the gate during some period of the day, other air carriers subscribing to the agreement may use the gate, as long as its use does not interfere with upcoming operations from the preferential carrier. Preferential-use agreements are typically signed by one carrier that has moderate levels of service at the airport, and one or more carriers or charter aircraft that have relatively few operations. From an operational perspective, the overall number of aircraft utilizing gates under shared-use agreements depends primarily on the number of operations served by, as well as the typical turnaround time of, the preferential carrier. The greater number of operations and greater turnaround time of, the preferential carrier tends to lead to fewer numbers of aircraft using the gates over the course of an operating day.

Travel Agency and Tour Operator

Travel agency is a firm qualified to sell services pertaining to tours, cruises, transportation, hotel accommodation, meals, transfer, sightseeing and other elements to the general public. This business firm is set up for providing services and earning profits. The business of travel agency uses some of the important management practices like division of labor, hierarchical authority and responsibility. Travel agency plans, organizes, directs, controls, coordinates and sets all resources to get her in such a manner that it can achieve objectives. When the functional areas of management are linked with organizational objectives, travel agency makes profits after satisfying customers. For example, Thomas Cook or Cox and Kings have become leaders in travel agency business worldwide for their continuous efforts in ensuring quality for customer satisfaction and delight.

A travel agency is a business entity or firm that retails package tours or any other individual travel solutions to customers as a representative of airlines, hotels, tour companies, and cruise lines. In these days, travel agents have created separate department to meet the travel needs of leisure and business tourists. Generally, a travel agent gives advice to tourists about the climate, distance, culture and do's and donot's to follow at the destinations or cities. Presently, most package holidays are sold through travel agents. The modern travel agents always remember the contribution of the legendary Thomas Cook for many innovative practices and Sir Henry Lunn (Lunn Poly) for inventing skiing as a leisure activity.

Travel agencies should have dynamic and structured organization with operational experience to manage business efficiently. It is essentially important to examine the fixed and variable investment to run the business. Apart from being severally affected by the seasonal nature of business, other external factors like natural calamities, outbreak of diseases, ethnic wars, etc do affect the prospect of business negatively. Travel agents make the booking tickets for air, rail, sea or road travel and arrange hotel reservations or guest houses, hire taxis etc. Besides domestic air ticketing, travel agents make international flight bookings and other bookings for special business tours or conferences.

On the contrary, tour operators deal with the bulk travel arrangements and management of FIT and GIT travel. It is recognized as principal agent or wholesaler. It offloads the responsibility to the ground handling agents to take care of receiving and dropping the guests at the airports/railway stations along with sightseeing arrangements. Importantly, tour packages are mostly promoted by tour operators through travel agents. Tour operators also offer special packages like deep-sea diving, snorkeling, Himalayan trekking and camel safaris.

Types of Travel Agencies

Travel agencies are broadly divided into wholesale and retail travel agency for the distribution of sale of tourism services. In addition to this classification, travel agency can also be classified as implant agency, conference organizer, meeting planners, trade fair organizer, etc.

1. Wholesale Travel Agency: The business of wholesaling in tourism industry is no way different from the wholesaling in the commodity market. A wholesale travel agency assembles different components of services to design tour packages for catering FIT and GIT customers. A wholesaler is one who initiates the process of forming organized tours or sells the individual components directly or indirectly through franchise or retail agents. For example, a wholesaler of Singapore airline or Taj Hotel or Sterling Time Share Group is authorized to sell the airline tickets or hotel rooms on behalf of the principal service providers. A wholesaler may be a consolidator or a manufacturer of tours or General Sales Agent (GSA). It buys service components in bulk from different suppliers and it designs package and sells or resells these components together.

If it is tour wholesaler, the process starts from the research development followed by itinerary preparation. The most critical role of a tour wholesaler is the pricing of package that positions the product in the market. On the other hand, a wholesale travel agent is appointed to promote the sales of outbound package tour in a particular region. Many retail travel agents are also authorized to retail the outbound package tour in smaller cities and towns. The commission is paid to retail agents periodically. It however depends on retailer agencies to promote the products. Wholesaler travel agents may also directly sell to the customers through their own retail divisions. For example, Thomas Cook has its own network of branch offices in big cities to directly sell tour packages to customers. In many cases, Thomas Cook appoints retail travel agents. It generates revenues through volume discounts from principal services providers such as hotels, airlines, railways, car rentals, coach operators, ground handlers etc.

2. Retail Travel Agency: Retail travel agencies are defined as "a business that performs the following functions: quotes fares, rates, makes reservations, arranges travel tickets and accommodation, arranges travel insurance, foreign currency, documents and accepts payments". Are tail travel agency is one that sells directly to customers at several small locations in cities or towns. Retailer gets commission from the gross sale of hotel rooms, airline, train, bus and cruise tickets, insurance, foreign exchange, etc. Commission is the primary source of its revenues. A two-way selling method, that a large travel agent practices, includes commission and mark-up price. A marked-up price refers to mark up of cost of tour. It is sold on a higher price. Further, market-up price is obtained from the difference between retail price and the wholesale cost. The role of retail travel agencies is crucial when majority of principal service providers have no choice to increase the sale without the help of retail travel agents. Thus, there is a mushrooming growth of retail travel

agents dealing with the booking of hotel rooms, airlines seats, cruise line seats, etc. They consider in reaching the customers through retail agents or getting the hotel or airline promoted through retailers easy, reasonable and sustainable.

3. Full Service Agency: It is a type of travel agent that deals with all kinds of services. It may be called as complete travel agents. Apart from being an accredited agent of IATA or any other principal service providers, this full-service travel agent owns the transport fleet sand charter flights and cruises.

4. Commercial Agency: It is a category of unconventional travel agency that deals with business travel. It books convention centers and stalls in exhibition center. It also arranges venue for conducting small and large meetings.

5. Implant Agency: It is a type of travel agent that is located in the premises of corporate offices to maketravelarrangementsofemployees.Itisaregisteredtravelagentappointedasperthe agreements.

6. Group/Incentive agency: It is an emerging form of travel agency business that a specialized category of agent acts as intermediary to deal with bulk bookings for employees and clients of corporate houses.

7. Online Travel Agency: It resembles an offline travel agency in all its services. It operates on the internet through a website connected to a global distribution system. The OTAs apply the operational mechanisms of ecommerce and transact online with their customers. The OTAs offer information, bookings of hotels, cars, reservation of seats in airlines, railways, ships and buses. They sell package tours; customize tours and take enquiries. Transaction of payment is also done online using online payment modes such as credit/debit cards, internet banking, pay-pal etc.

Roles and Services of Travel Agency

The volume of business has increased so much and the areas of business operation have also been expanded in the post globalization period. With the operation of more scheduled airlines in domestic and international sector, the scope of business of travel agency is more in terms of receiving benefits and returns. Customer satisfaction and delight is given top priority. A high degree of professional accuracy is needed to survive in the business. It is otherwise difficult to stay in the business. Most of the essential services are primarily provided by travel agents include transport (road, rail, air and water), accommodation, passport, and visa procuring facilities, foreign exchange and also guidance and information about the places of travel. Many travel agents sell packages on commission basis offered by inbound operators. These are the following important roles and responsibilities of a large travel agent:

- It works as a retailer and sells package tours on behalf of wholesaler. The sale of package tours involves the rate of commission fixed on the agreement.

- It ensures horizontal integration for the purpose of achieving bumper sale.

- It is an intermediary between tour operators and tourists in terms of selling package tours in case of outbound tours and conducting sightseeing tours in case of inbound tours.

- It follows tour itinerary and it does not have anything to do with itinerary.

- It acts as a local agent to confirm and reconfirm the services reserved by the tour whole-salers.

- It sorts out problems as per the directions of tour wholesalers.

- It negotiates the terms and conditions for commission with principal suppliers.

- It recruits trained manpower from time to time.

- It procures advanced technology for operation of business.

- It collects feedback from suppliers and consumers.

- It shares information and knowledge.

Tour Operator

Tour operator links between customers (tourists) and primary service providers. This acts as a major destination promoter and this is also called as wholesaler. It is a professional agent with the capacity of buying services in bulk and distributing through the channel in methodical and organized manner. It is essential to understand the meaning of tour operator. It is an organization and firm or company with the experience and capacity to buy individual travel components separately from different suppliers and assembles them into attractive packages by adding mark-up. It is sold in different price tag to customers directly or through the middlemen (Travel Agent).

Tour operator is largely responsible for delivery of services as per the contract in tour itinerary. Tour operator is a professionally managed company with expertise and experience in planning and operation of pre-paid and pre-planned packages for vacationers or business travellers. Tour operators generally provide the services independently and tours are conducted at the cities where the offices are located. However, these services can be arranged though the other suppliers at various places. Package tours are retailed through travel agencies or directly to customers. However, at our operator may have ready-made or tailor-made packages as per the trends of market. The distribution of package tour business passes through various stages.

Dominant Roles of Tour Operators

Tour operator buys (or owns in some cases) a high volume of travel services like carriers, accommodation and services. These services are then assembled into packages for purchase by consumers. Packages are sold via travel agents (independent or owned) or through the phone and internet.

Nature of Primary Activities of different Tour Operators

- Inbound: Describing places of important of the country.

- Outbound: Highlighting holidays about other countries.

- Domestic: Specializing on domestic holidays within country.

- Specialist: Special interest travel to destinations.

- Independent: Specialized in specific holiday.

- Integrated: Business Conglomerate.

- Mass-market: Targeting more sales.

The following services are provided by the tour operates in the package tours:

- Airport and hotel transfer.

- Arrangements for traditional reception at the arrival points.

- Arrangements of luggage transfer in the airport and railway stations.

- Arrangements of guided sightseeing tours.

- Options and selection for worldwide destination.

- Comprehensive itinerary planning.

- Appropriate hotel selection & reservation.

- Meeting, conference and meeting arrangements.

- Exhibition and factory visits.

- Theme parties, events & sightseeing.

- Air tickets & travel documents like passport, VISA, health certificate and currency, insurance and permits for entry into the restricted areas.

- Foreign Exchange & Travel Insurance.

- Experienced and professional tour guides, escorts, interpreter and tour managers.

- Personalized services at destination.

- Coordination with local tourist organizations at destination.

- Domestic and international air travel.

- Business/trade delegations.

Types of Tour Operator

Tour operators are classified as they do tour business and area of operation of package tours. Each category of tour operator is unique in their own ways of providing services. This classification is suggested to distinguish difference of meanings and functions. They are called as inbound tour operators, outbound tour operators, domestic tour operators, specialist tour operators and ground tour operators. Figure presents travel trade intermediaries that include types of travel agency and tour operators.

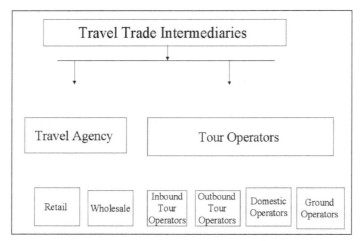

Inbound Tour Operator

They handle inbound foreign tourists in the host country. They provide them various services on their arrival and departure such as transfer, accommodation, transportation, sightseeing, entertainment, currency, insurance services etc. They are known as inbound tour operators or incoming tour operators as they specifically operate for handling incoming foreign tourists or guests. Inbound tour operators make tour packages individually or in collaboration with foreign tour operators. An inbound tour operator prepares package tours on their own and conducts tours through ground operators at host destinations. Reception upon arrivals and departures of guests and arrangements of stay and sightseeing are some of the functions of inbound tour operators.

Outbound Tour Operators

They sell package tours highlighting the destinations in foreign countries. These operators are specialized in designing and promoting multi-national tours. Like inbound tour operator, outbound tour operator sells a package tour to an individual or a group of people of a country to another country or a number of countries for a temporary period. They arrange travel documents, transportation and hotels and sightseeing, inbound tour operators/ground operators provide accommodation, transportation, local sightseeing and other services. For example, a group of American visitors have bought packages to visit Singapore, Thailand and Bangkok from Cox and Kings Office in New York. The Cox and Kings New York office takes care of the ground arrangements at these countries through an inbound tour operator. Generally, outbound tour operators appoint inbound tour operators/ground operators to make arrangement of services. They receive the guests at airport, transfer group from airport to hotel and arrange local sightseeing for business or leisure oriented customers.

Domestic Tour Operator

Domestic tour operator is one which conducts tour within the country. Domestic tour operators operate within the boundary of home country and cater the diverse needs of individuals and group travelers like inbound and outbound operators. They promote tour packages both through their own outlets and other retail travel agents.

Ground Handlers/Operators

Ground operator is otherwise known as reception operator or destination management operator or handling agencies. These operators are generally expected to provide arrangements and ground logistics at a particular destination. Thus, a ground operator provides the services required by large tour companies and they do not have a local branch/office. They do not deal with the principal suppliers such as hoteliers, transport operators, car rentals, entertainment organizations and so forth. The operator coordinates, supervises and handles accounts/payments of all services related to tour. Thus, inbound as well as outbound operators must look into the following aspects before the selection of a ground handling operators:

- Convenient Location.

- Size of business.

- Professional staff.

- Length of business.

- Reputation and membership with International and national travel and tourism associations.

- Credit facilities.

The wholesale tour operators primarily depend on ground operators for the following reasons:

- Introduction of new product or plan to promote these exotic destinations.

- Lack of control over the government regulations.

- Lack of personal contract.

- Language of barrier.

- Unfeasible to maintain own branches at each destination.

Special Interest Tour Operator

This type of tour operator offers and promotes the special interest package tours. They mostly do direct marketing for the packages or through the retail agents. These are the wildlife and ecotourism tour operators and they design wildlife and ecotourism packages for group in the niche market. This type of tour operator does not plan for mass market as buyers are limited in number. When the company plans for dealing with specialized areas, there must be potential buyers for the package tours as the nature and cost component is relatively higher unlike the conventional package tours. The specialist tour operators only organize tours in the pleasant climate and the business is mostly seasonal in nature. In the recent years, many specialist tour operators are moving towards corporate travel, incentive travel, MICE travel, ecotourism, rural tourism and cultural tourism. They are also called as personalized or customized tour operators as package tours are made on the choice and suggestions of tourists. These are the following activities that specialized tour operators carry out during the tour:

- Arrangement of visit of fairs and festivals venues.

- Arrangement for shopping and exhibitions grounds.

- Provision of hiring equipments for sports and games (Golf, winter sports and water sports).

- Provision for scholarly interpretation of objects with the help of experts at the museums.

- Arrangements for host community interaction.

- Organizing special cultural programmes in the palaces.

- Special amenities for the tourists in the train or bus journey.

Roles and Characteristics Tour Operator

In this package tour market, tour operators showcase destinations though their unique package tours. Thomas Cook, American Express and Cox and Kings follow the customer-driven approach for designing package tours to cater the demands of customers. Roles of tour operators are given below:

- It is a wholesaler as it assembles packages as per the trend of market and capacity of distribution channel.

- It deals with customers directly as a principal agent or foreign travel agent without off-loading tours to ground handling agents.

- Tour operator has liberty to amend the tour itinerary and program if it warrants.

- It invests much of time and resources to chart out delightful and value added tour itinerary for meeting the demand and expectation of tourists.

- It gives much stress on selling the tour than the conducting the tour.

- Tour operators are mostly located in the mega cities or in the cities with the international airlines services for the strategic advantage of controlling the package tours.

- It mostly provides international transfer from hotel to airport and vice-versa, if offices of tour operators are located.

- It deals with both the tourists and primary service providers as direct intermediary.

- Tour operators design the tours in such a way that handling agents may not get extra excursion tours directly from tourists.

- It is committed to work as a responsible partner in the tourism industry to popularize destinations and explore new potential destinations through their package tours.

Linkages and Integration in Travel Trade

A Travel agent or tour operator is an intermediary in the travel trade. Linking customers with service providers is the primary job of a professional travel agent or tour operator. Unlike the travel agents, the relationship of tour operators with principal service providers is linked in the form of selling the primary services to customers. Tour operator or travel agent is a linking point or connecting place that provides travel information and confirms hotel rooms, airlines, train, ferry and bus tickets and other ground services. Tour operator designs itinerary for organized package tours for which it requires travel information from hotels, airlines, bus and car rental companies, cruise companies, tourism office, etc. It establishes forward and backward linkages with the service providers to design the packages. These linkages can be horizontal and vertical to seek the ways of keeping competitors behind. Linkages can be direct or indirect between travel intermediaries and principal service providers depending on the nature of business. Integration between tour operators and principal service providers is essential for mutual benefits.

Meaning of Linkages and Integration

Integration is an approach of doing things together. Business integration is a means of combining generic talents and resources to produce best products or delivery quality services. It is very common in manufacturing sector and it has become usual business strategy to prefer integration for marketing and sales of products or producing products in minimum costs. The primary objective of integration is to maximize output with least costs. Cost cutting measure is one of the ways of reducing production cost. This leads to lower the final price of products. Lowering the price can increase the market share. Business integration is essentially important in travel and tour operation business as each provider of service cannot provide complete services on its own. Thus, linkages and integrations are common business practices in tourism business. A tour operator maintains integration with another tour operator in another city for use of common resources.

A tour operator wishes to establish business link with hotels, airlines, railways, transport operators, etc. for optimizing resources. Integration enables a travel agent or tour operator to increase its market share. It simultaneously reduces the risk of loss and fear of competitive forces. There are horizontal and vertical integration in travel trade. The former is meant for business linkage between airlines or among airlines and the latter is known for linkage between airline and hotel or between tour operators between cruise lines. There are benefits of integration as well as risks of doing integration. These are the following benefits:

- Economics of Scales: This concept is very common in business and it would be more appropriate in tour operation and travel agency business. The volume of productions and sales would be more that leads to providing more profits. The cost of production can be drastically minimized with the help of integration. For example, a tour operator can take care of marketing, sales and customer care of an airline or hotel operator or they can jointly do the marketing.

- Avoidance of Middlemen: Integration can link the tour operator with primary service provider directly. Consolidation of Market: Integration can increase the market share and it simultaneously helps in dominating the market.

- Control over Supply for More Bargaining Power: Merger and acquisitions can help travel agency and tour operator to have more control over supply of package tours in market. At the same time, tour operator can secure some bargaining power for booking hotel rooms and airline seats.

- Horizontal Integration: It involves two tour operators or two travel agencies or two hotels and two airlines for amalgamation of competitive product through merger or acquisitions. This integration helps the players offer complementary products and minimize unfair competition.

- Vertical Integration: It is a type of integration that links between airline and hotel or tour operator and airline or hotel for mutual benefits. Big corporate airlines and hotel companies have owned travel agencies at key destinations for increasing the volume of business and gaining competitive edge over other competitors. Needless to say, travel agency and tour operation business is facing cut-throat competition due to the rising number of small players entering into the package tour market.

- Linkages for Effective Distribution of Services: Tour operator is a partner of a dynamic travel distribution channel through which buying and selling of package tours is possible in a long-term basis. The vertical integration establishes continuous relationship with many direct and indirect providers of services to tourists. Tour operators bring the principal suppliers to a common network. These principal suppliers are transport operators, airlines and charter flights, cruise line companies, railways and car rental companies, hotels and event mangers. They are selected on the basis of location, existence, service quality, physical facility, credit facility, etc. Tour operators make the final contacts with these service providers on the conditions that tourists are served at the destinations. When tour operators are ready with package tour to be promoted in market, they prefer to promote it through organized channels and in certain cases clients buy directly from them. What tour operators plan for the sale of package tours is that they open new branches in big cities and appoint several retail travel agents in the smaller cities. The detail distribution network is given in figure below.

Distribution Networks of Tour Operation Business

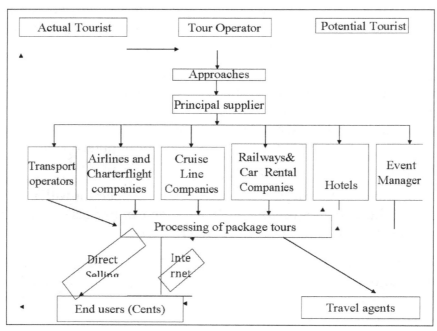

In the manufacturing sector, supply chain management is a significant area in the distribution of finished products in the market. Tour operators are the travel intermediaries who negotiate and sell the services of primary producers to tourists. It is almost difficult both in case of tourists and principal service providers to contact separately on selling the products. This is a dynamic In the manufacturing sector, supply chain management is a significant area in the distribution of finished products in the market. Tour operators are the travel intermediaries who negotiate and sell the services of primary producers to tourists. It is almost difficult both in case of tourists and principal service providers to contact separately on selling the products. This is a dynamic mechanism to make the products reachable at the consumer doors from the place of production. Neither the producers nor the consumers confront in the final stage of sales because there is a very active linkage system to deliver the product in the market area. Both the producers and consumers are controlled by the distributing agencies. In similar case, you may compare the relationship of tour operators with the producers of tourism products and services like transport companies, accommodation providers and destinations agencies. These are the following services that tour operates seek to strike integration with the principal service providers for deigning the conventional package tours.

- Airline: Airline is a major segment in the tour operation business network. Tour operators maintain alliance with domestic and internal airlines for the bulk reservation of seats for a particular season. The role of airlines in the channel of distribution in tour operation business is significant. Air travel is an important component and airlines prefer the sale of air tickets in bulk through tour operators. The sale of air tickets is done as per the conditions.

- Car Rental Companies: Tour operators procure ground transportation for the purpose of airport transfer and drop from recognized car rental companies. Car rental companies provide luxury car services on the terms and conditions with tour operators. They sometime work on the annual contact and fixed rate or sometime work on the fixed commission.

- Railways: Tour operators take the help of railway companies for booking seats and other amenities at the railway stations. Journey in train gives different pleasure and experience than other modes of communication. Thus, tour operators sign contract with railways companies for the reservation of special coach issue of special tourist pass.

- Cruise Companies: The size of market of cruise travel is growing due to the preference of new-age tourists for experience. Cruise package is now very affordable. Cruise companies have designed packages suiting the needs of lower, middle and upper segment of customers. Tour operators block and book the seats in large numbers. They work on the commission and sometime special discount also along with complementary cruise travel. In the travel trade distribution network, cruise operators take direct help of tour operators and travel agents for bulk sales of cruise packages.

- Luxury Coach Operators: A coach operator is a primary service provider in tour operation business distribution network. Tour wholesalers appoint coach operators on the basis of competitive rates and quality of transport and services. Coach operators send quotations for transfer, sightseeing, and excursion trips to tour operators or wholesalers during May and June every year. Each tourist coach must have elevated bucket seats, white window glass, microphone, air condition system and refrigerator. The service quality is measured in terms of punctuality, safety, flexibility, and adaptability.

- Accommodation Operators: Accommodation operators maintain conventional and non-conventional type of accommodation. Tourists may have choices of selecting accommodation depending on budget, facilities, locations and comfort. It adds value in package tour. Room, restaurant and cock tail services along with duty-free shopping, doctors on call, beauty parlor, fitness center, etc. make a guest feel at home.

- Event Management Companies: Tour operator may be an event management company to deal with MICE activities. There are specialized event management operators like Creative Tours and Travel. Booking venues, food, conference kits and post & pre-conference sightseeing programmes are the functions of Event Management Company. Tour operators negotiate with the event management companies on the flat rate basis. Even management companies maintain the inventory of essential items for conduct of mega events for which tour operators establish integration with them.

- Authorized Foreign Exchange Dealer: Tour operators also deal with foreign currencies as they receive for the sale of inbound package tours. Payment is also made through foreign currency for booking of hotel rooms, transports, guide services and other services in case of outbound package tour. Authorized foreign exchange agents or authorized money exchangers deal with foreign currency is an important part of travel trade linkage and integration. Endorsement of foreign currency, more importantly Dollar or Euro or Great Britain Pound in passport of clients is mandatory in foreign travel.

- Insurance Company: Travel insurance is an important area of business for tour operators. Most of the package tours are insured and insurance companies working with tour operator. Tour packages are insured for compensation to the tour operators or guests in the event of cancellation. Customers also prefer for insuring health and luggage insurance. Tour operators get commission from the insurance companies.

- Destination Management Operators or Ground Handling Operators: Ground handling operators work for tour operators to provide ground logistics services. It includes the luxury car or bus services, guide and language interpreter services, entrance fees, reception upon arrivals, etc. Ground operators are located at the major tourist destinations and they work as per the directions of tour wholesalers or tour vouchers. However, adventure tour operators or special interest tour operators arrange most of the ground services. Tour operators collect transport tariff and information about the destinations from the ground operators during the off season.

References

- History-of-travel-agency-and-tour-Operation: uou.ac.in, Retrieved 07, January 2020
- Tourist-attractions, USA-US: planetware.com, Retrieved 12, May 2020
- Top-rated-tourist-attractions-in-Europe: planetware.com, Retrieved 26, August 2020

International Travelling

The movement of people from one geographical location to another is termed as traveling. It can be accomplished through various means such as automobile, boat, bus, foot, ship and airplane. The diverse aspects of traveling such as travel behavior and travel technology have been thoroughly discussed in this chapter.

Travel

A statue dedicated to the traveler in Oviedo, Spain.

Travel is the movement of people between relatively distant geographical locations, and can involve travel by foot, bicycle, automobile, train, boat, airplane, or other means, with or without luggage, and can be one way or round trip. Travel can also include relatively short stays between successive movements.

Etymology

The origin of the word "travel" is most likely lost to history. The term "travel" may originate from the Old French word *travail*. According to the Merriam Webster dictionary, the first known use of the word travel was in the 14th century. It also states that the word comes from Middle English *travailen*, *travelen* (which means to torment, labor, strive, journey) and earlier from Old French *travailler* (which means to work strenuously, toil). In English we still occasionally use the words *travail* and *travails*, which mean struggle. According to Simon Winchester in his book The Best Travelers' Tales (2004), the words travel and travail both share an even more ancient root: a Roman instrument of torture called the tripalium (in Latin it means "three stakes", as in to impale). This link reflects the extreme difficulty of travel in ancient times. Also note the torturous connotation of the word "travailler." Today, travel may or may not be much easier depending upon the destination you choose (i.e., Mt. Everest, the Amazon rainforest), how you plan to get there (tour bus, cruise ship, or oxcart), and whether or not you decide to "rough it. "There's a big difference between simply being a tourist and being a true world traveler," notes travel writer Michael Kasum. This is, however, a contested distinction as academic work on the cultures and sociology of travel has noted.

Purpose and Motivation

Train travel – Passengers on a train on a bridge of the Nilgiri Mountain Railway, between Mettupalayam and Ootacamund, in Tamil Nadu, India.

Reasons for traveling include recreation, tourism or vacationing, research travel for the gathering of information, for holiday to visit people, volunteer travel for charity, migration to begin life somewhere else, religious pilgrimages and mission trips, business travel, trade, commuting, and other reasons, such as to obtain health care or waging or fleeing war or for the enjoyment of traveling. Travel may occur by human-powered transport such as walking or bicycling, or with vehicles, such as public transport, automobiles, trains and airplanes.

Motives to travel include:

- pleasure

- relaxation

- discovery and exploration

- getting to know other cultures

- taking personal time for building interpersonal relationships

Geographic Types of Travel

Travel may be local, regional, national (domestic) or international. In some countries, non-local internal travel may require an internal passport, while international travel typically requires a passport and visa. A trip may also be part of a round-trip, which is a particular type of travel whereby a person moves from one location to another and returns.

History of Travel

Once difficult, slow and dangerous, travel has tended to become easier, quicker, and more frivolous in the course of history. The evolution of technology such as horse tack and bullet trains has contributed to this trend.

Travel Safety

Travelers in a British Airways 747 airplane. Air travel is a common means of transport.

MS Skania ferry in the port of Szczecin.

Authorities emphasize the importance of taking precautions to ensure travel safety. When traveling abroad, the odds favor a safe and incident-free trip, however, travelers can be subject to difficulties, crime and violence. Some safety considerations include being aware of one's surroundings, avoiding being the target of a crime, leaving copies of one's passport and itinerary information with trusted people, obtaining medical insurance valid in the country being visited and registering with one's national embassy when arriving in a foreign country. Many countries do not recognize drivers' licenses from other countries; however most countries accept international driving permits. Automobile insurance policies issued in one's own country are often invalid in foreign countries, and it is often a requirement to obtain temporary auto insurance valid in the country being visited. It is also advisable to become oriented with the driving-rules and -regulations of destination countries. Wearing a seat belt is highly advisable for safety reasons; many countries have penalties for violating seatbelt laws.

There are three main statistics which may be used to compare the safety of various forms of travel (based on a DETR survey in October 2000):

Deaths per billion journeys	Deaths per billion hours	Deaths per billion kilometers
Bus: 4.3	Bus: 11.1	Air: 0.05
Rail: 20	Rail: 30	Bus: 0.4
Van: 20	Air: 30.8	Rail: 0.6
Car: 40	Water: 50	Van: 1.2
Foot: 40	Van: 60	Water: 2.6
Water: 90	Car: 130	Car: 3.1
Air: 117	Foot: 220	Bicycle: 44.6

Bicycle: 170	Bicycle: 550	Foot: 54.2
Motorcycle: 1640	Motorcycle: 4840	Motorcycle: 108.9

Pilgrimage

David Teniers the younger: Female Pilgrim.

A pilgrimage is a journey or search of moral or spiritual significance. Typically, it is a journey to a shrine or other location of importance to a person's beliefs and faith, although sometimes it can be a metaphorical journey into someone's own beliefs. Many religions attach spiritual importance to particular places: the place of birth or death of founders or saints, or to the place of their "calling" or spiritual awakening, or of their connection (visual or verbal) with the divine, to locations where miracles were performed or witnessed, or locations where a deity is said to live or be "housed," or any site that is seen to have special spiritual powers. Such sites may be commemorated with shrines or temples that devotees are encouraged to visit for their own spiritual benefit: to be healed or have questions answered or to achieve some other spiritual benefit. A person who makes such a journey is called a pilgrim. As a common human experience, pilgrimage has been proposed as a Jungian archetype by Wallace Clift and Jean Dalby Clift.

The Holy Land acts as a focal point for the pilgrimages of the Abrahamic religions of Judaism, Christianity, and Islam. According to a Stockholm University study in 2011, these pilgrims visit the Holy Land to touch and see physical manifestations of their faith, confirm their beliefs in the holy context with collective excitation, and connect personally to the Holy Land.

Bahá'í Faith

Bahá'u'lláh decreed pilgrimage to two places in the Kitáb-i-Aqdas: the House of Bahá'u'lláh in Baghdad, Iraq, and the House of the Báb in Shiraz, Iran. Later, `Abdu'l-Bahá designated the Shrine of Bahá'u'lláh at Bahji, Israel as a site of pilgrimage. The designated sites for pilgrimage are currently not accessible to the majority of Bahá'ís, as they are in Iraq and Iran respectively, and thus when Bahá'ís currently refer to pilgrimage, it refers to a nine-day pilgrimage which consists of visiting the holy places at the Bahá'í World Centre in northwest Israel in Haifa, Acre, and Bahjí.

Buddhism

Ancient excavated Buddha-image at the Mahaparinirvana Temple, Kushinagar.

Tibetans on a pilgrimage to Lhasa, doing full-body prostrations, often for the entire length of the journey.

There are four places that Buddhists make pilgrimage to:

- Lumbini: Buddha's birthplace (in Nepal).

- Bodh Gaya: place of Enlightenment.

- Sarnath: where he delivered his first teaching.

- Kusinara: (now Kusinagar, India) where he attained *mahaparinirvana* (died).

Other pilgrimage places in India and Nepal connected to the life of Gautama Buddha are: Savatthi, Pataliputta, Nalanda, Gaya, Vesali, Sankasia, Kapilavastu, Kosambi, Rajagaha, Varanasi, Sabari mala.

Other famous places for Buddhist pilgrimage include:

- India: Sanchi, Ellora, Ajanta.

- Thailand: Sukhothai, Ayutthaya, Wat Phra Kaew, Wat Doi Suthep.

- Tibet: Lhasa (traditional home of the Dalai Lama), Mount Kailash, Lake Namtso.

- Cambodia: Angkor Wat, Silver Pagoda.

- Sri Lanka: Polonnaruwa, Temple of the Tooth (Kandy), Anuradhapura.

- Laos: Luang Prabang.

- Malaysia: Kek Lok Si, Cheng Hoon Teng, Maha Vihara.

- Myanmar: Bagan, Sagaing Hill.

- Nepal: Boudhanath, Swayambhunath.

- Indonesia: Borobudur.

- China: Yung-kang, Lung-men caves. The Four Sacred Mountains.

- Japan:

  - Shikoku Pilgrimage, 88 Temple pilgrimage in the Shikoku island.

  - Japan 100 Kannon, pilgrimage composed of the Saigoku, Bandō and Chichibu pilgrimages.

    - Saigoku 33 Kannon, pilgrimage in the Kansai region.

- Bandō 33 Kannon, pilgrimage in the Kantō region.

  - Chichibu 34 Kannon, pilgrimage in Saitama Prefecture.

- Chūgoku 33 Kannon, pilgrimage in the Chūgoku region.

- Kumano Kodō.

- Mount Kōya.

Christianity

Pilgrims

Christian pilgrimage was first made to sites connected with the birth, life, crucifixion and resurrection of Jesus. Aside from the early example of Origen in the third century, surviving descriptions of Christian pilgrimages to the Holy Land date from the 4th century, when pilgrimage was encouraged by church fathers including Saint Jerome, and established by Helena, the mother of Constantine the Great.

Old lady climbing Mount Ara on foot on a pilgrimage to Tsaghkevank on Ascension Day.

Pilgrimages were, and are, also made to Rome and other sites associated with the apostles, saints and Christian martyrs, as well as to places where there have been apparitions of the Virgin Mary. A popular pilgrimage site is along the Way of St. James to Santiago de Compostela, in Galicia, Spain, to the shrine of the apostle James. Chaucer's *The Canterbury Tales* recounts tales told by Christian pilgrims on their way to Canterbury Cathedral and the shrine of Thomas Becket.

Hinduism

Bathing ghat on the Ganges during Kumbh Mela, Haridwar.

Pilgrimage to Kedarnath.

Pilgrims on their way to Manikaran, Himachal Pradesh, India, in 2004.

According to Karel Werner's *Popular Dictionary of Hinduism*, "most Hindu places of pilgrimage are associated with legendary events from the lives of various gods.... Almost any place can become a focus for pilgrimage, but in most cases they are sacred cities, rivers, lakes, and mountains." Hindus are encouraged to undertake pilgrimages during their lifetime, though this practice is not considered absolutely mandatory. Most Hindus visit sites within their region or locale.

Kumbh Mela: Kumbh Mela is the largest pilgrimage recorded in history. Kumbh Mela is also credited with the largest gathering of humans in the entire world. The location is rotated among Allahabad, Haridwar, Nashik, and Ujjain.

Char Dham (Famous Four Pilgrimage sites): The four holy sites Puri, Rameswaram, Dwarka, and Badrinath (or alternatively the Himalayan towns of Badrinath, Kedarnath, Gangotri, and Yamunotri) compose the *Char Dham* (*four abodes*) pilgrimage circuit.

Old Holy cities as per Puranic Texts: Varanasi formerly known as Kashi, Allahabad formerly known as Prayag, Haridwar-Rishikesh, Mathura-Vrindavan, Pandharpur, Paithan and Ayodhya.

Major Temple cities: Puri, which hosts a major Vaishnava Jagannath temple and Rath Yatra celebration; Katra, home to the Vaishno Devi temple; Three comparatively recent temples of fame and huge pilgrimage are Shirdi, home to Sai Baba of Shirdi, Tirumala - Tirupati, home to the Tirumala Venkateswara Temple; and Sabarimala,where Swami Ayyappan is worshipped.

Shakti Peethas: Another important set of pilgrimages are the *Shakti Peethas*, where the Mother Goddess is worshipped, the two principal ones being *Kalighat* and *Kamakhya*.

Islam

Muslim pilgrims circumambulate around the Ka'aba during the Hajj.

Supplicating pilgrim at Masjid al-Haram (Mecca, Saudi Arabia).

The pilgrimage to Mecca (*Hajj*) is one of the five pillars of Islam and a mandatory religious duty for Muslims that must be carried out at least once in their lifetime by all adult Muslims who are physically and financially capable of undertaking the journey, and can support their family during their absence. The gathering during the Hajj is considered the largest annual gathering of people in the world.

Another important place for Muslims is the city of Medina, the second holiest site in Islam, in Saudi Arabia, the final resting place of Muhammad in Al-Masjid al-Nabawi (Mosque of the Prophet).

The Ihram (white robes of pilgrimage) is meant to show equality of all Muslim pilgrims in the eyes of God, that there is no difference between a prince and a pauper. Ihram is also symbolic for holy virtue and pardon from all past sins.

Arba'een

Arba'een (Arabic: الأربعين, "forty"), Chehelom (Persian: چهلم, Urdu: چہلم, "the fortieth [day]") or Qirkhi, Imamin Qirkhi (Azerbaijani: İmamın qırxı, امامین قیرخی, "the fortieth of Imam") is a Shia Muslim religious observance that occurs forty days after the Day of Ashura. It commemorates the martyrdom of Husayn ibn Ali, the grandson of Muhammad, which falls on the 20th or 21st day of the month of Safar. Imam Husayn ibn Ali and 72 companions were killed by Yazid I's army in the Battle of Karbala in 61 AH (680 CE). Arba'een or forty days is also the usual length of mourning after the death of a family member or loved one in many Muslim traditions. Arba'een is one of the largest pilgrimage gatherings on Earth, in which up to 31 million people go to the city of Karbala in Iraq.

Imam Reza

The second largest holy city in the world, Mashhad attracts more than 20 million tourists and pilgrims every year, many of whom come to pay homage to the Imam Reza shrine (the eighth Shi'ite Imam). It has been a magnet for travelers since medieval times.

Judaism

While Solomon's Temple stood, Jerusalem was the centre of the Jewish religious life and the site of the Three Pilgrimage Festivals of Passover, Shavuot and Sukkot, and all adult men who were able were required to visit and offer sacrifices (*korbanot*) at the Temple. After the destruction of the Temple, the obligation to visit Jerusalem and to make sacrifices no longer applied. The obligation was restored with the rebuilding of the Temple, but following its destruction in 70 CE, the obligation to make a pilgrimage to Jerusalem and offer sacrifices again went into abeyance.

The western retaining wall of the Temple Mount, known as the Western Wall or 'Wailing' Wall, remains in the Old City of Jerusalem and is the most sacred and visited site for Jews. Pilgrimage to this area was off-limits to Jews from 1948 to 1967, when East Jerusalem was under Jordanian control.

Jews at the Wailing Wall in Jerusalem during the Ottoman period, 1860.

There are numerous lesser Jewish pilgrimage destinations, mainly tombs of *tzadikim*, throughout the Land of Israel and all over the world, including: Hebron; Bethlehem; Mt. Meron; Netivot; Uman, Ukraine; Silistra, Bulgaria; Damanhur, Egypt; and many others.

Sikhism

The Harmandir Sahib (the Golden Temple) in Amritsar.

The Sikh religion does not place great importance on pilgrimage. Guru Nanak Dev was asked "Should I go and bathe at pilgrimage places?" and replied: "God's name is the real pilgrimage place which consists of contemplation of the word of God, and the cultivation of inner knowledge."

Eventually, however, Amritsar and Harmandir Saheb (the Golden Temple) became the spiritual and cultural centre of the Sikh faith, and if a Sikh goes on pilgrimage it is usually to this place.

Zoroastrianism

In Iran, there are pilgrimage destinations called *pirs* in several provinces, although the most familiar ones are in the province of Yazd. In addition to the traditional Yazdi shrines, new sites may be in the process of becoming pilgrimage destinations. The ruins are the ruins of ancient fire temples. One such site is the ruin of the Sassanian era Azargoshasb Fire Temple in Iran's Azarbaijan Province. Other sites are the ruins of fire temples at Rey, south of the capital Tehran, and the Firouzabad ruins sixty kilometres south of Shiraz in the province of Pars.

In India the cathedral fire temple that houses the Iranshah Atash Behram, located in the small town of Udvada in the west coast province of Gujarat, is a pilgrimage destination.

Meher Baba

The main pilgrimage sites associated with the spiritual teacher Meher Baba are Meherabad, India, where Baba completed the "major portion" of his work and where his tomb is now located, and Meherazad, India, where Baba resided later in his life.

Travel Technology

Travel technology (also called tourism technology, and hospitality automation) is the application of Information Technology (IT) or Information and Communications Technology (ICT) in the travel, tourism and hospitality industry. One form of travel technology is flight tracking.

Since travel implies locomotion, travel technology was originally associated with the computer reservations system (CRS) of the airlines industry, but now is used more inclusively, incorporating the broader tourism sector as well as its subset the hospitality industry. While travel technology includes the computer reservations system, it also represents a much broader range of applications, in fact increasingly so. Travel technology includes virtual tourism in the form of virtual tour technologies. Travel technology may also be referred to as *e-travel / etravel* or *e-tourism / etourism* (eTourism), in reference to "electronic travel" or "electronic tourism".

e Tourism can be defined as the analysis, design, implementation and application of IT and e-commerce solutions in the travel & tourism industry; as well as the analysis of the respective economic processes and market structures and customer relationship management.

From a communication science perspective, eTourism can be also defined as every application of Information and Communication Technologies (ICTs) within both the hospitality and tourism industry, as well as within the tourism experience.

Travel technology is increasingly being used to describe systems for managing and monitoring travel, including travel tracking and flight tracking systems.

In other contexts, the term "travel technology" can refer to technology intended for use by travelers, such as light-weight laptop computers with universal power supplies or satellite Internet connections. That is not the sense in which it is used here.

Applications

Travel technology includes many processes such as dynamic packaging which provide useful new options for consumers. Today the tour guide can be a GPS tour guide, and the guidebook could be an audioguide, podguide or I-Tours, such as City audio guides. The biometric passport may also be included as travel technology in the broad sense.

XML-based technologies have become increasingly important for the travel industry. XML can be used to support air reservation booking or to implement optional services and merchandising functions in the booking process. Another important application of XML is the establishing of direct connections between Airlines and Travel Agencies. In order to create a generally accepted XML-standard, the Open Axis Group was founded.

Internet

The Internet has a powerful impact on hospitality and tourism. For many businesses and locations, the experience starts long before a traveler arrives--it begins with the first visit to the website, when a person sees photos of the location and gets a sense of what to expect. In the hospitality and tourism business, effective use of Internet technologies can improve revenue. Websites, blogs, online advertising, social media, online ordering and information repositories all help convince customers to choose a location or business. Reservations Systems.

Booking engines to allow easy access by consumers and travel professionals; the systems enable individuals to make reservations and compare prices. Many, like Expedia and Orbitz, are available through online interfaces. Booking engines cut costs for travel businesses by reducing call volume and give the traveler more control over their purchasing process.

Computer Systems

Because many tourism businesses are large and dispersed, they use computer systems to stay connected. Computer systems allow communication between branches and locations which makes it easier to streamline reservations and cross-company policies.

They are also used internally to keep all of the staff on the same page and make it easier to access information that can improve the guest experience: guest preferences, house-keeping information and reservation details can all be kept on a single system.

Mobile Communication

Many travelers take some form of mobile communication device with them on the road, whether it is a tablet computer or a mobile phone. To keep customers advised of changes many tourism and hospitality businesses use mobile communication; they send delay notices, offer deals and sponsor location-based advertising. Depending on the type of business the communication might happen through emails, text messaging or GPS tagging, for example.

Travel Behavior

Travel behavior is the study of what people do over space, and how people use transport.

Questions Studied

The questions studied in travel behavior are broad, and are very much related to activity analysis and time-use research studies.

- How many trips do people make?

- Where do they go? (What is the destination?)

- What mode do they take?

- Who accompanies whom?

- When is the trip made? What is the schedule?

- What is the sequence or pattern of trips?

- What route choices do people make?

- Why do people travel? (Why can't people stay at home and telecommute or teleshop?)

Other behavioral aspects of traveling, such as letting people get off before entering a vehicle, queueing behavior, etc.

Data

These questions can be answered descriptively using a travel diary, often part of a travel survey or travel behavior inventory. Large metropolitan areas typically only do such surveys once every decade, though some cities are conducting panel surveys, which track the same people year after year.

That data is generally used to estimate transportation planning models, so that transport analysts can make predictions about people who haven't been surveyed. This is important in forecasting traffic, which depends on future changes to road networks, land use patterns, and policies.

Some years ago it was recognized that behavioral research was limited by data, and a special data set was developed to aid research: The Baltimore Disaggregate Data Set which is the result an in depth survey, ca. 1977. Its title indicates today's emphasis on disaggregated rather than aggregated data. This particular data set is believed lost. A small program to preserve and make available on the web these travel behavior surveys, the Metropolitan Travel Survey Archive, is now under way at the University of Minnesota. There is also the National Personal Transportation Survey (later National Household Travel Survey), conducted every five years or so, but with much less spatial detail.

Travel Behavior and Activity Analysis

Analysis of travel behavior from the home can answer the question: How does the family participate in modern society. Consider two non-observable extremes. At one extreme we have the non-specialized household. It does everything for itself, and no travel is required. Ultimate specialization is the other extreme; travel is required for all things. Observed households are somewhere in between. The "in between" position of households might be thought of as the consequence of two matters.

1. There is social and economic structure – the organization of society. To participate in this society, the household specializes its occupations, education, social activities, etc.

2. The extent to which members of the household specialize turns on their attributes and resources.

Moore (1964) has observed that increasing specialization in all things is the chief feature of social change. Considering social changes, one might observe that 100 years ago things were less specialized compared to today. So we would expect lots of change in household travel over the time period. Data are not very good, but the travel time aspect of what's available seems contrary to the expectation, travel hasn't changed much. For instance, the time spent on the journey to work may have been stable for centuries (the travel budget hypothesis). Here are some travel time comparisons from John Robinson (1986).

Table: Minutes per day spent in travel				
	Men		**Women**	
Activity	1975	1985	1975	1985
Work Travel	25	31	9	17
Family Travel	33	31	33	33
Leisure Travel	27	33	21	23
Total	85	94	63	73

Most travel behavior analysis concerns demand issues and do not touch very much on supply issues. Yet when we observe travel from a home, we are certainly observing some sort of market clearing process – demand and supply are matched.

History of Travel Behavior Analysis

Analytic work on travel behavior can be dated from Liepmann (1945). Liepmann obtained and analyzed 1930s data on worker travel in England. Many of the insights current today were found by Liepmann: time spent, ride sharing, etc. Most academics date modern work from advances in mode choice analysis made in the 1970s. This created much excitement, and after some years an International Association for Travel Behaviour Research emerged. There are about 150 members of the Association; it holds a conference every three years. The proceedings of those conferences yield a nice record of advances in the field. The proceedings also provide a record of topics of lasting interest and of changing priorities. Mode choice received priority early on, but in the main today's work is not so much on theory as it is on practice. Hagerstrand (1970) developed a time and space path analysis, often called the time-space prism.

Gender Difference In Travel Patterns

On November 18–20, 2004, Transportation Research Board (TRB) held its third conference in Chicago, Illinois, with an interest in advancing the understanding of women's issues in transportation. One of the presented studies, conducted by Nobis et al., revealed that the gender difference in travel patterns is linked to employment status, household structure, child care, and maintenance tasks. They found that travel patterns of men and women are much similar when considering single families; the differences are greater once males and females are compared in multi-person households without children; and are the highest once they live in households with children. Over the past two decades numerous studies have been conducted on travel behavior showing gender as an influential factor in travel decision making.

References

- Varozza, G. (2015). 501 Time-Saving Tips Every Woman Should Know. Harvest House Publishers. p. 214. ISBN 978-0-7369-5951-3

- Long, Matthew (2011). Islamic Beliefs, Practices, and Cultures. Marshall Cavendish Corporation.

p. 86. ISBN 978-0-7614-7926-0. Retrieved 02, August 2020

- Nobis, C.; B. Lenz. (2004). "Gender Differences in Travel Patterns: Role of Employment Status and Household Structure". Research on Women's Issues in Transportation, Report of a Conference,Vol. 2: Technical Papers. Retrieved 27, June 2020

- Egger, Roman; Buhalis, Dimitrios (2008). Etourism Case Studies: Management and Marketing Issues. Amsterdam [etc.]: Butterworth-Heinemann. ISBN 978-0-7506-8667-9

- Tesone, Dana V. (2005). Hospitality Information Systems and E-Commerce. New York: John Wiley and Sons Ltd. ISBN 978-0-471-47849-2

- Cantoni, Lorenzo; Xiang, Zheng (2013). Information and Communication Technologies in Tourism 2013. Berlin – Heidelberg: Springer. ISBN 978-3-642-36309-2

- Benckendorff, Pierre J.; Sheldon, P.J.; Fesenmaier, D.R. (2014). Tourism Information Technology(Second Edition). Wallingford, UK: CABI. ISBN 978-1-7806-4185-0

- Fatemeh Baratian-Ghorghi; Huaguo Zhou (2015). "Investigating Women's and Men's Propensity to Use Traffic Information in a Developing Country". Transportation in Developing Economies. Retrieved 20, June 2020

- Buhalis, Dimitrios (2003). Etourism: Information Technology for Strategic Tourism Management. Harlow, England: Financial Times Prentice Hall. ISBN 978-0-582-35740-2

- Zhou, Zongqing (2004). E-commerce and Information Technology in Hospitality and Tourism. Clifton Park, NY: Delmar Learning. ISBN 978-0-7668-4140-6

- Mosher, Lucinda (2005). Praying: The Rituals of Faith. Church Publishing, Inc. p. 155. ISBN 9781596270169. Retrieved 18 September 2014. Technology(Second Edition). Wallingford, UK: CABI. ISBN 978-1-7806-4185-0

- Fesenmaier, Daniel R.; Wober, Karl W.; Werthner, H. (2006). Destination Recommendation Systems: Behavioural Foundations and Applications. Wallingford, UK: CABI. ISBN 978-0-85199-023-1

Diverse Aspects of Destination Management

The process which involves synchronized actions in order to control the different aspects of a particular tourism industry is termed as destination management. Some of its major aspects are destination life cycle, destination visioning and destination marketing. This chapter has been written to provide an easy understanding of these varied aspects of destination management.

A destination is both a site and an event, and these two factors are the attractions. In a site attraction, a location exercises appeal. With an event acting as a pull, tourists are drawn' to a particular place because of what 3s happening at that location. Where both site and event are attractions, the success of such a destination multiplies. Destinations can be spread over a wide geographical area. The attraction to a destination lies in the image it has or the attractions it offers.

Primary and Secondary Destinations

All destinations are not created equal some have more potential than others to draw visitors. Primary Destinations influence a traveler's decision about where to go, are often the main reason for visiting an area, and are closely linked to the image of the destination as promoted in marketing campaigns. Secondary Destinations are those that enhance the tourist experience, but are not part of the major destination selection process.

Concept and Characteristics of Tourism Destination

In the conceptual estimation of destination, different standing points can be followed. In the whole, destination is a physical location where the tourist is spending at least one night. It is containing tourist attractions, products, relating services that are necessary to meet the stay of a tourist on the place at least for one day. Destination has physical and administrative limits, which are determining its management, and has an image and perception. It includes a lot of elements being concerned, it is capable for constructing a network, a cooperation and to become a bigger destination; the determination of destination is made from the point of view of the tourist. To become a tourist destination the location, the region has to have the factors that determine the tourist destinations. These factors are determinants in the bordering, determination of the core area destination; their development is essential by the increase of the competitiveness of the specific destinations determinants of the destination are as follows:

- Tourist attractions: Natural factors, factors made by human being, heritage, special events, etc.

- Approachability: The entire traffic system, including roads, traffic means, etc.

- Tourist services: Accommodation, host services, other tourist services, etc.

- Product packages.

- All kind of activities that can be run by the tourists during their stay; public-utility services, e.g. banks, telecommunication, hospitals, etc.

Definition of destination, summarizing the aspects regarding the nature of destination and its determining factors; the characteristics of destination can be summarized as follows:

- Area target that is chosen by the tourist as the target of his travel.

- Receiving area that is providing services for the tourist and people living on the spot.

- It is defined from the point of view of the tourist.

- A place/region that is confinable physically and geographically.

- A place/region that is containing tourist attractions, products, services and other background services being necessary for spending at least one day.

- The tourist is spending at least one night here.

- It is containing a lot of persons being concerned who are cooperating with each other.

- It has an image.

- It has perception (it means that each of the tourists can form an opinion about a destination through his own "screen" subjectively).

- It is providing integrated experience for the tourist.

- In a wider sense it is a tourist product that is competing with other tourist products (destinations) on the market of tourism.

- A kind of a complex and integrated system that is taking the existence of a modern tourism controlling and management system to the successful operation for granted.

- It is a system being built from below and supported from above.

Not all locations, regions can become a tourist destination. There are such kind of basic criterions that has to be met so that a location, region could become a tourist destination. The above mentioned are only the most basic criterions. The determination and bordering of the destinations or the core area destinations are supposing the development of a special system of criterions that is made according to preferences, expectations, points' of view of the tourist first of all.

Features of Tourism Destination

Features of destinations include quality, authenticity, uniqueness, drawing power, and activity options. It is the combination of these elements that sets destinations apart from one another.

- High Quality is a key guiding value in tourism development. For any attraction this means having a pleasing clean appearance, offering smooth customer oriented operations and procedures, resource protection, friendly hospitality.

- Authenticity, being real, matters. It means letting the distinctive local flavor of a community shine through in ways that create and produce a "sense of place".

- Uniqueness is the "edge" that sets an attraction in your community apart from the competition somewhere else.

- Drawing Power is measured in terms of the number of visitors who will travel a specified distance to visit your community and whether they will return for repeat visits.

- Activity Options are important characteristics of destinations. The first impulse is to concentrate on buildings, sites, facilities. But, it is important to remember the activities that provide resident and visitors things to do.

Development of Tourism Destination

The destinations as the organizational systems developing on the regional concentration and cooperation have to be taken into connection with the economic processes in the world; one basic principle of which is that the durable industrial and business competitive advantages are appearing concentrated geographically more and more. In the competition there are not taking part separate persons of the market but the basic units of the market competition, the companies, enterprises and regional institutions. The establishment and operation of these systems are helped by the government schemes and supporting resources as well. The regional concentration principle is playing a determinant role in the effective operation of the destination as well, which is generating competitive advantages. The tourist target areas are worth settling to a regional concentration being significant from the point of view of tourism, based on definitive basic principles, so that the economic potential of the region can be increased.

Determinant factors of the tourist competitiveness of each region are the development and operation of the management system with the effective, suitable competences and calculable financing and organizational background. Modern tourism management and operation, that is the revaluation of the current traditions, are needed to the development of an effective management system organized on the basis of the regional concentration principle. The integrated planning, management and operation of tourism are needed on all levels of tourism. Development of the system is taking for granted such kind of regional and organizational planning basic principles are:

- Revaluation of cooperation, development of consciousness in the cooperation, development, planning, organization, operation of the forms of cooperation.

- More close cooperation with other regions, branches in the processes of planning and development originating from the multiplier effect of tourism.

- More complex approaches in the development of the service system of tourism: beside the development of the tourist infra- and superstructure the development of the background infrastructures, the supporting factors have to be emphasized too.

- The use of innovative, modern, up to date technologies in the processes of development.

System of Destination and Tourism

The place of destination in the system of tourism is demonstrated by the system of tourism. Destination can be found on the side of the supply (the product) from the two sub-systems of the tourism system. The tourist supplies are consisting of the factors of the receiving area that is used by the tourist during his stay. Central element of the supply is the tourist product that is containing the services meeting the demands of the tourist. Tourism is an integrated, open, complex system operating dynamically each element of which (its micro- and macro environment) there is in a mutual dependence with the others. It can be understood from the following figure, from the factors forming the two sub-systems of the tourism market, the supply (tourist product) is consisting of the following elements: attractions, accessibility, services, safety, hospitality, etc.

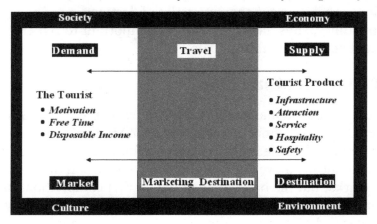

The elements of the tourist destination run as follows: tourist attractions (natural and made by human being, special events, etc.), accessibility, tourist services, product packages, active activities, and public services. One can say that the elements and combination of the factors of the supply and the ones forming the destination are the same. However there is a difference because the tourist product can be only one product or some services or even a pile of services meeting the demands of the tourist being away from his home. From the point of view of the tourist only the pile of complex services is meaning a product because it has to meet all of his demands.

The product can be only one or several products as well; however destination can be characterized as a set of complex services and attractions related to each other. Some scientists put an equal mark between the tourist product in a wider sense and the tourist destination: e.g. destination is just like a tourist product that is competing with other products on the tourist market. Destination management system being responsible for the tourist destination controlling and management is forming a connection with the poles of demand and supply.

Characteristics of Tourist Destination Management

On the basis of some definitions summing up the point of the tourist destination management organization:

- The tourist destination management organization takes the entire responsibility for the tourist products of the whole destination, for their development through controlling, encouraging and other means and for the development of a partnership that is able to provide positive experience for the tourists.

- Its main role, function is the establishment of the cooperation and coordination between the non-profit and private characters of tourism. Its purpose is to increase the tourism, the tourist income of the specific area and to strengthen the image of the territory.

It usually introduces the tourist supplies of a specific area for the tourists and the branch of tourism on a way free of competition. According to the tourist destination management model the tourism destination management and its organizational characteristics can be understood from the following table.

Dimension	Characteristics of destination management
Character	• Directing. • Management. • Coordinating activity.
Mission	• To establish the sustainable and competitive tourism in a specific area through the comprehensive creation and operation of the system of tourism.
Purposes	• To meet the demands of the tourists. • To ensure the profitability of the branch. • To get the local community take part in the processes of development, to improve the quality of life. • To protect and take care of the environment.
Means	• Tourist planning. • Development. • Monitoring. • Business federation (and lobby activity).
Main working practices	• Establishment of the communal partnership. • To get to know the demands and interests of the characters (tourists, inhabitants, authorities, partner organizations, tourist enterprises).
Structure	• From the bottom to the top (at the same time it is supported from the top), it means that the organizations with regional level are forming the small regional and regional co-operations.
Characteristics of organization	• Prepared professionally, skilled organization. • Decisions are made with the contribution of the persons being interested. • Has the suitable independence (own resources and means) needed to the execution of its decisions.
Financing	• Self-maintaining (provided by the characters). • Supported from the top.

Destination Life Cycle

Butler's life cycle model highlights and explains six possible stages to a tourist destination's life cycle. The sixth stage in his model, however, has two probable scenarios attached to it.

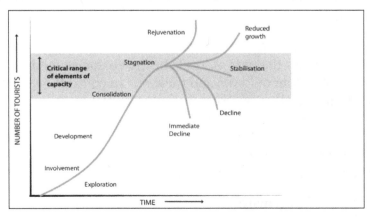

Exploration Stage

The exploration stage is characterized by small number of tourists Plog's Allocentric and Cohen's explorers who have been attracted to the area by its unique and considerably different natural and cultural features. At this stage, the tourism area sees a small number of visitors, making arrangements for them and not sticking to a regular schedule. Some of these tourists might be non-local visitors who have been drawn to the destination by its unique features. These tourists are likely to use local facilities and to have a high level of interaction with locals. This is because at this time, the tourism area wouldn't have specific facilities to cater to the needs of visitors. Tourism would have a relatively insignificant effect on the economic and social atmosphere of the area. As the numbers of visitor increase, and as their visitations take on more regularity, local residents will begin to see the potentials of the area, and then progress to stage 2, which is the involvement stage.

Involvement Stage

As the numbers of visitors increase and assume some regularity, some local residents will enter the involvement stage and begin to provide facilities primarily or exclusively for visitor. At this stage, local residents will start to offer services meant mainly for visitors. There will still be high levels of interactions between local residents and visitors. Expectations at this stage of the life cycle include:

- Advertisements, to get the attention of visitors.

- An initial primary market area for tourists can be established at this stage.

- A tourism season will probably surface, and local residents can be expected to make changes in their pattern of their social lives to suit the season.

- Sustained pressure on the government to provide organized transport systems, and other infrastructures for tourists.

Development Stage

The development stage reflects a well-defined tourist market area, shaped in part by heavy advertising in tourist-generating areas. As this stage progresses, local involvement and control of development will decline rapidly. Some locally provided facilities will have disappeared, being superseded by larger, more elaborate, and more up-to-date facilities provided by external organizations, particularly for visitor accommodation.

At the development stage, a well-structured tourist market area is easily recognized. This is due in part to intensified advertising on the part of locals in the visitor-generating sites. With advancement in this stage, the involvement of locals and their role in controlling development will diminish. Large, modern and more elaborate structures constructed by external interests will replace former facilities provided by indigenous residents. Furthermore, the cultural and natural appeal of the destination will be enhanced and specifically marketed for tourism. There will be observable changes in the tourist area's appearance, and local residents might not agree with some of these changes. Some other reflections of the development stage include:

- More involvement (both regional and national) from the government in the provision of structures and facilities for visitors. Local residents might not necessarily welcome this involvement.

- At the peak of tourist seasons, the number of visitors should be expected to equal or even surpass that of the indigenous population at the destination.

- Tourists at this stage are also likely to be the institutionalized tourist.

Consolidation Stage

As the consolidation stage is entered the rate of increase in numbers of visitors will decline, although total numbers will still increase, and total visitor numbers exceed the number of permanent residents. A major part of the area's economy will be tied to tourism. Marketing and advertising will be wide-reaching and efforts made to extend the visitor season and market area. Major franchises and chains in the tourist industry will be represented but few, if any, additions will be made. The large numbers of visitors and the facilities provided for them can be expected to arouse.

As a tourist destination progresses to the consolidation stage, the increase in the proportion of tourists is expected to stall, and then start to decline, although the total number of tourist at the site will still rise, and the their numbers will still likely be more than that of the local population. Efforts will be made, through promotion and advertisement, to prolong the duration of the tourist season. Big franchises and brands in the tourism industry will by now have businesses at the destination, and very few changes, if any at all, will be made. The large size of the visitor population, and the structures and services offered to them, will prompt dissention and discontent among some of the local populace, especially those not directly involved with tourists. Restrictions might then be placed on the activities of these ones. At the consolidation stage, tourist destinations are also expected to now have well-structured commercial centers/quarters, and former facilities may now be seen as below average and undesirable.

Stagnation Stage

As the area enters the stagnation stage the peak numbers of visitors will have been reached. Capacity levels for many variables will have been reached or exceeded, with attendant environmental, social, arid economic problems. The area will have a well-established image but it will no longer be in fashion. There will be a heavy reliance on repeat visitation.

As the tourist destination progresses to the fifth stage of the life cycle, the stagnation stage, the numbers of visitors will have peaked. The carrying capacity limits will have been reached, and, or exceeded, with implications for the social, environmental, and economic situation of the tourist destination. The area's well established and well-known public image will no longer be as desirable as it was before. The tourist area will start to lean heavily on conventions and repeat visitations from past tourists. The facilities provided to serve visitors will become surplus, and efforts will be concentrated towards retaining past levels of tourist visitations. Man-made facilities are likely to have replaced the original cultural and natural attractions of the tourist site. Development, if it happens at all, will occur at the outskirts of the tourist destination and onsite facilities are likely to undergo regular changes in their ownership. The majority of visitations to the area at this stage will be the Psychocentric, or the mass tourists. The Sixth Stage of Butler's tourist life cycle presents two probable scenarios: decline and rejuvenation. Butler offered five possibilities that fit between the decline and rejuvenation options. These are:

- Successful restructuring leads to the revitalization, and subsequent growth of the tourism business.

- Some changes to the capacity limits of the destinations lead to a moderate growth of the tourism business.

- Stabilization is achieved by cutting the tourist area's capacity levels.

- Sustained overuse of facilities leads to eventual decline in the attraction of the tourist area.

- Catastrophic phenomena like war or disease cause the tourism business to fold up completely.

Decline Stage

In the decline scenario, the tourist destination's popularity reduces and it is unable to compete with newer attractions and destinations. The tourist area will have lost its allure to visitors and will only be used for day and weekend visits, if it has large enough facilities. The maintenance fee of properties will be high as less and less visitors use them. As the tourist area moves away from tourism, tourist facilities might eventually be superseded by structures not related to tourism. At the decline stage, more local involvement in tourism is expected. Locals are able to buy tourist facilities at giveaway prices, as the tourism business falters. Hotels and other resort facilities may be transformed to retirement homes, and apartment buildings. Since these structures are fitted with adequate facilities, they become appealing as places of permanent residence, especially for the elderly. A tourism destination in decline might eventually lose its tourism label completely. During growth and maturity, management of change is the priority, in order to prevent deterioration or decline.

Rejuvenation Stage

The rejuvenation stage is the only other alternative to decline for a tourism destination at the sixth stage, although rejuvenation may not be achieved without a total overhaul of the past foundations upon which tourism is based. Butler presents two ways of achieving rejuvenation:

- The installation of artificial attractions. Adding a unique man-made feature may boost the appeal of a tourist destination. The downside is that the feature is bound to lose its uniqueness as soon as other sites and destinations start using it.

- Alternatively, natural and cultural attractions at the destination that had up till now not been explored may now be tapped. The establishment of new facilities may help revitalize the old trade.

- The joint effort of both the government and private sector is necessary for rejuvenation in most cases. It should be expected that even the new additions to the tourist destination will eventually lose their appeal. They may only retain their attractiveness, only when they are truly unique and even then, the taste and preferences of visitors will likely change.

Rejuvenation of destinations does not and cannot occur by accident. It can only be the result of planning, consultation, and the application of specific strategies.

Destination Visioning

Vision is foresightedness, where imaginative future image is being formulated by the various visionaries. Vision is often believed to be the image of future. Vision is image of excellence in the best possible future created by person, team or organizations. Vision acts as a catalyst which gives 'SHAPE' to the future of the company. Development of Vision is a part of Strategic management, wherein the four basic elements are: environmental scanning, strategy formulation, strategy implementation and evaluation and control. Vision and mission statements are a by-product of strategy formulation. It not only develops the vision and mission statement but also develops strategic objectives.

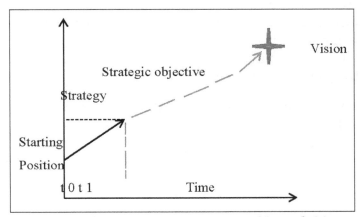

Relationship between Strategy, Strategic position and vision.

The strategy leads us to a strategic position, which is defined as our strategic goal of our direction at particular time, which in turns lead to the final position which is been viewed or designed in the vision statement.

How is Vision and Vision Statement Developed?

1. Strategic Management: Vision is developed keeping in mind the future dominant environmental factors which may create monopoly in the market or might be able to create the best of image in the minds of end users that they prefer to purchase our products over the others. Hence, vision becomes an essential ingredient in the success of an organization. It becomes a driving force for the organization to motivate itself to bear the growing pain in the future so as to achieve the desired vision or goal.

2. Development of Vision: Vision is being developed by the Visionaries, who analyze the present and predict the future in the best possible environment. There are various ways to develop vision:

- Vision through intuition,

- Team Approach,

- Rational Approach.

Using the intuition is considered to be the most traditional view of formulation of vision where generally the visionaries are the founders of the organization. Such visionaries have different orientation towards the achievement of goals; they tend to lead the organization in the required direction.

Two Heads are Better than One

Working in teams is considered good in many ways and so as in the development of vision. Many minds give many ideas which in turn become helpful in the formation of vision because it not only leads to the development of vision but also helps in the understanding of various other outlooks which may affect the strategies in long run. Every individual has a different identity which out brings different ideas, different possibilities and hence the results of such groups are more effective. Last but not the least, rational approach relies more on analysis and synthesis, comparison, deduction and other techniques of empirical investigation. But this approach has its own drawbacks, like this approach never lets vision to be more creative or more radical vision because it works on the analysis of the information of the past. So it is also named as conservative approach as it restricts the creativity of the human mind.

Vision statement may or may not convey the whole idea so we need good leaders too who can orient all the resources in the required direction. Vision statements require having:

- Motivational,
- Easy to understand,
- Inspiring,
- Easy to remember,
- Future oriented,
- Challenging,
- Attractive,
- Involves all organizational interests,
- It is not a one-time thing, which can be achieved and discarded.

Adapting from other organization may happen that the group of visionaries of the organization might be inspired with the vision of some other organization and would try to mould it to fit it in their organization.

Vision is Centred on Three Major Questions

- Where are we now? Discussion should be regarding the current situation of the business and the current external and internal factors favoring or hindering the business.

- Where do we want to be? Creating a hypothetical goal that is to be achieved in the future, which will foster the business.

- How do we get there? Generating the action plans for meeting the desired goals using the present resources and keeping in mind the constraints that will restrict the growth.

Importance of Vision in an Organizational Strategy

- It is the most critical element in the building of strategy for any organization.

- It acts like a guide in the foundation of the organizational objectives.

- Based on vision strategic and tactical plans are formulated.

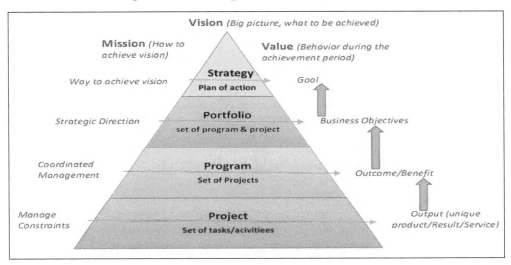

Strategic Visioning Concept

In an organizational set-up, a vision is viewed as a practically achievable picture of the organization in the future and is considered as an important ingredient in the strategic planning. The main objective of vision development is to bring the people in the same locus has been defined in the vision with the help of which the strategic plans are formulated. In strategic planning, planning means formal, structured and logical exercise which is the major responsibility of the executives. Also, vision development was considered as a responsibility of the leaders of the organization. On the contrary, strategic vision is a total opposite of strategic planning. In strategic visioning, the strategies are developed over a period of time which is a iterative process of observing, analyzing and acting. Visioning process is developed with the group of leaders which should be active enough to participate in the discussion for the development of the vision which is considered to be the collective idea of the group representing the future of the organization.

Strategic visioning concepts are applied in the community planning as its stems are originating from corporate. Strategic visioning is identified valuable for the community planning because it incorporates divergent options from the different stakeholders which come to a consensus about the future direction for the growth of the destination and its community too.

Strategic Visioning and Destination Planning

It is believed that the destination visioning is possible only when the objectives and policies of the sustainable development of the destination are kept in mind. It's been observed that in the absence of the vision, sustainable development of tourism is not possible. Researchers have encapsulated visioning approach with the principles of the sustainable tourism development.

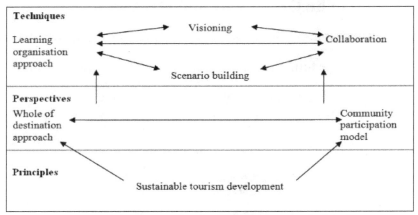

Framework for the Destination Management and Planning.

Visioning as a process requires a major shift from consulting to the more meaningful engagement of the different stakeholders in the decision making.

Visioning and Destination Life Cycle

For the strategic development of the vision it becomes really important to understand the various changes and the developments in the destination. By integrating tools of the strategic planning with the long term perspectives stated by the different stages in the life cycle of the destination, it will help in the development of the management strategies for destination as they progress in the various stages of the life cycle.

Strategic planning works on integrating the marketing and planning approaches to a higher order so as to formalize the planning approach. Characteristics of the strategic planning approach are:

- Considering the long term perspectives.

- Creating integrated plans to control the process of change through the goal formation.

- Creation of formalized decision process which prepares the destination for the future action plans.

The application of strategic planning is bit complicated in the case of destinations compared to the commercial organization. Some gaps in the implementation of strategic planning in the tourist destinations:

- In the case of destinations, there is a constant shifting of stakeholders and so as the value system. Every group of stakeholder then has a different perspective towards the growth of the destination and hence the action plans may differ from one group of stakeholder to the other. Therefore, the implementation of one single action plan is not possible.

- That the tourism sector is a seasonal business, so the management lacks the expertise to maintain a balance between the public and the commercial sectors.

- Depending on the stage of the life cycle, planning methods or the motives differ for the destination. Like we can say that if the destination is in the early stages of the life cycle then the planning is made keeping the long term growth of the destination. Whereas, in the later stages of the life cycle then the planning is being rationalized keeping cost as a major factor in mind.

- Performance of the destination is often measured in terms of the volume of the tourist, which is the most traditional method of looking at the performance but the sustainability is not tangible in the context of tourism's impact on the environment and society.

Tourism being the growing sector in many economies has not only increased the flow of tourist but has also opened ways of generating revenues. With the increase in flow of tourist, sustainability of the destination is of bigger concern. A tourism activity has many positive impacts on the destination but due to the lack of proper planning frameworks has proved it to be a detriment of many destinations around the world. So the guidelines are required to make the destination sustainable. The involvement of various stakeholders in the process of creating a vision for a destination is of bigger concern because bringing major stakeholders on one platform is an issue of concern. Though the importance of creating a destination vision is known to all but including the stakeholders in the process of designing the same is still not appropriate. Academics and non-governmental institutions have supported the idea of including all the parties involved in the sector to be a part of the destination planning and decision making activities.

One of the widely used methods of including the stakeholders is the process of building a strategic vision. Building a strategic vision for a destination will not only include the business players in the process but will also call the local communities of the destination to bring in their inputs in the process of building the vision for the destination. So we can say that in the process of designing the vision of the destination three key elements are required:

- Vision should include the views of the local community and the various other stakeholders.

- Vision should meet the needs of the future.

- Vision should clearly define the long term goals for the destination to grow sustainably.

Residents of the communities or the regions involved in the tourism activities are demanding to be involved in the decisions affecting their development. Hence it can be said that the destination visioning is a community based strategic planning approach where the responsibility lies in the hand of the local communities, government and travel agencies.

Destination Marketing

Destination marketing is a form of marketing, in which a destination is promoted to potential visitors, in order to increase the number of people that travel to that location. The destination can be fairly specific, as is the case with town or city marketing, or much broader, as is the case with region or country marketing. Ultimately, the purpose of destination marketing is to make your location or destination seem more attractive than the main alternatives, boosting the number of people who travel there and assisting the local travel industry. It is also about increasing awareness of the destination, with a view to raising demand and improving its reputation.

Importance of Destination Marketing

To attract travellers to a certain destination, it is important that the plus points of that destination are highlighted. This is especially crucial when one destination is competing with another for the same tourists or visitors. An example of this would be both the Caribbean and the Great Barrier Reef offering excellent diving experiences. The goal of most destination marketing is to promote your destination as superior to alternatives, by highlighting the things that make it unique, or the things that make it a desirable place to travel to. Successful destination marketing can then be of huge benefit to the local tourism industry, including hotels, restaurants, bars, airlines and related suppliers.

Responsibility for destination marketing typically falls on a dedicated destination marketing organisation (DMO), or tourist board. These organisations represent the community or destination being promoted and attempt to drive interest in the region amongst travellers by using a range of different marketing techniques. In many ways, a DMO also serves as a link between the visitor and the destination, encouraging the visit in the first place, but also providing important visitor information. Hotels, local businesses, attractions and their owners are often members of a DMO, and funding tends to come from government sources and/or membership fees.

A number of different marketing strategies can be used for destination marketing purposes, helping to boost overall awareness of a destination and increase the number of people who actually visit.

Define the Unique Selling Points

Arguably the single most important step for any organisation engaging in destination marketing is to take the time to clearly define what makes your destination unique. There are huge range of ways a destination can stand out, such as unique activities to offer visitors, or unique natural features, like mountains, beaches or volcanoes. It could be that your location has a fascinating history, or unique landmarks, like the Eiffel Tower, the Empire State Building, or the Great Wall of China. Perhaps the culture of the location is its unique selling point and visitors would want to travel to experience local events, museums or sports clubs. Try to identify as many USPs as possible.

Define Target Audience and Market

Another of the best destination marketing strategies involves identifying your target audiences. Think about who is likely to want to visit the destination and for what reason. Often, you will need to break this down into several different audiences, who each may have different reasons for wanting to travel to your location. For instance, it could be that your destination appeals to youngsters on a gap year, and elderly couples enjoying their retirement. It might be that it appeals to people who enjoy outdoor sporting activities and people who want to relax on the beach. You also need to consider the different groups, such as tourists, business travellers and students. Finally, think about whether certain markets are more likely to be interested than others. This could mean people in nearby countries, if you have excellent transport links, or people who speak the same language.

Utilise Data for Analytics

Destination marketing organisations can potentially obtain and utilise vast amounts of data, for a number of different purposes. As an example, the organisation's website can allow you to use tools like Google Analytics to find out about your visitors, who they are, where they came from and what their motivation was. Offline, you can find out information about existing visitors, such as the average age, whether your destination appeals more to men or women, and what methods of transport they use. Once you have gathered sufficient data, you can analyse it to identify the best people to reach out to, the best ways to reach them and the best messages to push.

Brand your Destination

Branding is a technique used by businesses, in order to make them easily identifiable. The concept of branding can include logos, colour schemes and other design principles, as well as slogans or repeated use of certain terminology. Ultimately, branding is about being recognisable and standing out from others. This principle can be fairly easily applied to a destination. Try to come up with a coherent colour scheme, use a tagline that says something about the destination itself, create hashtags for people to use on social media, and try to be as consistent as possible with your promotional messaging, so that people become familiar with it.

Involve all Stakeholders

A significant component of destination management involves looking out for the interests of various stakeholders, in order to establish trust and facilitate engagement. The stakeholders might include officials from your country, city, village or state, as well as hotels, attractions, restaurants, shopping venues, travel agents and tour operators. Try to come up with destination marketing strategies that actually encourage these various parties to participate and support your destination. See if you can get stakeholders to agree to use some of your wider destination branding, and to run their own advertising or marketing campaigns, in order to maximise visitor interest.

Create an Amazing Destination Website

Regardless of their reasons for travelling, the majority of travellers now use the internet to research their destination before booking. A destination website is the ideal place to showcase unique selling points, communicate directly with your target audience(s) and promote your destination through images, videos and virtual reality tours. You can use the website to provide travellers with all of the information they need ahead of their trip, and to promote accommodation options, attractions, events, places to eat and drink, and more. It is important that your website is optimised for mobile users, while an on-site blog can help to encourage people to keep coming back.

Search Engine Optimisation

When people use search engines like Google to look for things related to your destination, or features that your destination can offer them, you want to make sure your website is near the top of those search engine results pages. The best way to do this is to create a comprehensive search engine optimisation strategy. This involves researching keywords, creating content that targets those keywords, and using a range of other techniques to improve your placement. You can also use SEO principles to promote videos and images too. An on-site blog can be beneficial here too, as it will give you plenty of fresh content to optimise with strategic keyword usage.

Experience Marketing

Most travellers are motivated by experiences, so it makes sense to market a destination this way. Instead of showing attractions, use promotional material to show how people experience them. One way to do this is to stimulate the sharing of user generated content, so that people share their own moments on your website and on social media. When you achieve this, you turn your own visitors into ambassadors for your destination. Word of mouth promotion can be extremely successful, because it is considered more trustworthy than hearing from an organisation with a clear motive. On top of this, VR 360 tours can be a great way to allow online users to enjoy their own experiences.

Video and Virtual Reality Marketing

Both video marketing and virtual reality marketing can go a long way towards boosting your destination marketing efforts. Video content can be easily shared across platforms like Facebook, Twitter, Instagram and YouTube. These videos can promote local places of interest, or can feature local people speaking about your destination. Virtual reality marketing goes a step further and provides ways for your target audience to actually experience aspects of your destination from the comfort of their own home. This could be a virtual tour of a local hotel, a virtual travel experience of a nearby entertainment venue, or 360 degree tours of attractions or landmarks.

Social Media Strategies

Social media platforms like Facebook, Twitter and Instagram serve as an ideal means to reach people and promote your destination. In truth, the destination marketing strategies on offer here are almost endless, from simple promotional posts, images and video content, through to competitions and even viral content or memes. Additionally, most social media platforms offer paid marketing opportunities, such as advertisements or sponsored posts. These can boost the visibility of your social media marketing efforts and can be aimed at very specific demographics, meaning you can target people based on age, gender, location and even their online browsing habits.

Work with Influencers

Many modern internet users have a natural distrust for direct advertising and other overt marketing methods. However, many of these people may be able to be reached indirectly, through influencers. In simple terms, influencers are people with an established following on platforms like Instagram, Twitter, YouTube, Facebook or their own blog. Their followers tend to be loyal and tend to trust the influencer's opinions more than they would trust an organisation. By partnering with influencers, you can promote your destination across different platforms, even to niche audiences, who are then significantly more likely to react positively to the message that is being promoted.

Promote your Destination on Travel Websites

In addition to having your own destination website, it is important to be able to reach people who do not have existing awareness of your destination. Travel websites provide a perfect solution and this can include international travel websites, as well as local websites, or websites aimed at specific demographics. There are various ways you can use travel websites to promote your destination, including posting images, publishing stories, creating video content and even promoting virtual reality tours. You can also use travel websites to monitor reviews, respond to criticism and improve feedback over time.

Online Advertising Strategies

The information and data you have gathered about your visitors and your target audience can be used to inform your online advertising. Using this information, you can target search advertising to specific regions, pay for display advertising on the right platforms and promote content on third-party websites your target audience use. In addition, re-marketing allows you to reach out to people who have previously engaged with your destination website or your DMO's social media channels. This gives you the ability to remind people of your destination, knowing that they have already previously shown interest, which can be great for encouraging them to commit to a visit.

Offline Promotional Strategies

Once you know your target audience, what they are looking for and where they are coming from, you should also be able to identify when they are likely to travel. For instance, some destinations attract visitors in the summer months, while others attract people for winter sports. Some might hold greater appeal at Christmas, or another holiday. This then makes it easier to devise a comprehensive offline promotional strategy. Some of the offline methods you use might include television advertising, radio advertising and promotion within newspapers and magazines. With the latter two examples, you could pay for advertisements, write features on your destination, and target specific local publications in areas where your target audience reside.

References

- Destination-Planning: pondiuni.edu.in, Retrieved 09, January 2020
- Destination-marketing: revfine.com, Retrieved 15, July 2020

Hotel Management and Lodging

All the diverse elements related to the management of a hotel fall under hotel management. Lodging comprises renting a place for a short term stay. A few different types of lodging are homestay, bed and breakfast, guest house and boarding house. This chapter discusses in detail these types of lodging as well as the different elements of hotel management.

Hotel

Hotel is a place to stay day or night by payment of its rent.

Hotel is such a place where the accommodation system to stay night with the facilities food and beverage is available.

Or,

Where the facilities of sleeping accommodation, food and beverage service available and guest or client pay the rent for staying day or night in the room and for taking those facilities is called Hotel.

Special Qualities of Hotel

- A Hotel is an establishment, which is established on some point and facilities below:

Held out by a Proprietor

Maximum Hotels are run by some Proprietors. But many Hotels are running by many proprietors, its mean one hotel is running by about 10 to 15 proprietors.

Offering Facilities

Hotels are always offering many important facilities like Food, Drink, and Sleeping Accommodation etc. peoples go to any hotel to spend their night safely. If you went any far place and if you have no relative there then you will choose to stay in a hotel to stay the day or night.

Without any Contract to any Traveler

You can stay in any hotel as long you want. If you want to stay one night, it is okay and if you want to stay more than one night then it also okay. That is mean hotel cannot make any contract with you to stay in the Hotel. Example: Hotel never contract with you that you have to stay 2 or 3 day or night in the Hotel. Hotel gives their facilities without any contract to any traveler.

- A hotel is an Enterprise, which is running with some special ability, performance and options, Like below:

Created by People

A hotel is created by peoples and for the peoples. Because peoples will be utilized a hotel.

Managed by Skilled Peoples

A hotel cannot run with little skilled or non-skilled persons. Hotels always manage its management and its service with good skilled peoples.

Management and Service

Hotels are organizing many occasional festivals by order, making good marketing & selling of production and service.

Basically, Hotel is a right place to sleep or stay day or night without self-home and by pay rest to stay their. Moreover, Hotel offers good facilities of Food and beverage and sleeping accommodation by taking money from client or guest.

Eco hotel

Part of the joy of going on holiday is finding the perfect place to stay. And though there seem to be options abound when looking into top destinations around the world, most hotels have yet to incorporate sustainability into their mission.

If sustainability is part of your travel decision-making process, you might not want to stay in accommodation that's detrimental to the environment and the community.

That's where eco-hotels come in! Eco-hotels (also known as "green" hotels, or environmentally friendly hotels) are properties that embrace environmental sustainability and have a positive impact on the community they operate in.

Waterfall Villas in Dominical, Costa Rica, a wonderful example of a great Eco-hotel.

But what does an environmentally friendly hotel look like? What does it do? And most importantly, how do you go about finding one?

Unfortunately, there is no easy way to find eco-hotels around the world. Search engines like booking.com have not yet incorporated a "green hotel" filter in their system. So in many cases, eco-conscious travelers are forced to rely on their own research when deciding whether or not the property they are considering is "green."

A simple Google search for "Eco hotel" or "green hotel" in the destination of your choice will often reveal a few options. But we've come to realize that there are some great responsible accommodation options that simply don't highlight this information on their website.

Evaluating an Eco-hotel

If your search has led to a few potential options, start by browsing the hotels' websites searching for sections dedicated to sustainable commitment or environmental practices. Below you'll find a list of helpful questions to keep in mind.

Sustainability Practices does the Hotel have in Place

- Was the hotel built with consideration of the local climate?

- If the hotel has central heating/cooling, is there a thermostat in each room to allow guests to adjust the temperature to a reasonable level?

- How often do housekeeping clean rooms during your stay?

- Do they stress the importance of conserving water and reuse of bathroom towels?

- Does the hotel provide disposable toiletries or offer shampoo/conditioner in refillable containers instead?

- Does the hotel food/beverage services use reusable products (glass cups, ceramic plates, cloth napkins, etc.)?

- Is there a recycling program?

- Is there a solar energy system in place on the property?

- Does the hotel have a water separation system on the property?

- If the hotel has grounds, are the plants being treated with pesticides or natural fertilizers?

Ways by which the Hotel Utilize the Local Environment and Support the Local Community.

- Is the food locally sourced?

- Are the hotel staff locals?

- If the hotel offers tours of the area, are the tour guides local?

- Does the hotel embrace the local culture?

- Does the hotel offer bicycles for guests? Alternatively, does the hotel have information available for guests about public transportation in the area?

Grant the hotel a point for every "yes" to the questions above and choose a hotel that truly "walks the talk" when it comes to sustainability practices.

If you've tried to find an eco-hotel in the destination you are planning to visit but couldn't settle on a good option, don't be discouraged. Use the opportunity to spark a conversation with the staff at the hotel about sustainable accommodation, and some simple practices they can put into place to immediately make the property more environmentally friendly.

Here are some of our suggested conversation starters:

- Start a recycling program on the property – start with separate bins for paper/plastic/compost/general waste in the lobby and kitchen, and then expand to guestrooms.

- Switch from buying individually packaged guest room toiletries to buying in bulk with reusable containers for shampoo/body wash/hand soap.

- Switch to non-toxic cleaning products.

- Switch to manual gardening instead of motor-powered tools (If hotel has grounds).

- Consider adding solar panels to the roof or grounds of the hotel for water heating.

- Eliminate individual bottles/cans in restaurant/bar of hotel and to minimize plastic use.

And there are so many more. Once you've started to do your research about sustainable accommodation, you'll have a better idea of what to look for in green hotels and what to suggest to hotels that aren't there yet.

Remember, the more guests ask about it, the more likely it is that hotel management will consider incorporating sustainable practices into the hotel's business model.

Capsule Hotel

Capsule hotels are one of Japan's best known and unique types of lodging. They are usually found around major train stations in large cities and target individuals looking for a low budget, single night's stay. Capsule hotels provide their guests with private, enclosed beds and basic amenities for less money than regular or business hotels. They usually charge between 3000 and 4000 yen per night. Recently a few premium and themed capsule hotels have been opening around Tokyo, Kyoto and Osaka with slightly higher prices.

While capsule hotels traditionally cater mostly to business men, these days many places also accept female guests and offer gender segregated sleeping floors or separate buildings for men and women. Capsule hotels are also popular with foreign travelers and are increasingly offering English websites and booking systems.

The typical capsule includes a TV and wifi internet inside,
and a privacy curtain or door to cover the entrance.

The standard capsule is a fiberglass unit built around a single size futon mattress, measuring roughly 1.2 meters wide, two meters long and one meter high. They are usually stacked two units high and lined up side by side along the corridor. Sheets, blankets and pillows are provided, and each capsule also comes outfitted with a light, alarm clock, TV and radio unit built in. A curtain or door can be closed in front of the entrance for privacy. In addition, most places provide power outlets and free wifi internet inside the capsules.

All of the other facilities at the capsule hotel, such as washrooms, toilets and showers, are shared among the guests. Many capsule hotels also commonly provide large communal baths where you can enjoy a soak before bed. In addition, they may also have restaurants, vending machines, laundry facilities, internet kiosks, lounges, entertainment rooms, game rooms or manga libraries within the facilities.

Capsule hotel guests relax in the lounge.

The procedure to stay at a capsule hotel may seem intimidating at first, but it is essentially the same at most capsule hotels and only differs slightly from other types of accommodations in Japan. Some places even provide English check-in instructions at the counter or may have English speaking staff. It typically goes as follows:

- Remove your shoes and place them into a locker. Take the key to the check-in counter.

- When checking into a capsule hotel, you are assigned a capsule number and given a key to a corresponding locker where you can store your belongings. The lockers are not usually very large, so most places have an additional luggage room or coin lockers to store suitcases and other large items. Do not store valuables inside of your capsule unattended as they usually cannot be locked.

- Most people start with a bath and then change into a fresh set of clothes. Shampoo, soap, towels and other toiletries are usually provided. Sometimes yukata or other nightwear is also provided.

- Many capsule hotels offer lounges, restaurants or other entertainment areas where you can relax by yourself or spend time with friends. Eating and smoking are generally not allowed inside of the capsules.

- Once you retire to your capsule, close the curtain or door for privacy.

- Check out in the morning. While it is possible to stay for consecutive nights, most capsule hotels require you to check out and remove all of your belongings from the hotel during the day.

Business Hotel

A great business hotel can make or break a business travel trip. If you're staying in a great hotel that caters to the specific needs and hectic schedules of business travellers, it does make doing deals on the go that much easier. Luckily, many hotels have recognized the need to satisfy professional travellers and a crop of business-friendly stays have popped up across the globe.

From incorporating innovative services to the rise of tech-savvy amenities, here are nine features to look for before booking your next business stay.

In-Room WiFi

This is perhaps the biggest must-have for any hotel hoping to draw business travellers. With so much work to be done on the fly, it's imperative that corporate guests be able to log-on in their rooms. Slowly but surely, hotels across Australia are catching on to the all important presence of WiFi and are increasingly offering in-room access. The really great hotels are taking it a step further by offering complimentary access.

Work Desk

Work desks have long been a staple of the standard room, but these days hotels are revamping this in-room workspace. It's not uncommon to find more stylish desks with an increase in surrounding space, providing a comfortable spot to finish off those last few emails or presentation notes. Ergonomic designs with office-style chairs are replacing the tired furniture of old, while tech savvy additions can include power panels as well as docking stations for all your gadgets.

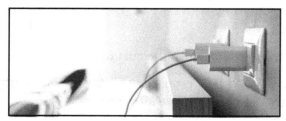

Outlets Galore

Speaking of outlets, there's nothing more frustrating than walking into your room and having to scour the walls for an outlet only to find that you'll have to sacrifice your bedside lamp to top up your mobile battery. Thankfully business-friendly hotels are offering up more power outlets, whether it's a power panel such as those found at Hyatt Place hotels in the US, or simply more available wall outlets. Some hotels even go as far as providing adapters for overseas guests.

A Top Business Centre

Outside of firing off a quick email or two at the end of the day, many corporate guests would prefer not to work in their rooms. Enter the hotel business center. A great business hotel will always offer a 24-hour business center with comfortable seating, online access, computers and a number of other office services such as copying and printing.

Fitness Centre

A sound mind and body is a sure way to reduce stress while on the road, which is why fitness routines should never fall by the wayside. This is especially true for international travellers trying to cut down on jetlag. 24-hour fitness facilities are a must for business travellers hoping to stay healthy while adhering the to the demands of a busy schedule. While 'fully-equipped' may be asking a little too much, the basic machines and a pool should be accounted for.

Concierge Services

If you're not familiar with the Concierge, you could be missing out on a valuable source of information. Sure they can book a taxi for you, but they can also provide you with expert recommendations, offer directions to just about anywhere you want to go or book a last minute reservation at your destination's hottest restaurant. The good ones can even secure tickets to sold out shows. Good hotels have them and smart travellers use them.

Communal Spaces

Stuffy hotel lobbies are a thing of the past. At least they should be. New hotel designs favour open, flowing spaces that encourage guests to hang out. Perhaps a symptom of design meeting the expectations of younger generations, these communal spaces are great for business travellers. Not only do they provide a change in scenery if you'd like to get a little work done, they can also be great networking spots where you can mingle with like-minded travellers.

Express Check-in/Check-Out

If you've ever struggled with managing a busy schedule while on a work trip, express check-in and/ or express check-out can be a God send. Luckily more hotels are integrating this service, particularly hotels that cater to business travellers. Double check to see if your chosen hotel offers such a service. You'll be happy you did if you happen to be running a few minutes late.

Location

One of the first things you should look into when booking a great business hotel is the location. You don't want to be stuck in peak hour traffic en route to the office because you booked a room on the wrong side of town. This is where the help of your FCBT Travel Manager can come in handy. All you need to do is let them know where you need to be and they can provide a few suggestions on top hotels within convenient proximity.

Airport Hotel

An Airport Hotel is a hotel near the airport. The hotel does not have to be connected to the airport (although some are) or even adjacent to it; it could be located up to five miles away. Most airport hotels have a shuttle to and from the terminals.

Benefits of Airport Hotels

Convenient Location and Fresh Start

If you have an early morning departure or a long drive to the airport, staying at an airport hotel eliminates the stress of having to wake up too early in the morning - something no-one should have to do when leaving for a relaxing holiday. This is a huge help for parents who are taking their kids on holiday - you won't have to mobilize your little ones at three in the morning, when they're tired, grumpy and uncooperative. The two hours you'd spend getting ready and driving to the airport could be better spent dreaming about the Greek sunset and waking up at a reasonable time.

If you're due to travel during the morning rush hour, you need to factor the inevitable delays and extra time into your journey. By staying in an airport hotel the night before you fly, you get to avoid the stress of rushing to get to departures on time. Even if your hotel isn't within walking distance of the terminal, transfers to the airport are either prearranged, scheduled through the hotel or available on request. Your shuttle will have you there in minutes, so there's no risk of getting stuck in morning traffic.

Rather than arriving at the airport feeling ratty and stressed, you will have enjoyed a good night's sleep and will be ready to enjoy yourself. For special occasions, when you're travelling to a business function, a special wedding or to an event, the extra hours of rest will go a long way to improving your overall experience.

Often Cheaper than Parking Alone

It's hard to believe, but booking an airport hotel with parking can work out cheaper than paying for official parking at the airport on its own. It's one of the best money saving features of airport hotels, so keep your eyes peeled for bargains out there. All of the hotels that offer parking do so with full confidence in the security of your vehicle - you can expect a high level of security.

Points to Consider when Booking

Distance from airport - Choose from an airport hotel that is practically inside the terminal, or something a little bit further away, for a more country-feel.

Star Rating/Price Range - Airport hotels range from two star budget facilities with few amenities, going all the way through to luxury, five star accommodations.

Lowest Price Guarantee - Get the best deals available anywhere on the net. If you can find the same room for a cheaper price elsewhere, we'll cover your stay ourselves.

It is worthwhile booking an airport hotel. This hassle-free service will give you plenty of time to enjoy the more pleasurable aspects of travel at your leisure, such as a glass of freshly squeezed juice with breakfast before departure.

Suite Hotel

It doesn't matter if it came with origami swans, a cutely wrapped candy and a bottle of champagne, a room is not a suite. And not all suites are created the same either. So if not for the all the fancy schmancy, how is a suite different from a room?

Hotel Room vs Hotel Suite

A standard room is the most commonly booked type of accommodation – 80% of the time to be exact. You get a single room with one or more king, queen, full, or twin beds, a work desk, a bathroom, and maybe a closet, TV, and a dresser. A suite is a much larger accommodation. It usually has an attached bathroom, a living area, and most times, includes a dining area as well. Think of it as a furnished apartment-like stay that can be anywhere between 400 sq. ft to 3000 sq. ft (or more!).

Junior Suite

Interestingly, not all suites are made the same, and some people end up getting a glorified room when they book a 'luxury suite'. That's why it's important to know what kind of suite you're getting, ask questions and see a lot of photos of the suite. A suite can mean one of these:

1. The Suite: A large apartment-like layout with separate living area, one or two bedrooms with attached bathrooms and/or powder rooms and most times, a dining area as well. Most of these suites have living rooms and bedrooms separated by a solid partition like a door. These are the most common suites and are typically preferred by families with young kids or one or more couples traveling together.

Empire Terrace Suite, Andaz 5th Avenue.

2. The Junior Suite: Junior suites are smaller than a regular suite but more importantly, typically don't have a solid separation between the bedrooms and living area. These suites have small living areas that are an extension of the bedroom space and don't come with dining areas. The good part of junior suites is that they're priced lower than regular suites and often have sofa beds so you can accommodate more guests.

Viceroy Junior Suite, New York.

3. The Residential Suite: These are fully-furnished suites in every sense of the word. Not only do you get a separate living room, dining room and one or more bathrooms, some suites also come with wet bars, fully stocked kitchens, in-suite washer dryer units and even patios and terraces.

Residential One Bedroom Suite at AKA Times Square.

4. The Presidential Suite: The absolute best suite in any hotel. Most hotels would usually carry only a few presidential or penthouse suites. Typically housed on the top floors, this is your ultra-lavish-architecture-digest-fancy-af suite with everything you can think of. Fabulous panoramic views, high-end toiletries, jetted tubs in bathrooms that look like spas, expansive living, dining and bedroom areas, entry foyers, private terraces and sometimes even private butlers.

Penthouse Suite at The Time New York.

5. The Connecting Suite: Available only on Suiteness, connecting suites are suite configurations where more than one bedroom is connected to the living area of a suite. Some of these also feature one suite that connects to another suite. You see, most hotel suites are built with an attached room or suite that has a separate private entrance. Sadly, hotel reservation systems are outdated. So while these suites and rooms are attached, they can only be sold separately and never together as a connecting suite. Until now, that is. A connecting suite is essentially the same as a regular full-sized suite that has more than one attached bedroom only, less expensive. You're looking at anywhere between a $100 to even $1,000 difference between a regular two-bedroom suite and a connecting two-bedroom suite. See what staying in a connecting suite is like with this virtual tour.

The Best Suite

Well the question should be, which is the best suite for me? Because it depends on your budget and needs. We've seen that regular one-bedroom suites are a big hit with families with babies or toddlers who specifically need a door that can be closed between the living area and bedroom. But our star-sellers are connecting suites, booked 3.3X more than their non-connecting counterparts and are huge with group travelers of up to 10 guests.

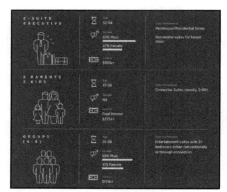

Quick snapshot of the typical Suiteness customer.

The Advantage of Connecting Suites

It's not too surprising why people love connecting sites; they offer a great balance of value, space, and quality. For example, the median price per night per person for a connecting suite in a 4 or 5-star Vegas hotel is $80. We've seen large groups of eight or more snag a two-bedroom luxury hotel suite on the Strip for under $500 – and that's weekend pricing. With suites, in a lot of cases, there is also a difference between actual occupancy of the suite and maximum occupancy. With connecting suites, for example, we've seen that the average suite occupancy is 5.9 guests while the average number of guests is 3.5. What this means is that while a suite might be able to sleep only up to 4 guests, because of the limitation of beds, it has the space to accommodate up to 6 or 8 guests for a get-together or party. Usually, when this happens, our guests accommodate overflow by booking additional rooms nearby.

The Right Time to Book a Suite

Suite prices seldom ever come down closer to your travel dates. In fact, Suiteness suites are booked an average 54 days in advance. Connecting suites are best booked 2-3 months in advance for better pricing and more importantly, better availability.

Just like anything else that's travel-related, suite prices are subject to seasonal trends. So the usual suspects like summer, holidays, and spring break are peak season when demand is high. Depending on the city you're visiting, steer clear of conference dates and wedding season as well.

So, if you're traveling with a big group, or are a family with kids, or need upgraded options for a special occasion, go for a suite. It's probably better than booking a vacation rental if you consider the amenities and hidden charges. It is best to look at different options by comparing the number of beds you're getting, included amenities, any add-on services and of course, the price.

All-suite Hotel

An all-suite hotel is one that includes all room types and at least a suite. A hotel suite typically connects other additional rooms, which is often a luxury and upscale type accommodations. A "suite" also generally means a separate living room area, like a sofa or chairs, and may include a kitchen-ette or even a full kitchen. Suites generally offer a bit more room to spread out than the average hotel room and may include a sofa bed for an extra guest.

All-suite Hotel Brands

Properties at hotels like the Ritz Carlton or Marriott may designate certain suites as their hon-eymoon, presidential, or royal suite. Premium suite rooms with special amenities are often mar-keted to couples and newlyweds with heart-shaped tubs, romantic flair, and other unique fea-tures. Locations with only suits are also often suited for business travelers who need additional space for client meetings and entertainment. Upper and middle-class brands that include suites as part of some of their hotel locations include Embassy Suites, Hilton Garden Inns, and Home-wood Suites. Those that are more likely to use the latter include budget-friendly families and vacation goers.

Rio All-Suite Hotel & Casino

Located in Las Vegas, Nevada, this 4-star all-suite hotel is popular for its casino area, El Burro Baracho restaurant, pool, and free shuttle to the strip. Travelers find that the rooms are large and well-equipped with comfy beds, Wi-Fi, and non-smoking rooms.

The hotel also includes a breakfast buffet and has been recognized for its GreenLeaders Silver level award for participating in green practices like tracking energy use and implementing a towel reuse program.

Coconut Cove All-suite Hotel

This family-friendly all-suite hotel in Clearwater, Florida is rated about 2.5 stars.

The non-smoking hotel has free Wi-Fi and free parking and offers a heated pool with a waterfall. The suite rooms are big and often accompanied with a balcony. Visitors can expect a middle-class hotel experience with friendly staff members, an Italian restaurant next door, and the beach just being a few minutes of a walk away.

Hilton Garden Inn New York

The Hilton Garden Inn on West 35th street is a 3-star hotel that offers a breakfast buffet, free Wi-Fi, a restaurant, and many air-conditioned suites. The beds are comfortable with updated bedding despite the rooms leaning toward the smaller side. The location is great for travelers, being right near popular destinations including Fifth Avenue, the Empire State Building, and Macy's.

Cambria Hotel & Suites Chicago Magnificent Mile

This 4.0-star hotel in downtown Chicago is accompanied by a restaurant and a rooftop bar. The lo-cation is a top favorite among guests, reasonably priced, and very cleanly. The size of the room and bathroom leans on the spacious side. Guests will also be delighted to find out that they can enjoy the famous Chicago pie with Gino's pizza being conveniently located right next door.

Extended Stay Hotel

Good hotels used to promise guests everything but the kitchen sink. Nowadays, they're throwing that in as well.

Fully equipped kitchens are just one of the many extras being built into a rapidly growing segment of the hospitality industry: extended-stay hotels. These lodgings target guests planning a longer-than-usual hotel stay—anywhere from four days to four months—and offer amenities ranging from CD players to dual phone lines to full-size refrigerator or freezers. Some of the units resemble studio apartments, with one large room and a galley kitchen; others offer multiple bedrooms and baths, kitchen and dining areas, and extensive in-room business equipment.

It's a market, hotel developers say, that's waiting to be served. According to D.K. Shifflet & Associates, a travel industry research group, hotel guests who stay five nights or longer accounted for 265 million rooms in 1995, compared with 215 million rooms in 1993 and 1994.

And it's a market that continues to grow, offering opportunities, primarily in site selection, for commercial real estate professionals who understand what chains, real estate investment trusts (REITs), and other extended-stay developers are seeking.

One facet of the market is easily recognizable: Workers who are relocating or in town for long-term projects or training, who prefer to stay in a more home-like environment where they can cook a dinner and spread out their spreadsheets. But while the upper-priced tier of extended-stay hotels has established itself by catering to these businesspeople, competition is heating up in the middle- and lower-priced segments of the market as well. These newer chains aim to attract guests traveling for business who also like a homey atmosphere, but who are watching expenses. However, they also appeal to families who are visiting resort areas or individuals who simply are making a transition between homes or relationships.

Price Versus Features

Extended-stay hotels are categorized as limited-service facilities, but the service that guests do get depends on what they pay. The upper-priced tier, dominated by Marriott's Residence Inns, includes other chains such as Hawthorn Suites, Homewood Suites, Summerfield Suites, and Woodfin Suites. Individual rooms may contain apartment-like features such as separate living and sleeping areas, kitchens, and even fireplaces. But the properties also offer many traditional hotel services such as swimming pools, free continental breakfasts, and meeting rooms—as well as amenities geared specifically toward extended-stay travelers, such as free grocery shopping services and weekly social hours. Rates run anywhere from $70 to $105 a night, depending on the length of the stay. While most guests are likely to stay for at least a week, the hotels welcome guests who are staying only a night or two.

The lower-priced groups—Extended StayAmerica (which includes Extended StayAmerica Efficiency Studios as well as Crossland Economy Studios and StudioPlus Hotels), Homestead Village, Lexington Hotel Suites, Suburban Lodge, and Villager Lodge—more closely resemble small apartments with simpler rooms, less-frequent housekeeping service, and fewer extras. The hotels market themselves more as extended-stay lodging—in some cases, charging by the week rather than the night—and rates can dip as low as $25 a night in some areas.

Hotels in the mid-priced niche, such as Candlewood Hotels (started in 1995 by DeBoer in a joint venture with Doubletree Hotel Corporation); Homegate Studios and Suites, MainStay Suites, operated by Choice Hotels; and Marriott's TownePlace Suites, hover in the $40- to $60-per-night range, and their features fall between the upper and lower ends—swimming pools and exercise rooms show up in some cases; twice-weekly maid service in others.

Occupancy rates at extended-stays tend to be higher than standard hotels. Gregory Hartmann, managing director of the Boulder office of the hotel consulting firm HVS International, says that industry-wide, extended-stays enjoy an occupancy rate of only about 5 percentage points higher—85 percent versus 80 percent for a standard hotel. But that average is lowered somewhat by statistics from the inclusion of more leisure-oriented markets, he says, where extended-stays face the same seasonal concerns as standard hotels.

Where extended-stays really excel, Hartmann says, is in more commercial markets; there, extended-stays keep their 85-percent rate, while other hotels drop to 70 percent. This is due in large part to the same problem that standard hotels face everywhere—weekends. A standard hotel in a commercial area generally isn't filled on weekends. But extended-stay guests have longer-term commitments—and it's not always necessary for them to check out of their rooms, even if they go home for weekends and return the next week. As a result, extended-stays simply are booked for longer periods of time. Hartmann adds that because they face fewer vacancies on weekends, they also don't have to drop weekend rates to attract guests.

And, adds Patrick Ford, CCIM, president of National Hotel Realty Advisors in Portsmouth, New Hampshire, extended stays often welcome one- or two-night guests, which widens their customer pool. Travelers—business travelers in particular—may find that for just a little more money, they can end up with much more spacious facilities than a traditional hotel room offers, Ford says.

Costs Vary

Because extended-stay properties are constructed differently from conventional hotels, development costs differ as well. "Keep in mind the square footage you're building is substantially larger than a traditional hotel room," Webb says. At the same time, extended-stays tend to eliminate many of the public areas associated with standard hotels—extras such as restaurants, lounges, spacious lobbies, meeting rooms, on-site dry cleaners, and parking garages. Therefore, Webb says, "to compare construction costs, it's more relevant to compare an extended-stay hotel to a one-bedroom apartment than to a traditional hotel."

Overall, Hartmann says, extended-stays cost about $10,000 more per room than standard hotels. One factor driving up costs, he says, is the inclusion of kitchens in the units. But, he says, because the units are larger, each hotel simply will have fewer units per parcel—and that can increase the per-room figure as well.

However, the difference in building time, he adds, is minimal—"maybe two weeks." Where developers might face delays, though, is before building starts—in the approval process. If municipalities aren't familiar with extended-stays, he says, they may take longer to approve the projects because of fears about the hotels turning into transient apartments. This is a problem that may ease, Hartmann says, as more extended-stays are built and municipalities can better study their track records. And currently, he adds, in markets where planning commissions are more familiar with extended-stays, they may be more willing to speed up the approval process because they see the hotels as filling a new niche—particularly if the hotels cater to more upscale guests.

Costs also vary according to the brand. According to Tim Sheldon, brand vice president for Marriott's TownePlace Suites and Residence Inns, a TownePlace Suites development generally costs $45,000 to $47,000 per room without land; a Residence Inn development costs $62,000 to $68,000 per room. Part of that cost, Sheldon says, stems from the increased size of Residence Inn facilities; guest rooms tend to be 20 percent larger, and the hotels also may include meeting rooms. Land costs, he adds, also can be higher for Residence Inns because they tend to be located in more-visible areas.

Whatever the price tier, the economics of operating extended-stay properties are significantly different from those of traditional hotels, Ross says. Generally, he says, a conventional hotel employs large numbers of people because it provides extras such as daily housekeeping and food service. An extended-stay hotel, though, only has a front desk, and it doesn't provide room service or daily maid service, so it can run with far fewer employees. The Extended StayAmerica properties are a case in point: The chain says a typical Crossland Economy Studios property with 120 to 140 guest rooms is staffed by three full-time and three to five part-time employees. Its top-of-the-line segment, StudioPlus Hotels, has five or six full-time employees at an 80- to 100-studio site.

Extended-stay hotels also can cut costs by using more flexible staffing. Sheldon says that TownePlace Suites uses a self-managed service team, where staff members fill in for each other. Although the hotels are staffed 24 hours a day, the cross-training reduces the number of front-desk personnel as well as housekeeping staff. The result: a 100-unit TownePlace Suites can run with a full-time staff of seven; a similar-size Residence Inn—because it offers more standard hotel amenities—generally needs 22 to 25.

Setting Sights on Sites

Site selection offers the greatest opportunity for brokers interested in working on extended-stay properties—"There's more consulting or land-sale function for all levels of these properties, versus resale of existing properties," says Dewey Struble, CCIM, president of Trident Real Estate in Reno, Nevada. "Right now, there just aren't very many of them—and now there's money to build new."

Site-selection criteria illustrate extended-stays' hybrid characteristics. "The physical needs of the property are very similar to an apartment complex," Webb says; "However, they have retail needs like a hotel." A site should have reasonably good visibility and access, he adds, "but it doesn't have to be a premier-hotel site."

In fact, a nontraditional hotel site sometimes can be very effective, says Jeffrey Fisher, chief executive officer of Innkeepers USA Trust. Such locations "feed into what guests want," Fisher says. "If you were staying somewhere for three weeks, would you want to sit on the side of a highway?" Instead, he says, Innkeepers looks to acquire properties with "a more wooded, residential feel."

An extended-stay property, however, does need proximity to its market; if it's targeting corporate clients, it should be close to businesses and office parks whose employees and clients are the most likely potential guests. Struble says economy-priced properties can be a little more flexible, locating in more-residential areas as well as areas where conventional motels might operate. Support services, like restaurants and grocery stores, also should be convenient.

Evaluating the Competition

Site selection also should include evaluation of the competition—and not just other hotels. "Corporate apartments really are the competition for the extended-stay hotel," Ross says. Oakwood Corporate Housing, for example, operates more than 17,000 extended-stay corporate apartments in the United States. The company offers customers a variety of personalized amenities, including packages for kids and for business travelers. The units are marketed as fully furnished apartments and are meant for stays of a month or longer.

But developers should keep an eye on the local rental market as well. "If a particular market has any strong extended-stay demand characteristics, then local apartment complexes can become flexible and start renting on a short-term basis—maybe monthly leases—and satisfy that demand. So you should also look at the local apartment market to evaluate potential competition," Ross says.

"Most markets where extended-stays are successful are communities that are experiencing high growth, have strong economic factors, are strong in migration, are healthy, vibrant, and can also support the addition of residential apartment units," he adds.

Understanding Segmentation

Brokers working on site selection need to clarify for themselves the various products' distinctions, Webb says. "It's important to understand the product that you are representing to sellers—particularly in sites where there are multiple pads for multiple products; you may have someone wanting to put in three hotels in an office park. It's extremely important to understand what you're bringing to the site—not only its physical requirements, but the caliber, quality, and image that it's going to generate for that particular park or hotel center."

In fact, the slight differences between extended-stays and apartments as well as other similar kinds of lodging could be a drawback to extended-stays in their current stage. "The hospitality industry has blurred all the lines," Webb says. "There are too many brand segments in the market, and the consumer doesn't understand them. It's difficult enough for someone who deals with them every day to understand. We now have at least three and maybe four tiers in the extended-stay line alone—and probably seven or eight only slightly different tiers of quality in the hospitality industry overall in just the general hotel line. I think it's very confusing for consumers even to the extent that when they pull up to the front door, they don't know exactly what services that facility may be offering to its guests."

The lines particularly may be blurry when comparing extended-stays to suite hotels. "There is potential confusion in the marketplace as to what is really included in a suite property," Struble says. "You may get a studio, but you'll have a kitchen—versus a lower-priced product that may have one or two bedrooms and no kitchen—but they'll still call it a suite because it's more than one room." Extended-stay can be a differentiating factor, he adds, but a suite hotel may need to add amenities to call itself such.

"I liken it to what happened eight or 10 years ago where we saw a great proliferation of segmentation in the hotel/hospitality business," Struble says. Then, he points out, the difference in products was based more on service and amenities in conventional hotels. "What we're seeing now is a different kind of segmentation—it's a different product rather than a different price point."

In the meantime, the chains aim to clear up consumer confusion with careful marketing. "The medium and upscale range are corporate products," says Webb. "They're often marketed directly to corporations to garner the relationship. I don't see an awful lot of traditional hotel advertising as you might for tourism." Marriott's Sheldon, for instance, says that TownePlace Suites will build on Residence Inn's experience of direct sales, emphasizing such sales even before the facilities open. He adds that TownePlace Suites' general managers are expected to spend five to seven hours a week in sales.

Other chains position themselves simply by the amenities they offer. Extended StayAmerica hotels also are marketing themselves toward corporate travelers, so their rooms offer free voice mail and computer data ports, but the hotels lack pools and other features that might be more attractive to families.

Extending Extended-stays

Most of the players in the extended-stay market have ambitious plans for the next five years. As of September 1997, Candlewood, for example, had five company-owned hotels open, 24 under construction, and 34 sites under contract. It also had five franchised hotels open or under construction. (It expects that eventually its hotels will be roughly 50 percent company-owned and 50 percent franchised—with Wichita-based Candlewood managing about half of the franchised properties.) Extended StayAmerica—founded in 1995 by Blockbuster Entertainment's H. Wayne Huizenga and George Johnson—operates 134 properties under its three brands and has another 90 under construction and options to purchase 120 more sites for development. The company aimed to have 181 properties open by the end of 1997 and more than 540 by the year 2000. Marriott launched TownePlace Suites in March 1997 and plans to open 35 of them by the end of 1998, with 130 projected by 2000.

Are developers being too optimistic? Hartmann thinks the market is good. "If you look at the numbers, travelers staying five days or more are about a third of the market—and extended-stay hotels are only about 4 percent of the market." If the economy stays strong, he says, true extended-stay hotels won't be affected by the growth of new supply.

Struble is more cautious. "There is concern in some peoples' minds, that in an area that has never really been previously defined, if we've reached saturation—or are we beyond saturation already? Nobody really knows," says Struble. What could be troubling, he adds, is "that the hospitality market has been on such a high the last couple of years, we don't know the shakeout of that, which will eventually come. It's a very cyclical business, and the hospitality market cycles tend to be shorter than other cycles in the real estate business. And whether the part of it will help drive that or whether it's immune from it—we don't know, because most of this extensive new development of these properties has happened since the last down market. It's all been occurring in an up market, so we've never seen a shakeout of the market."

The future also might bring brokers future opportunities aside from site selection, Ford says. "The real brokerage opportunities may come four or five years down the road," he says, when the properties have matured and are riper for resale, and a particular market is "developed out."

Consolidations also may affect extended-stay lines. StudioPlus Hotels is part of Extended StayAmerica as a result of its merger with the Fort Lauderdale-based company in April 1997; Promus Hotel Corporation, which owns Homewood Suites, merged with Doubletree Corporation in September 1997.

The hotels' identities also will affect their success. "I think what you'll see is more consistent branding much like what you have in the traditional hotel industry," says Webb, "where you have, for example, Marriott product lines that target different tiers of the market." Consumers, he adds, then will begin to identify with a limited number of names.

In any event, brokers interested in hopping on the extended-stay bandwagon now should know what they're undertaking. "You either have to have expertise in the hospitality business or align yourself with someone who does," Struble advises. "It's a different animal. Many things are the same, but they have different labels in the hospitality business—it's a little different language."

And, he adds, "be comfortable working in a corporate environment. You'll get involved in that either because it's a company-owned product or because they're almost all franchised. You have to be comfortable working with corporate real estate people."

Marriott's Sheldon agrees. "It's a growing market, and lots of people want to play in this arena," he says. "But you have to have a clear understanding of what it is."

Casino Hotel

Whether you're a frequent traveler, heading overseas with your family, or planning a trip for the first time, Casino hotels have started popping up all over the world. And with casino tourism continuing to trend, booking an onsite hotel is a pretty sure bet.

These are luxury hotels and resorts, which are owned or attached to the casino, and with cheap rates, central locations, and access to a range of entertainment, this is a great idea for accommodation, even if you don't plan on gambling.

But when it comes to staying at a casino, there are a few necessary things you should know, because these are not your average hotel.

Things you Need to Know About Staying in Casino Hotels

The Tightest Security you'll See at a Hotel

One of the biggest concerns among travelers these days is security, so a fantastic thing about casino hotels is that security is very tight. You'll probably find that casinos have the tightest security of any hotel.

In the interest of protecting their gaming licenses, many casinos employ independent security, and some may even have a police presence. Even the slightest hint of suspicious or questionable activity will be cut off, and anyone acting in an abusive manner will be removed from the premises.

As a guest, this means you can sleep safely, but it also means you should keep your behavior (and drinking) in check. Also, be aware that there are cameras absolutely everywhere. You probably shouldn't do anything stupid while staying there.

Tipping

The country you're traveling to will depend on whether you're expected to tip or not. For instance, in Australia there is no culture of tipping, and the price you pay includes all service charges.

But if you're visiting a country like the United States, where tipping is customary, it's important to remember that dealers, cocktail waitresses, hotel valets, housekeeping etc, are all paid minimum wage, and make their living almost entirely from your tips.

In this case, it's usually standard to leave a tip of $1 per drink, or 15 – 20% of a restaurant food bill. If driving and using the hotel valet, a $2-5 tip is normal for handling your car.

Plan on giving a couple of dollars to the bellman, and leaving the same for the housekeepers who service your room. Pay the concierge $10 for special requests, and if you do visit the tables, $5 per hour for the dealer is an average tip.

Check the Gambling / Drinking Age

Just as the culture of tipping varies depending on country, so too does the gambling and drinking age. You should be aware of this before you travel, so you don't land yourself in legal trouble overseas. Remembering too that casino hotels have tight security.

The legal age for drinking in the United States is 21, though when it comes to gambling, each state determines their own minimum age. In some states, it's 18, though in most parts of the USA (especially if it's an alcohol-licensed casino) it's 21 to match the drinking age. As a general rule, in Canada you must be 19 to enter a casino, though in Australia, the UK and most parts of Europe you must be 18.

This doesn't mean that you can't stay at the hotel if you're underage, or traveling with children, however you won't be permitted in the gaming areas, and you will not be permitted to drink.

An Attraction in their Own Right

Most Casinos double as Entertainment Complexes, and have a range of trendy restaurants, night-clubs and bars, well as theaters and resort amenities like water parks and swimming pools onsite.

Off course there are plenty of activities you'll want to take in offsite, perhaps the Cheltenham Festival where you can get in some Cheltenham betting, but the complex is usually an attraction in it's own right, and chances are you're already planning on heading there at some point. Why not make transport easy by staying onsite.

For instance, Crown Casino Melbourne pulls more visitors to Australia each year than the iconic Sydney Opera House. With an annual 10.9 million visitors compared to the 8.2 million who check in at the Opera House, well known tourist attractions don't even come close to seeing the type of tourism numbers that Australian casinos do.

Some Offer Free Rooms

If you're a high roller, or planning on spending a lot of money at the casino, you might be able to get your room for free. The most expensive rooms at many Casino hotels are usually set aside for VIP's. Though even if you don't fall into that category, the room rates at casinos are often a lot cheaper than other luxury hotels.

The idea behind offering ridiculously discounted or free rooms for travelers is that the property will make back the money on the casino floor. Casinos don't really care about the profits from their hotels, and they're really not interested in whether or not you book an expensive room.

What they do care about is convincing you to open your wallet where it really counts – the casino floor – so will often use cheap accommodation as a lure. Before you travel, join the email list of the casinos you're thinking about visiting to receive alerts about promotions, and follow them on social media to hear about last minute deals.

Boutique Hotel

Since the beginning of the 21st century, the lodging industry has become increasingly over-supplied with big monopolies of hotel brands. These brands, predominantly based in North America, succeed in selling consistency across the nation and, for some, around the world. These lodging facilities publicize the meaning of "hotel" through the truly traditional definition: a lodging accommodation for travelers.

Nevertheless, travelers nowadays expect more than simply comfort and convenience. An increasing number of travelers prefer to be "surprised" — positively, needless to say. When planning trips, they seek properties that are noticeably different in look and feel from branded hotels. Although many travelers claim to seek lodging facilities that coincide with the traditional hotel concept, boutique hotels are becoming more and more of a social manipulation: those who do not stay in boutique hotels are categorized as unfashionable and un-hip.

Boutique hotels are believed to have been invented in the early 1980s. Two of the first boutique hotels in the world opened their doors to the public in 1981: The Blakes Hotel in South Kensington, London (designed by celebrity stylist Anouska Hempel) and the Bedford in Union Square, San Francisco (the first in a series of 34 boutique hotels currently operated under the flag of one of the most eminent players in the boutique hotel world today, the Kimpton Group). In 1984, Ian Schrager opened his first boutique hotel in Murray Hill in New York City: the Morgans Hotel, designed by French stylist Andrée Putnam.

The definition of a boutique hotel varies, especially among the hotel industry's primary players. However, the majority of boutique hotel operators, creators, and owners can all agree on the following primary features of boutique hotels:

- Architecture and design Style, distinction, warmth, and intimacy are key words in the architecture and design of boutique hotels, which seem to attract a niche of customers looking for a special and differentiated property able to fulfill their individual needs. Boutique hotels are not boxed into standards; the definition and expression of a theme is a crucial path to success. Many boutique hotels introduce different themes in each guestroom, making every single stay unique, even for their repeat guests. For example, the Library Hotel in New York City offers a different theme (from romance to music) in every guestroom. Many hotel owners are revitalizing older hotels, repositioning them as boutique properties. While true modernism and newly born design generally become "hip" in no time, it is usually those properties that succeed in combining historic details with chic elegance that outlast the fads.

- Service: The question that blurs the meaning of boutique hotels is, "Does size matter?" Most boutique hotel "celebrities" insist that it does, and that boutique hotels are properties that do not exceed 150 rooms. They believe that what distinguishes boutique hotels from standardized hotels is the connection that hotel guests experience with members of the hotel staff. Most of these hotels impose the acknowledgment of guest names by all hotel staff members, an experience that is clearly difficult to achieve in a large-scale hotel. Nevertheless, Ian Schrager, founder and president of Ian Schrager Hotels, which currently comprises approximately 3,000 guestrooms in nine properties, is among those who do not believe in this commonly accepted facet of the typical boutique hotel. With creative people as his target market, he defines "boutique" as an approach and attitude, with no regard to hotel size. Personalized service does not appear to be important at Schrager properties, especially in his "biggies," such as the Paramount Hotel (594 rooms) and the Henry Hudson Hotel (821) rooms. Instead, Schrager hotels place the emphasis on entertaining their guests by creating a theatrical atmosphere that attracts all senses: through architecture, design, colors, lighting, art, and music.

- Target MarketBoutique hotels generally target customers who are in their early 20s to mid-50s, with mid- to upper-income averages.

Although no standard definition of boutique hotels has been agreed upon, and the sizes of these types of hotels vary considerably, most boutique hotels do share some common characteristics. As with any other hospitality product, the success stories of boutique properties begin with fundamentals such as location, product quality, market demand, a clearly defined marketing approach, and effective distribution/reservations coverage. In light of these factors, boutique hotel creators detach their creations into two branches:

- Boutique hotels in city destinations In city destinations, location still ranks number one on guests' priority lists. Good locations for boutique hotels are not determined only by manner of convenience, but also by the "trendiness" and "chic-ness" of their respective neighborhoods. Accordingly, most existing city boutique hotels are located in vivacious cities such as New York, London, San Francisco, and Miami. Ian Schrager, for example, claims to only open his hotels in cities with enough depth — i.e., big fashion and media capitals. Nevertheless, more and more companies are targeting less cosmopolitan cities that are believed to have strong potential for boutique hotels: cities with vibrant economies and high-end residential areas, but bland, characterless hotel inventories. Both the style and the design of city boutique hotels are unlike the traditional resort boutique hotels. Cooler notes, modernism, and the interpretation of the 21st Century — at times matched with historical components and art — are considered modish, and are found in most successful city boutique hotels. Technology strongly relates to these factors, whether it is technology that enhances the ambience and promotes emotional contact between the guests and the hard attributes of the building (such as lighting and music), or technology that is provided for the convenience of hotel guests (such as in-room DVD players, flat-screen television sets, cordless phones, and computers with high-speed Internet access and the latest monitor genres). Entertainment in boutique hotels is an important dynamic in creating a lively, chic and trendy mind-set. However, in the boutique hotel concept, entertainment is not limited to events such as live music and performances; the idea of a boutique hotel is entertainment in its own nature: a hip restaurant, lounge, and bar; an exceptional theme; and visually spectacular decorations.

- Boutique hotels in resort destinations Boutique hotels in resort destinations are exotic, small, and intimate. These boutique hotels give their guests a chance to explore the local feel without sacrificing luxury. Although location is just as important in resort destinations as it is in city destinations, the word "trendy" has a different designation in this matter; if location should be central in the case of city boutique hotels, trendy resort boutique hotels are generally well-hidden, tucked away in deserted corners of the islands or the mountains. The more difficult it is to reach the destination by means of common transportation, the more fashionable the location is considered. Successful boutique resort hotels unite traditional architecture with the comfort and luxury of modernism, without losing the personality of the local community. Each boutique hotel must develop its own recognizable flavor, with sumptuousness and excellence as the only similarities among boutique resort hotels. In boutique resort destinations, service is generally more important than it is in boutique city destinations. Exotic amenities take the role of technology in city destinations; in fact, boutique resort hotels actually promote the non-existence of electronics and communication devices in guestrooms as a competitive advantage. Traditional spas, rose petal baths, private individual plunge pools, honeymoon packages, and art and painting sessions are just a few examples of boutique amenities offered in resort destinations.

Marketing Boutique Hotels

Most guests stay in boutique hotels because it is fashionable to do so, not because of the facilities the hotels offer. In this regard, boutique hotels are being marketed in a manner that is similar to many other goods, where the experience and the image are sold, rather than the product itself. Marketing an independent boutique hotel can be difficult, as there are generally financial restrictions and other resource restrictions. The main issue in marketing a boutique hotel or resort involves "sending a message" to the target market. Story development is more important than ever, which relates back to the special nature of the experience or location, or the history behind the creation of the hotel. The unique and easily related story must then be delivered through effective and affordable channels such as direct mail or direct sales, allied group marketing, affinity group travel planners, and public relations through press.

Boutique hotels bring certain benefits in terms of operations and profitability. Besides strong customer demand, the economics are favorable for operators. For example, boutique owners do not have to pay a franchise fee to become part of a larger chain. The hotel can survive and succeed without such costly amenities as restaurants and ballrooms/meeting spaces; however, these amenities, when styled in a boutique manner, can bring significant additional profitability to the hotel's room's revenue. Once established, boutique hotels also tend to have a higher percentage of repeat business compared to the industry in general, which may reflect a smaller degree of volatility when going through difficult economic times. Nevertheless, smart boutique hotels must continue to adapt to the incessantly changing needs, tastes, preferences, and fashions in order to remain competitive in the flourishing boutique hotel market.

Characteristics of Boutique Hotels

Size: Boutique hotels are typically small, with 10 to 100 rooms. They are intimate in scale, creating the ambiance of being a personal guest in a private home, rather than just a hotel occupant. They often have communal "living spaces" where guests can interact.

The Library Lounge, Esprit Saint Germain, Paris – recommended
by Josée Covington, President & CEO of Covington.

Individuality: Properties have a distinctive vibe and never have the "cookie cutter" feel of being one in a series. They are often operated independently and are not affiliated with a major chain. That said, the largest independent boutique hotel operator in the world, the Kimpton Hotel brand, is owned by InterContinental® Hotels & Resorts (IHG). Or they may be independently owned, but belong to a luxury hotel association, such as Relais & Chateaux or Small Luxury Hotels of the World.

The Saguro Palm Springs – recommended by
Jennifer E., Covington Online Specialist.

Design: The architecture and interior design of a boutique hotel is as unique as its operations, but always upscale and often combining historic details with chic elegance. The lines may be sleek and contemporary or quaint and homey – or even an artistic amalgamation. Boutique hotels convey a progressively forward style with fastidious décor. Guestrooms are individually decorated, and use upscale linens and exclusive amenities.

Character: Boutique hotels usually have an eccentric personality. They are fun and funky, trendy and offbeat. Their quirky sense of humor might be exhibited through creative guest offerings. For example the Hotel Monaco in Washington, D.C. will deliver a goldfish to your room if you're missing your own pet.

Location: Again, there is no hard rule, but many boutique hotels are located in the most hip and fashionable urban areas. You'll find them in lively, up-and-coming sections – they may well be one of the factors in the area's rejuvenation – and high-end residential neighborhoods that are away from the crowds, but convenient to city highlights. Trendy boutique hotels are also found in resort areas, generally well hidden from the main tourist throng.

Southern Ocean Lodge, Kangaroo Island, Australia – recommended
by Karen K., Luxury Vacation Advisor.

Culture: As an extension of the unique personality of each property, boutique hotels often celebrate the local flavor with a strong sense of place by incorporating locally-sourced materials and reflecting the locations heritage through color and art. Themed boutique hotels build the entire guest experience, from décor to services, around a particular subject such as art, fashion or sports.

Service: Highly personalized service is a hallmark of boutique hotels. Staff will know your name on the first day of your stay. Providing bespoke luxury amenities such as an extensive pillow menu and custom toiletries, as well as offering sumptuous spa services creates a very high-quality, individualized experience.

The Farmhouse Inn near Healdsburg, CA boasts a
Michelin-starred restaurant for fine country dining.
Recommended by Kim S., Covington Vacation Advisor.

Gastronomy: Like everything else about boutique hotels, their restaurants and bars tend to be hip, trendy and locally-sourced. High quality, authentic cuisine, and comfortable cocktail atmospheres make these dining and drinking spots popular with locals as well as guests.

Clientele: The types of travelers who are attracted to boutique hotels are as individual as the hotels themselves and tend to be just as hip. Guests from Millennials to Boomers who enjoy creative design, quirky character, and luxurious service will be right at home in boutique hotels.

Serviced Apartment

A serviced apartment is a fully furnished apartment, available for both short-term and long-term stays, providing amenities for daily use, housekeeping and a range of other services, all included within the rental price. Now, you might be thinking: "Sounds a lot like a hotel." But nope, they are actually two very different things. So what exactly is the difference between a hotel and a serviced apartment?

Hotels and Serviced Apartments – Comparing Apples and Oranges

Serviced apartments offer facilities much like a traditional hotel but with added space, convenience and privacy like home, so you can enjoy living like a local when travelling – and usually at a much lower cost.

Most online booking sites have long offered serviced apartments, but with no separate category – most are just labeled "apartment" and offered as another option alongside regular hotel rooms. The problem is, serviced apartments offer much more than just the physical dimensions of an apartment and shouldn't be compared to traditional hotel rooms either.

But the term is slowly becoming more well-known also outside the business travel space, also because more and more leisure travellers are finding that serviced apartments are available and offer a credible and cost-effective alternative. They are especially economical for longer stays and for group and family travel.

Your Home Away From Home

These days, especially business travellers are looking for alternative accommodation solutions when away from home in order to have a more comfortable stay. If you are a business professional who is continuously living out of a suitcase and staying in traditional hotel rooms, you will appreciate the features of a serviced apartment. They allow for space, privacy and comfort in your own surrounding and the freedom to do exactly the same things you would do at home.

Prepare your own meals in your kitchen, finish up work in the living room, throw your sports clothes in the washing machine after a run, then kick back and watch Netflix in your bedroom.

The advantages of a serviced apartment compared to traditional hotels in a nutshell:

- A serviced apartment is more of a home, with utilities that enable more freedom and comfort.

- A serviced apartment typically has more square meters than a traditional hotel room. We have room for your sports equipment.

- A serviced apartment is substantially cheaper than a hotel room when staying for a longer period of time. Both because of the actual cost of the apartment compared to a hotel room, but also because of the possibility to cook for yourself and not having to eat out on every meal.

- A serviced apartment resembles the culture of the specific area. It gives insight into what a real local apartment would look like, giving a more comprehensive immersion of the culture and values compared to hotel rooms, which usually all look alike.

Timeshare / Vacation Rental

Timeshares and vacation rentals are increasingly popular accommodation options. Here, we'll answer common questions about how they differ and highlight the pros and cons of each from both an owner and guest's perspective.

Vacation Rental

The Basics: The rental property belongs to an owner, who decides when to rent their space to guests. The owners are often limited by the rules of their condo board, homeowner's association, or local government, depending on circumstance and location. Some owners opt to hire a property management company to maintain the premises and handle guest communication. Since the rental is fully the owner's property, he or she can choose its decoration, amenities, and dates of availability.

Timeshare

The Basics: A timeshare's ownership is differentiated by the fact that its ownership is shared. Typically, each owner has a certain amount of time each year (usually broken down by weeks) that he or she can use the property. There are two common types of timeshare agreements:

Deeded Timeshare

Under a deeded timeshare, a buyer is granted a deed to the property and is consequently a partial owner of it. In the U.S., this can mean the owner has the right to sell their portion, give it away, or bequeath it in a legal will.

Right-to-use Timeshare

The right-to-use arrangement is more similar to a lease than an outright ownership. This type of agreement grants use of a property for a set week period over a set number of years, but as there is no ownership, the buyer can lose the right to access the property when the agreement expires or should the timeshare company go bankrupt, for example.

The timeshare arrangement you prefer depends on whether you want to invest in a property or simply rent one for a vacation.

For Buyers Considering Investing in a Vacation Rental or Timeshare

Buying a Vacation Rental

Vacation Rental Benefits for Owners

- You fully own a property.
- You can customize the decor and design it to appeal to certain demographics like pet owners or seniors.

- You can use a variety of methods to attract customers: personal sites, listing sites, even partnerships with local tourist organizations.

Vacation Rental Drawbacks for Owners

- You're liable for any damages or issues with the property.

- If you live out of the area, you may have to pay a property management company to take care of the property.

Buying a Timeshare

Timeshare Benefits for Owners

- It's less of an initial investment than a vacation rental.

- You have guaranteed time to use the property or sell that time to others.

Timeshare Drawbacks for Owners

- You don't fully own the property.

- You may have to pay maintenance fees and property taxes.

- You may have to use a special broker to sell your unused time, subject to the requirements of the timeshare contract.

For Guests Considering Booking a Vacation Rental or Timeshare

Booking a Vacation Rental

Vacation Rental Benefits for Guests

- Vacation rentals are available all over the world: cities, towns, resort areas, even the middle of nowhere.

- You can find a property that matches your specific needs.

- Owners are often willing to accommodate guests' needs, and guests might be able to get a better deal on their reservation.

Vacation Rental Drawbacks for Guests

- Owners may not maintain the property to your standards.

- Communication with the owner may be difficult if they are not located nearby.

Booking a Timeshare

Timeshare Benefits

- Timeshares are often located in desirable resort areas.

- Timeshare properties are held to a certain uniform standard of care, cleanliness, and amenities.

Timeshare Drawbacks

- Timeshares have restrictions on decor and modifications.

- You will have limited control over which specific timeshare in a resort you will get, as they are only available on unused weeks.

- You often have to book in week segments, limiting shorter or longer term booking availability.

Micro-stay

Built around the concept of capsule hotels, Micro stay options first appeared in Europe, and spread rapidly to other Western countries. Micro stay hotels have now debuted in India, and with more and more people discovering the convenience they offer, they are definitely here to stay. Catering to people looking for a place to relax in for a few hours, these posh-tels are a cost-effective way of adding comfort to any trip, whether business or personal.

Workings

A Micro stay is charged on an hourly basis, for durations ranging from 3 hours to 9 hours. The guests have a range of furniture and amenities to pick from depending on their immediate needs. From a place to sit and work in, to a bed for a quick nap, or a clean cubicle to shower in, a Micro stay serves a very specific purpose. Ideal for a short stay, it is a boon for travellers who are always on the go.

Why it is better than a conventional hotel?

Most conventional hotels have a specific checkout time, irrespective of when you check in, and a stay is billed on a 24 hour basis irrespective of how long you occupy it. Micro stay addresses this issue of overpaying for a short stay quite effectively by offering hospitality services for a few hours.

Micro Stay is for Everyone

Micro-stay has caught the fancy of every kind of traveler, be it an entrepreneur or a high-profile company executive or a backpacker or a pilgrim. Wouldn't you love to get into a hotel, have a refreshing bath or grab your forty winks in a comfortable bed and pay on an hourly basis? All this at a facility with all the conveniences of a hotel where on the other hand you would pay for a 24-hour stay, without using it for the entire duration.

Business travelers can take the late-night train or an early morning flight for a meeting, catch up on their sleep in a cozy room and wake up fresh and full of energy for that all-important presentation. It also allows a lot of flexibility with travel plans and saves money, a fact that entrepreneurs and corporates love dearly. It is surely better than spending time at a cramped transit lounge or a dingy waiting room. No more worries of reaching the client's office in a crumpled shirt, with sleep-deprived eyes or discharged gadgets! Micro Stays offer several amenities in addition to space, to ensure you can recharge your gadgets, and tuck into a delicious snack to keep you going.

Roadies and backpackers dig this kind of an arrangement as it becomes easy to avail all the necessary amenities of a hotel room without being saddled with a bill that could break their budget. It's a win-win situation for the guests and the hotel since they pay only for the few hours they've stayed. Generally, backpackers run a tight ship and cannot afford to let the budget run amok and this is where hourly booking comes in handy.

Corporate travelers are on the road for a major part of their work schedule, and organizations are conscious of the travel expenses they incur. With a facility where you can pay by the hour, your travel plans become quite flexible and you can pay less than half of the actual room rent. Get rid of that jet-lag in a jiffy.

Families and groups who are enroute pilgrimages can also make good use of micro-stay. It is quite easy on the pocket and they are assured of safety, cleanliness and comfortable accommodation while on the move.

Micro stays comes to the rescue when people staying in the same city need to entertain guests, but are unable to do so because of space constraints. It becomes a hassle-free and economical way of accommodating guests and creating a great impression. People who accompany patients for medical attention can use this option to take a break from the monotony of hospitals and stay here to rejuvenate them.

Destination Spa

A destination spa is somewhere where every guest has turned up to spa. Just that. You can stay at a destination spa for as long as your need or budget prescribes (anything from a few days to a few months). You can relax. Or have fun with a friend. A destination spa is not a hotel with a pool that's a nice base for touring the Cotswolds. It's all about the spa.

A destination spa can offer everything from beautiful surroundings to comfortable beds, delicious food, friendly service and the highest quality of facilities and treatments, which themselves can range from manicures to Tui Na (Chinese medical massage).

A destination spa aims to hit every "restore" button you have. People tend to visit because they want to relax and unwind, and the emphasis is often just as much on pampering as on health. If you want a wrap and to eat cake -- or even to wrap yourself in cake -- there'll be a destination spa for you.

Some destination spas are set in remote countryside or mountain areas, without telephones, TVs or other things that can distract you from your focus on well-being.

Destination spas often let people in just for the day, too. But the difference between a hotel spa and a destination spa is that, at lunchtime, everyone will be in toweling robes. They will be for breakfast, as well. These are people seriously chilling, not fitting in a gym spree or sauna after their management consultancy. They are here to put their own needs first.

Types of Destination Spa

There are several varieties of destination spa.

There's the just all-out gorgeous. Here the setting is not Spartan or forbidding. The focus in on you, looking after you, and doing what's best for you. These destination spas are often like well-appointed country-house hotels, with the difference that anyone not in a toweling robe looks odd -- not the other way around. When the day guests go, those staying congratulate themselves on their wise choice of putting off a return to the real world for at least another night.

To name a couple: Ragdale Hall Health Hydro and Thermal Spa, Leicestershire; Stobo Castle Health Spa, Peeblesshire.

Another type of destination spa is the health-focused retreat, beloved of so many. These spas take a "let's improve" approach to your health and well-being. Destination spas with a focus on health offer personal medical assessments, body and facial treatments, complementary therapies, and diet and exercise advice, all tailored to your individual needs. Quite often, people choose to visit because they want to lose weight or make permanent changes to their lifestyle.

Many of these destination spas aim to nurture you in a more thorough way than simply pampering. They offer an opportunity to look at your whole lifestyle, and to work on a range of different aspects of your self. The range of treatments on offer may sometimes be narrower, but a lot of energy goes into finding out about you, and your specific issues and needs. You're more likely to go for a series of visits or a residential stay so that you can have some consistent input into your overall health and well-being. Some holistic spas run meditation, yoga and other workshops and short courses that you can take when you're there, and take with you when you leave.

To name a few: Champneys Spas in Hertfordshire, Bedfordshire, Hampshire and Leicestershire, Lifehouse Spa Hotel in Essex and Grayshott Spa, Surrey.

There are also some dedicated spas which happen to be in the grounds of a family holiday resort. Which genius thought of that? Family holidays and a chance for pampering.

Resort spas offer a large range of activities and family experiences in extensive grounds. You'll find something for everyone in the family to enjoy, and get plenty of fresh air while they're doing it. Spa-ing is just one of the available options for pleasure. Which you can book in advance. For you. On your own. By yourself. Or with your partner.

To name a few: Aqua Sana Spas at Center Parcs in Bedfordshire, Cumbria, Nottinghamshire, Suffolk, and Wiltshire.

To Get the Most Out of your Visit to a Destination Spa

Choose your destination carefully; what do you want to get out of your trip. Pampering? Weight loss? Yoga before breakfast? All is on offer. Call ahead. If you get there and find activities or treatments you want are already booked up, you'll be disappointed.

When you arrive, do what you want to do. If that's to walk through natural surroundings for four hours every day before lunch, do it. If you want to eat alone, do that. Use your stay as a time to explore all the ways you can release your tension and stress. You can be as focused or as open as you want; you'll often find that, while you're there, there are opportunities to try out and learn about new things. Be honest about your lifestyle, and your priorities for your visit. The more you tell your therapists, the more appropriate their advice will be.

Hotel Management

A hotel manager is confident, approachable and adventurous. They aren't afraid to try new things. Excited to experience new cultures. And they know the importance of teamwork. If you want a career that's full of challenges, interesting people and exciting developments, hotel management could be just what you're looking for.

Managing a hotel comes with a range of responsibilities. You must be able to adapt to new challenges, help different departments and ensure the hotel maintains a standard of excellence. As a hotel manager, you will be responsible for overseeing and having a strong knowledge of finance, planning, service and organization. While you have a team of managers working alongside you, as hotel manager you have to lead rather than follow. You must also make sure your staffs are managing their time and departments efficiently, whether that be through improving their monthly profits or simply ensuring a guest's expectations are exceeded.

You must have strong attention to detail, leadership and teamwork skills. At some hotels, depending on the size and type, you may find yourself dealing with a lot more day-to-day tasks than you would at a more prestigious place. You may also have less contact with guests, but you'll spend time monitoring the business through regular meetings.

An Evolving Industry

The world of hospitality continues to expand. It is one of the world's fastest-growing industries, and will create over 80 million new jobs over the next ten years. The travel and tourism sector will account for one in nine jobs by the year 2026.

A hotel manager needs to know the current industry trends. They are aware that their hotel needs to evolve and change in order to stay current. At a recent Glion Luxury Conference, hospitality the audiences were told about what it takes to keep up-to-date. "To be successful, you have to create emotions," said Philippe Tardivel. "Whatever you create has to be extraordinary, and you have to go the extra mile.

Industry experts gave our students valuable info at our Luxury Conference

Skills Required for a Hotel Manager

You need a range of soft and hard skills to be a successful hotel manager. Furthermore, you also need to gain first-hand experience of the industry. Many future managers embark on internships to gain more experience, working at hotels of varying ranges, reputations and locations.

If you can, Open a Hotel

An excellent experience for any budding hotel manager is to take part in a hotel opening. It can be the new site of a leading brand or a boutique independent, either way seeing what it takes to get a hotel started gives you a true understanding of all the moving parts. Unlike taking a job at an established hotel, where you have processes in place to learn and master, at an opening hotel, you're responsible for installing or even creating those processes.

From registration cards to restaurant menus, the smallest and biggest elements, that you would usually take for granted, will need researching and creating, all to a deadline. It's usually all hands to the pump and it's a great opportunity to cross roles and gain experience in different departments as you take on duties outside your comfort zone. It may even be that you can't work in the hotel, as it's not finished, so you'll be doing all of this from a nearby office.

The skills you need to have included communication, teamwork and organization. However, you also need to understand and appreciate the challenges every department faces. It is important you spend time working or shadowing each part of a hotel, from finance to housekeeping. This ensures that you will have the awareness and experience to assist these departments when you become a manager.

Hotel Management Structure

Every hotel, whether it's big or small, needs an organizational structure to carry out its daily operations. It is used to help divide tasks, specify the job for each department, and delegate authority within and among departments. Effective job specifications will increase work productivity and efficiency. Each hotel organizes the workforce in different ways. Here shows a medium size hotel organizational structure.

It was basically segmented into six divisions: finance, front office, human resources, food and beverage, sales and logistics as the following organizational chart:

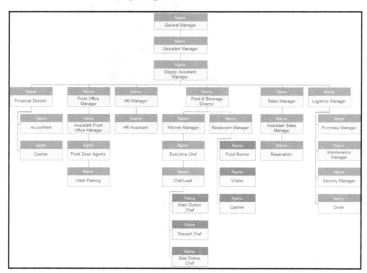

Financial

The financial department's role is to record financial transactions, prepare and interpret financial statements, and deal with cost accounting and cost control.

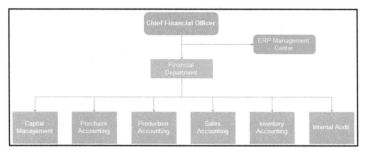

Front Office

The front office (room management) department handles customer service including front desk service, reservation, laundry, concierge, telephone, and housekeeping service. A hotel's front office is where guests are greeted when they arrive, where they get registered and assigned to a room, and where they check out. It's almost the most important department as it often offers contact with customers.

Human Resources

The human resources department is given the responsibility to handle employee recruitment, arrange staff training, make promotion and disciplinary decisions, and check staff attendance.

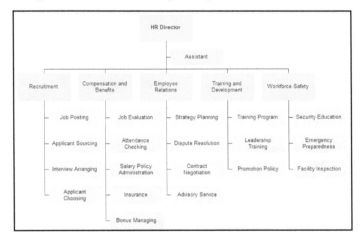

Food & Beverage

The food and beverage department is responsible for all of the dining rooms, restaurants, bars, kitchen, clean up services, etc. Here we basically divide F/B department into two parts: kitchen and restaurant. Kitchen department is responsible for food preparation including main food, dessert, side food, and beverage. Restaurant department's role is to provide dining room operation, waiter service, food runner, and clean up service.

Sales

The responsibility for the sales department is to sell the hotel facilities and services to individuals and groups. They sell rooms, food, beverage or special services such as massage and laundry to potential customers through advertising or direct contacts.

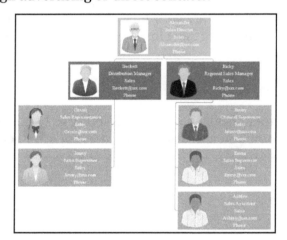

Logistics

The logistics department is responsible for tracking for daily supplies, purchasing appliances, and keeping security.

Hotel Energy Management

Hotels are large consumers of energy and fossil fuels to provide high quality services to guests. India's current growth potential for hotel construction will continue to result in an increasing energy consumption trend. There is also a misconception that correlates increased energy use with improved quality of services. Hotels can effectively reduce energy use without compromising the high quality of services for guests and in the process benefit from cost savings. Managing energy use in your hotel is the first step towards this. Energy management helps improve your bottom line and holds down operating costs. Controlling costs is a key to profitability in the hotel industry allowing your hotel to route resultant savings toward fulfilling other requirements including purchasing additional amenities, staff salary increases, etc.

Before any energy management program can be developed a dedicated staff team is required to ensure that accurate objectives are set and the right people will implement the plan. Identify a core team. This is the first step in initiating an energy management team. Identifying key staff members who will be involved in energy management activities and those responsible for overseeing the program is imperative for success. An effective team should include members from owner or management, the hotel staff, facility operations, engineering and someone who understands finance. A key group to have represented among the hotel staff is housekeeping. Commitment from top-level management and their involvement is vital to providing focus to energy management operations. The General Manager's attitude toward energy savings sets the pace for increased efficiency. Also, designate a mid level or upper level employee as "Energy Manager" to monitor energy saving activities and projects daily. Once the team is selected, plans organize a introductory session to start laying the groundwork for the program.

Identify and set specific objectives: Identifying the program goals and objectives helps establish a standard of comparison for success and also lays the path toward achieving desired results. For example, if you want to save 25% over the next 1-3 years you should consider the following:

- Have you defined the 25% as reduced consumption of energy or as reduced cost?

- What is the base you will measure against?

- How and when will the measurement be made?

Receive input from your team and plan workable goals and objectives to establish a baseline for your efforts. Use this phase to also identify related budget factors to achieve goals.

Develop a plan: Create an action plan to define the implementation of the pre-determined energy management goals and objectives. This plan will outline steps toward achieving desired results, delegate responsibilities, identify budget limitations and set targets for energy saving opportunities.

Communicate plan: Once the plan is established the success of the energy management program depends on the effectiveness of communicating it to the involved staff members and other individuals including guests etc. Use the plan to delegate responsibilities to key staff including housekeeping, front desk, and maintenance. Ensure that it is easy to understand and everyone shares the common goals and objectives of the program. Regular updates on program and visual tools to share progress are effective ways of building momentum within staff members.

Implement measures and monitor performance: Implementing measures identified and monitoring of measures and associated results is imperative for the program. Without regular monitoring of program it will be difficult to evaluate any savings. Follow up is also required to ensure that measures have been implemented properly.

Motivate staff members: The key to keeping people onboard with your energy management plan is having a reward and celebrating successes. Don't wait until the end of a two year program to announce results. Have regular milestones and incentives to meet them. Make people feel part of the program's success and it will take on a life of its own. Create an environment where people work together to get things done and enjoy the rewards of achieving success on a regular basis.

Determining Efficiency Targets

There are numerous variables that need to be considered while setting efficiency targets including occupancy rate, operating expenses, etc. The profitability of running a hotel must also be considered while identifying the appropriate variables. Operating expenses is one of the significant "constant" variables to be considered while determining savings objectives. Others like occupancy rate cost of materials and supplies will fluctuate based on external factors. Operating expenses are largely influenced by actions you can take and on average, the cost of energy accounts for 3% to 5% of the total operating expense. Through this guide, your hotel can aim to reduce energy costs by up to 20%.

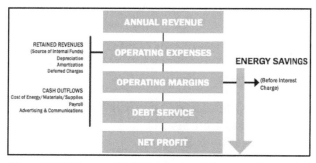

Figure: Factors involved in establishing profitability for hotel Source: "Managing Energy in Your Hotel".

Where is Energy Being Used

The first step in determining efficiency targets is to study where energy is being utilized within your hotel. Identifying areas of high and low energy use will help you target key areas for improvement and also areas that will provide maximum returns. Figure below highlights a typical hotel energy end use graph.

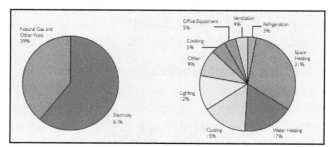

Figure: Typical energy end use in a hotel.

Facility Type	If Annual Energy Costs...	Estimated Annual Savings for reductions: Lighting by 20%		
		Lighting by 20%	HVAC by 20%	Water heating by 20%
50,000 sq. ft.	'$' 3,525,000	'$' 375,000	'$' 164,500	'$' 164,500
100,000 sq. ft	'$' 7,050,000	'$' 750,000	'$' 329,000	'$' 329,000
150,000 sq. ft.	'$' 10,575,000	'$' 1,125,000	'$' 488,800	'$' 470,000

Assumes facility uses electricity and natural gas and each are about 50% of the total energy consumption, and hotel includes on-site food service, laundry, and pool.

Conducting Energy Assessments

An energy assessment is an essential component of a successful energy management program. This will help you identify the present energy use situation within the hotel and flag energy costs. Energy saving opportunities can be identified based on the assessment report. The assessment will also help you develop a baseline for future comparisons of program success by comparing energy use before program implementation and after. Hotels can conduct either a basic walk-through energy assessment or a more detailed energy analysis audit. Hotels also have the option of carrying out the assessment as a first step to identify existing energy saving opportunities and implement the results followed by a more detailed analysis audit to derive more detailed measures for savings including capital intensive energy saving opportunities. This guide focuses on the walkthrough energy assessment process as a means for hotels to delve immediately into saving energy and improving their bottom line through less capital intensive measures. Hotels are encouraged if they desire to follow implementation of these measures with a more detailed audit to garner additional savings.

Integrating Energy Management into Hotel's Culture

New employee energy management training: At all departments in the hotel, employees receive thorough training in department norms and expectations, safety procedures, and office etiquette. Developing an energy management training and integrating it into new employee orientation will help instill energy management as a department-wide value and teach employees how to use energy more efficiently in their work areas. Reinforcing this orientation training with regular energy management seminars, brochures, or other visibility will ensure that the initial training stays with employees throughout their tenure at the hotel.

Tracking and reporting energy consumption to all employees: While most department heads receive some energy and water use data on a weekly/monthly basis, very little of this information is shared with the rest of the employees. Energy consumption at each department can serve as a tool for reinforcing the importance of energy management, since consumption spikes in energy and water use can be more quickly identified and resolved when employees are tracking weekly or monthly use. The engineering department at the hotel is already tracking the energy-use data for all departments but still there is a need to identifying best and worse performers so that best-practices can be recognized and shared. Creating a culture of continuous improvement.

Make energy efficiency an integral part of employee culture. Encouraging leadership and visibility, tracking energy use and offering incentives will help. These aspects are described in more detail below:

a. Tracking: All efficiency efforts at the employee level should be recorded, tracked over time, and evaluated. This process will help department heads evaluate their energy performance training, incentive programs, and visibility level of the program. A transparent data-driven program will allow the employees to see their individual and collective impact on energy performance and encourage them to actively participate in charting the impact of their activities.

b. Visibility: A simple method like using a dedicated whiteboard to track daily energy data could be useful. A whiteboard that is centrally located can be used to record energy data and any factors that may influence energy use, as well as strategies to reduce energy consumption. Engineering staff and department heads can conduct daily briefings to discuss the data and energy management strategies.

c. Incentives: The recognition of employee commitment to energy efficiency can have a strong impact on participation. The recognition can be formal or informal, ranging from something as simple as offering employees free CFL lights as a reward for reducing energy consumption by a certain percentage, to rewarding cash bonuses for identifying major energy savings and process improvements.

d. Recognition: Employees who take leadership positions in energy management initiatives should be recognized for their efforts—from turning off the lights at work each night to developing ways to make sure that equipments are switched off when not in use.

Lighting

The lighting system is the most visible energy user in the building. And while it's usually a hotel's largest energy consumer, lighting may well be the first place to look for energy savings. Some hotels report finding 20 to 50 percent savings in their lighting systems. These savings are some of the most rewarding to achieve because most are easy to make and cost little or nothing.

As you walk through the hotel, also note the type of lighting present. One of the keys to improved lighting efficiency is using the most efficient light source to produce light. Incandescent bulbs are least efficient and have the shortest lives, but have the advantage of low first cost, good color rendition and easy installation. Fluorescents are popular in general because they are 4 to 5 times more efficient and have 10 times the life expectancy of incandescent. High Intensity Discharge (HID) lamps, which were once used almost exclusively outdoors because of their poor color rendition, are more and more being brought indoors in color corrected versions due to their extremely high efficiency and long life.

Identifying Savings Opportunities within your Lighting Systems

Begin your lighting improvement project by determining how much light is really needed in the various areas of the hotel and its surroundings. Areas where people are walking as opposed to seated or working require very different lighting levels, but all too often are lit to the same high levels. Do a walk-through of the facility looking at the existing lighting in each area and the area's lighting needs. It's a good idea to use a light meter (lighting suppliers often lend them). You can then compare your present lighting levels to recommended levels for the tasks being performed.

Recommended Lighting Levels For Hotels

Hotel Area	Average Foot candles	Hotel Area	Average Foot candles
Hallways	10.0	Guest Rooms	20.0
Lobby	15.0	Front Desk	75.0
Dining/Function Rooms	15.0	Kitchen	75.0

First, Do Things That is Free

Remove unnecessary lamps. Because a number of hotels were designed and built in an era when energy efficiency was not a high priority, lighting levels often are higher than necessary. But be careful. If you remove lamps near windows, make sure there will still be enough light on overcast days or at night.

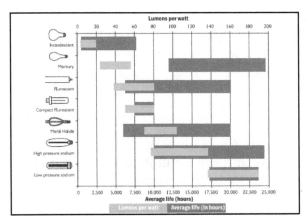

Make sure lights are turned off when an area is unoccupied. For the most part in hotels, that means getting employees on- board with the program. Use switch plate covers reminding people to turn lights off when leaving an area. In public places, guests and employees are hesitant to turn lights off without "permission," so signage is important. Wind-up timers, time clocks and occupancy sensors can help get lights off when they are not needed. Keep the fixtures clean to be sure you are getting all the light for which you are paying. Cleaning fixtures and reflectors can compensate for reduced light levels from de-lamping. Consider group re-lamping, which means changing all the lamps at once rather than as they burn out. Light output from lamps decreases as they age, so replacing them in a group assures you get full light output, and the practice can reduce the maintenance costs associated with lamp replacement by half.

Low - Cost and Low - Investment Projects

After doing the no-cost projects, consider modifying the lighting system. Many projects require only a small investment. Before investing, calculate the payback period and, for large expense projects, consider life cycle costs to see if the project will be a good investment. And, try an improvement in a small area before committing to major changes.

A. Retrofitting exit signs is one of the quickest payback projects in many hotels. The idea of replacing conventional exit signs with energy-efficient compact fluorescent ones has been widely promoted over the past ten years. Instead of two incandescent light bulbs that last a few months, compact fluorescent exit signs require only about 12 watts and generally last two years in continuous use. Converting to LED exit signs has become more popular. The light emitting diode, or LED meets electrical code requirements in most applications, uses minimal amounts of electricity and lasts up to 50 years. LED's are winners for cost savings and avoiding the inconvenience of replacing lamps.

S. N.	Cost Description	LED Lights	Incandescent Bulbs
1.	Lifespan	60,000 Hr.	800 Hr.
2.	Number of bulbs used in 60,000 hours	1	75
3.	Cost	'$' 1000.0	'$' 10.0
4.	Power dissipation	4 Watt	20 Watt
5.	Power savings per year*	140.0 kWh	-
6	Lifetime power savings	960.0 kWh	-
7.	Cost saving per year	Cost saving per year	-
8.	Lifetime cost saving	'$' 3360.0	-
9.	Payback period	2-years	-

* With one bulb in use for 24 hours and 365 days in a year. The power cost is '$' 3.50/kWh.

B. Retrofitting corridor fixtures are also a quick payback project in hotels. Attractive fixtures that house compact fluorescent lamps with color rendition similar to that of an incandescent are available. In most cases, no one will notice the difference.

C. Installation of more efficient lamps is one of the most effective ways to make lighting more energy efficient is to use the most efficient lamp possible. Here are some of the best examples:

Replace Incandescent Lights with Compact Fluorescents

The standard incandescent light bulb may seem inexpensive, but it is not a bargain. Not only is it extremely inefficient, it also has a very short life, which means it must be replaced frequently. One of the great advances in lighting technology is the compact Replace Incandescent Lights with Compact Fluorescents The standard incandescent light bulb may seem inexpensive, but it is not a bargain. Not only is it extremely inefficient, it also has a very short life, which means it must be replaced frequently. One of the great advances in lighting technology is the compact fluorescent lamp. Developed as a replacement for the common incandescent light bulb, the super energy efficient compact fluorescent is a spiral or miniature U-shaped fluorescent tube and ballast. Screw-in or pin holder compact fluorescents fit many of the fixtures where you previously used incandescent light bulbs. This makes it possible to replace an incandescent (15 lumens/watt, 800 hours life) with a more efficient and long lasting fluorescent lamp (70 lumens/watt, 6000 hours life). Consider that you can fluorescent lamp. Developed as a replacement for the common incandescent light bulb, the super energy efficient compact fluorescent is a spiral or miniature U-shaped fluorescent tube and ballast. Screw-in or pin holder compact fluorescents fit many of the fixtures where you previously used incandescent light bulbs. This makes it possible to replace an incandescent (15 lumens/ watt, 800 hours life) with a more efficient and long lasting fluorescent lamp (70 lumens/ watt, 6000 hours life). Consider that you can replace a 60-watt incandescent with a 15 watt compact fluorescent that will last 10 times as long and will deliver about the same amount of light for one quarter the energy. Compact fluorescents are more expensive than incandescent, but they will more than pay for themselves with savings in electricity, lamp replacement and labor costs. Payback is quickest when they are installed in fixtures that are used for many hours each day. Compact fluorescents are available in a wide variety of styles to suit most lighting needs, with reflectors and extenders that can make them fit and work well in many fixture types. They come either as one-piece screwing units that include the ballast or as modular units where the tube can be separated from the ballast when the lamp burns out. The compact fluorescent tubes have lifetimes of 10,000 hours, while the ballasts last 4 or 5 times that long.

Compact fluorescents can be used outdoors when they are protected by an enclosure. However, they have some cold limitations. For instance, they are dimmer for a short time when they start, until they get up to their operating temperature and may not start at all when it is very cold. Using an enclosed light fixture helps. Ask your supplier which would be the best option for your outside needs.

Fluorescent Ceiling Lights

Since some lighting systems in hotels are fluorescent, let's look at what can be done to improve their efficiency. There are four primary options:

1. Install lower wattage or more efficient lamps: When selecting new, more efficient fluorescent lamps, make sure they are compatible with the existing ballasts, although it may be cost-effective to replace the ballast as well. While some of the replacement lamps may yield slightly less light, this may be acceptable since in many areas you may have more light than you need. Furthermore, when clean new lamps are installed, and the diffuser and reflecting surfaces of the fixture are cleaned, there may be an increase in light output even with lower wattage.

2. Replace the ballasts: Replacing existing magnetic ballasts is often one of the most cost effective energy improvements. For instance, installing electronic ballast can reduce the energy consumption of a fixture with two 34-watt lamps from about 74 watts to about 59 watts, a 20% drop, with no reduction in light output.

3. Replace the fixtures: Fixture retrofits can involve changing out the ballast, replacing yellowed or hazy lenses, diffusers, and globes with new ones that will remain brighter and transmit more light, and installing reflectors that "bounce" more light out of the fixtures. New lenses and reflectors may enable you to use fewer or lower wattage lamps and still achieve acceptable lighting levels.

4. Rewiring or installing more efficient controls can be an effective investment, with a fast return.

D. Train cleaning and security staff twenty four hours of operation and varied occupancy schedules can result in lights and office equipments being left on in areas (offices, restaurants, kitchens, etc) where occupants are no longer in the building. Invariably, there will also be lights, computers, and other electronic equipment left on by employees who forget to shut down their workspace. Both security and cleaning staff can play an integral role in energy management by assisting in overall savings.

In most hotels, the house keeping staff provides two services to the guest rooms and they are responsible for getting the room cleaned and checked between the check out and check in. Most hotels have key cards for rooms, which is good to minimize wastages when guest is not in the room. It is recommended that to reduce the wastages, the house keeping staff should be trained to switch off all the lights and leave the curtains open after the morning service and close them at the time of providing evening service.

Only one bed side light and one bathroom light should be left on after they finish the evening service. This will minimize the wastages on lights during the day. Most guests do not bother to open the curtains and switch off the lights. E. Some Other Tips Control Outdoor Lighting. Most hotels have lights that are left on all the time for code compliance or to meet safety and security needs. While meeting code requirements, use only lighting necessary to do the job. It is recommended that the outside lighting should also be fitted with timers. Different timing should be set for summer and winter months. The alternative lights can be switched off after 11.30 pm. It is also recommended to create zones of every third lamp, and have each zone turn on 30 minutes apart, and turn off 30 minutes apart, instead of all at l once.

Rewiring. If your present switches don't give you enough control to turn off unneeded lights, you should consider rewiring and installing additional switches or dimmers.

Occupancy Sensors. In public areas where employees forget to turn lights off, an occupancy sensor may be the answer. These easy-to-install motion detecting devices turn lights on and off automatically in a space such as a restroom, storage area or stockroom. A sensor can be mounted on the wall where a light switch would normally go or can be installed in the ceiling or high on a wall. Occupancy sensors are activated when they detect motion, heat or both. Energy savings from sensors is greater the more hours the lights are off and the more watts controlled by the sensor. Savings from 20% to 40% are possible and even greater savings are possible when spaces are infrequently used. Consider installing occupancy sensors in the following: senior executive offices, conference rooms, employee locker rooms, restrooms, stockrooms, and storage areas. While providing the sensors in toilets it is important to note that WC areas should be kept out of the circuit to avoid inconvenience to the guests.

Use Task Lighting. Install desk lamps for close work at office desks and reception desks. This type of task lighting puts light where it is needed, when it is needed, and may permit ceiling lighting levels to be lowered.

Use Day Lighting. Day lighting is the practice of using free light from the sun during the day to supplement or even eliminate purchased light. Taking advantage of day lighting may require installation of blinds or shades to control heat gain and glare. Combining this with rewiring and installation of switches will enable you to save money by turning off lights when they are not needed.

HVAC

The hotel's heating, ventilating, and cooling systems are what create comfortable conditions inside the hotel. HVAC systems are large consumers of a hotel's energy. That means HVAC is an area likely to produce good returns on energy efficiency improvements. Finding savings of 20% or higher are quite often possible through more efficient operation and maintenance of the HVAC system. Much of the savings will come from simple things you can do yourself like keeping the system off when it is not needed, or operating it less by changing temperature settings. The remainder of the potential savings comes from making the system more efficient.

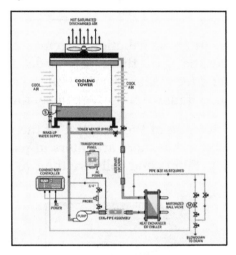

Use the HVAC checklists provided in this guidebook during your walk-through of the facility. In addition, here are some ideas to consider.

A. Keep system off during unoccupied times: The best time to save money in an area of the hotel is when no one is there. All too often energy is being wasted heating or cooling the air when nobody is there. Making matters more complicated, your occupancy hours are different for the various parts of the hotel building, like when there is a banquet in the ballroom or a convention in only one wing. Temperature can only be controlled for individual areas when there are separate heating or cooling units, zones, or thermostats.

B. Use ceiling fans: Ceiling fans can save you energy costs by making guests feel comfortable at higher temperatures in the summer. The fans create an evaporative cooling effect as they pull air over the skin. In winter, ceiling fans redistribute the warm air that collects near the ceiling to the lower part of the space for people's comfort. This can mean that heating thermostats need not be set as high.

C. Put locking covers on thermostats: Employees should not be given free reign on spending your energy money. Determine a reasonable setting and cover programmed thermostats in public areas with tamper-proof covers or look into replacing them altogether with ones that hold a fixed setting. Make sure to also check the accuracy of thermostats. At a time when your heating or cooling system has the hotel at a stable temperature, walk through with an accurate thermometer and see if the thermostats are accurately recording the temperature. If the thermostat says it is 70°F and the actual temperature in the space is 66°F, the cooling system may be running more than necessary.

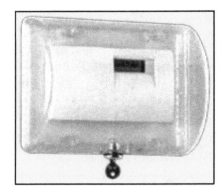

D. Inspect and repair duct leaks: In air distribution systems, take a look at the duct system as part of your energy check-up. Over the years, these systems deteriorate and can even get stepped on and damaged by contractors and technicians working in the area. Fix broken joints and other leaks, and be sure they are insulated if they run through unconditioned space.

E. Replace/clean filters & coils: It's one of the simplest of the conservation measures, and it's often overlooked. Take time to check that there are filters in place and see that coils and filters are cleaned and changed regularly. Filters and coils are the two most critical elements in HVAC system.

They are where the mechanical system interacts most directly with the environment it is trying to impact. It does not take much dirt and dust to degrade thermal transfer across the coils, and as filters get dirtier, air delivery to spaces and fan energy required to deliver air will suffer. Very aggressive cleaning schedules for coils and filters are always a part of the maintenance regime for buildings. It is very common to observe dirty filters and coils even when maintenance staff reports an aggressive approach. Often, teams will rely on pressure drop alarms in the BAS system to signal the need for filter cleaning. Our experience in the field indicates that this is not a proactive approach associated with capturing available low-cost savings.

The hotels do have regular maintenance schedules for their HVAC systems and for cleaning of coils and filters. But still it is recommended that the coils and filters be cleaned very aggressively and on schedule (preferably every month). Close inspection of coils and filters on a periodic basis will be the best initial indication as more aggressive schedules are set. The amount of dirt on the coils and filters can easily be determined by wiping the surface with a finger or clean cloth. As this measure is less popular with maintenance staff, motivation and oversight are required, which might result in a checklist that appoints a responsible staff person to ensure on time completion. Replaceable filters can be cleaned in batches to reduce labor associated with this measure, and pre-filters can be considered depending on local condition. Where coils and filters are difficult to access, it is important to document the process, appoint specific staff who can learn to do the job efficiently, and evolve cleaning techniques that are appropriate to the challenge. For example, if coils and filters are in terminal units above high end conference space, frequent cleaning with a liquid chemical solution may not be feasible compared to brushing, vacuuming, and forcing compressed air through the coils. The goal is to look at current conditions and practices and come up with a reasonable definition of an aggressive, sustainable approach. The estimated savings for this measure are difficult to calculate but with past experience it has been observed that this practice can save between 10-20 % of electricity use every year as very clean coils and filters are a fundamental part of excellent HVAC performance and should not be treated as an option to be weighed against others.

F. Chiller coil temperature reset: In hotels, chiller coils are operated at the temperature established during the design process to ensure adequate cooling during peak cooling conditions. They are designed to produce supply air temperature to meet set point temperatures under the most extreme loads anticipated the local climate and weather. This design coil temperature is lower than that required to meet building cooling loads under more typical, less extreme conditions. It is possible to slightly increase the cooling coil temperatures when cooling loads are not at peak, saving chiller energy. The EMS should be used to increase or decrease the coil temperatures in response to outdoor air temperatures. Even without using EMS, it is also possible to vary coil temperatures manually, and this can be done daily, weekly, monthly, or seasonally, the building engineering team is. More frequent adjustments produce greater savings. The load decreases by increasing the chiller coil temperature by even 10 C. This decreases the electricity consumption of the chillers by 10%.

G. Condenser water temperature reset: This initiative increases the efficiency of the chiller by reducing the condenser water temperature supplied from the cooling towers. Instead of a standard fixed condenser water supply temperature, water as cool as possible is supplied to the condenser side of the chiller based on manufacturer's recommendations and the continued ability to meet interior temperature set points. It is assumed that the cooling towers can produce a minimum condenser supply water temperature equal to 880 F above the outside air wet bulb temperature. This can be applied to the condenser water depending on how motivated loop with temperature set points as low as 750 F. It is recommended that the hotel should determine how much decrease in condenser water temperature is possible, while still meeting manufacturer's recommendations and interior set point temperatures. Vary condenser water temperatures depending on the outdoor conditions either by programming the EMS to automatically adjust temperature or by training staff to adjust the temperature manually based on outdoor air conditions. More frequent adjustments result in more energy savings. The estimated savings from decreasing the condenser temperature can exceed 10% of annual chiller energy and the payback is immediate if controls or manual approaches can be implemented without outside assistance.

H. Adjust temperature set points: Different sections of the hotel have different expectations for interior temperatures associated with seasonal climatic temperature conditions. About 1°C reduction in interior temperature settings during the winter months (October to February) can save as much as 5% in energy costs during these months. By carefully selecting seasonal set points that meet but do not exceed comfort expectations, considerable energy can be saved and guest satisfaction can be maximized.

I. Plan ahead: People rarely plan for an equipment failure, and when one occurs you will be under pressure to get it up and running right away. This makes it difficult to shop and plan for energy efficient replacements. So, prepare in advance for likely units that may fail, particularly in guestrooms, and check on the price and availability of efficient units. HVAC systems last a long time, so your hotel will live with the replacement for many years to come.

J. Buy energy efficient equipment: There are laws in place that require manufacturers of HVAC equipment and appliances to meet minimum efficiency levels and to label each product with its efficiency rating. Check with your local utility or HVAC Service Company for what is recommended for your area.

K. Heat exchangers: Consider installing heat exchangers to move fresh air in and stale air out of your hotel while exchanging 50% to 70% of the energy between the two air streams. In humid climates, heat exchangers with desiccant capability can control the humidity in the hotel. This is a good application where ventilation requirements are high, such as lounges, fitness rooms, smoking areas and cafeterias or where waste heat is being exhausted, for instance, by a kitchen hood. In some cases, chiller condenser waste heat can be used. Look into Cool Storage. When chilled water is used as the cooling medium, installing a cool storage system allows you to save on your electric bills by paying lower, night time, off-peak electricity rates to create and store the cooling you will need for the next day.

A cool storage system can save a lot of money, but you will need professional advice to valuate your situation.

L. Consider heat pumps: Heat pumps are electrical devices that move heat from one place to another. A heat pump can provide both heating and cooling. Most heat pumps are air-to-air systems. In the cooling mode, the heat pump operates like a window air conditioner, removing heat from inside air and moving it to the outside air. In the heating mode, it operates like an air conditioner in reverse that moves heat from the outside air and pumps it into the building. Water source heat pumps take heat from or reject it to a water pipe or connecting loop. Heat is rejected from the loop to a cooling tower or is provided to the loop by a boiler if the loop temperature falls. In addition to being highly efficient, heat pumps often have lower first cost, lower maintenance, and space savings compared to two separate heating and cooling systems. However, air-to-air heat pumps are not designed for severe cold. If the temperature drops too low, its heating effort may need to be supplemented by other sources of heat, either electric resistance or fuel-fired system. Most heat pumps have electric resistance heating elements for backup, but there are also dual fuel heat pumps that use gas for heating below a certain temperature.

Hotel Management Practices

Customer service, especially during the busy season, is crucial to the success of any hotel. Today there are more ways than ever to attract guests, however it is essential that hoteliers don't lose sight of customer service best practices. We've compiled the following 8 proven practices that are sure to help your staff woo and retain guests:

- Focus on face time: While a strong digital online presence is often what makes the first impression on customers, it's face-to-face communication that guests value the most once they check-in. A warm welcome, enhanced by personal connections throughout their stay, will remain with your guests long after they depart your property.

- Keep your staff happy: A happy (and educated) staff translates into happy guests. So, hoteliers should make a concerted effort to continually educate their staff about the importance of customer service and empower (and reward) them as they achieve customer satisfaction goals. Some hotel brands make the education process fun by using gamification techniques that truly engage employees in the training process. Whatever the approach, invest in the development of your staff. As Bill Marriott once said, "take good care of your people and they'll take care of the customer; and the customer will return."

- Know your customer: Are the majority of your guests traveling for leisure or business? What are their preferences? Hoteliers have a myriad of tools at their disposal, including online surveys and more sophisticated tracking tools that help gauge customer habits. Use these tools to keep "on trend" with your guests in order to achieve optimal customer satisfaction.

- Create a "wow" factor: What sets your property apart? Give guests the visual "fodder" that they will want to post and share on their social media channels! Invest in some eye-catching artwork for your property or host themed social hours in your lobby. In essence, provide that "wow" factor that will resonate with guests and leave them wanting to share their cool experience with others.

- Go above and beyond expectations: Today's guests have elevated expectations, so hoteliers must continually look for ways to elevate the customer service experience. Take the customer's experience to the next level by providing unexpected touches and amenities not already being offered by your competitors. If your competitor is offering a free breakfast buffet, why not up the ante by offering up complimentary room service for an extended stay or something else truly unique and of value to your customer base?

- Address guest input quickly: When it comes to customer satisfaction, timeliness is key! Bottom line, by addressing guests quickly, a hotel will have less complaints. A quick turnaround on everything from a request for an extra pillow, to a response to a TripAdvisor complaint, can make all the difference when it comes to keeping customers happy.

- Keep the dialogue going: Don't check-out when your guests leave. Online platforms give hoteliers the ability to proactively reach out to guests to get feedback about their stay and keep them in-the-loop on hotel news and happenings that will entice them to return.

- Learn from the best: Big and small hotel brands alike can learn from the best practices of others. Take Westin, for example, whose focus remains on the fact that their hotel's primary product offering is a good night's sleep. As such, they upgraded their standard beds to the Westin Heavenly Bed and immediately saw an incredible customer response. Monitor the best practices of hotel industry peers and adapt their programs into best practices of your own.

Hotel Toilet Paper Folding

This is seen in some upscale hotels where the cleaning staff will fold the first sheet of toilet paper into a triangle. The triangulated toilet paper informs the guests that the cleaning staff has been there, and has finished cleaning the room. The act of folding the first sheet of toilet paper into a triangle has spread to many hotels and to many countries.

Some hotels and resorts have taken toilet paper origami one step further by making more elaborate folds:

- Left: classic triangulated toilet paper origami.

- Middle: pleated toilet paper inspired by HotelChatter.

- Right: pleated-tuck toilet paper inspired by P O'Brian.

Folding toilet paper into a triangle is so prevalent that an elderly Japanese gentleman invented an automated toilet paper folding machine called "Meruboa". With the push of a lever, Meruboa will fold the first sheet of toilet paper into a perfect triangle. Manufacturers plan to make over 10,000 Meruboa holders per month, valuing over one billion yen per year.

Bed-making

Type of Sheets

Always buy 300 thread count Egyptian cotton sheets. A higher thread count than this will mean that the sheets will soon wear thin and could rip, and a lower thread count does not make for very soft sheets.

We always use flat sheets, never fitted. You can never press a fitted sheet flat enough, nor can you stretch them creaseless over the mattress.

Type of Bedding

We recommend 300 thread count white linen for duvet covers. Goose feather and down is the softest for duvets and pillows (and also the warmest). We use 13.5 tog king size duvets accompanied by four extra-large feather and down pillows.

Ways to Look after the Sheets

1. Try to change your sheets weekly, and wash them at 60°.

2. Dry your sheets outside if at all possible, because drying them in a tumble dryer always makes them harder to press.

3. The best way to iron sheets is with a roller iron but, at home, fold your sheet or duvet cover in half and press one side and then the other.

Ways to Make the Bed

Step 1: Make sure the sheet is central on the bed with the same amount hanging evenly over all the edges.

Step 2: Standing at one side of the bed, pull the sheet as tight as you can and tuck it under, then do the same to the other sides. Hospital corners (the tight diagonal fold used on hospital beds) are a must at Claridge's.

Step 3: Always shake the duvet to distribute the filling evenly.

Step 4: Lay the duvet cover on the bed. Put two of the corners of the duvet inside the top end of the cover, and then tuck in the rest of the duvet. Give it a good shake.

Step 5: Pull the duvet up until it's two inches from the headboard, and smooth it out to ensure there are no wrinkles.

And the finishing touches.

A cashmere throw placed across the end of the bed is a lovely way to finish making the bed. If you use decorative cushions, ensure the zip is facing down.

Towel Animal

Cruise ship stewards on Carnival Cruises and other cruise lines decorate the cabins each evening with creative towel animals that delight cruise passengers. As can be seen in the photo above, not all the animals are relegated to the cabins. These towel creations adorned the pool area on the Carnival Breeze. The crew went wild and decorated the pool deck and chairs with a whole zoo of towel animals.

Carnival Towel Animal - Rabbit.   Carnival Towel Animal - Swan.   Carnival Towel Animal - Elephant.

Lodging vs. Boarding

Boarding refers to a place where one gets accommodation as well as regular meals for a payment. Boarding is generally used by students, as they need both accommodation and food when they are staying away from home for a long period. According to the Oxford Dictionary, boarding is "the arrangement according to which pupils live in school during term time". A boarding place/house is usually used for a longer stay. The phrase, "boarding a plane" is also related to the accommodation and meals provided on the plane. A hostel (in a school) is an example of a boarding place.

Lodging

Lodging is a facility that provides only accommodation and some other basic facilities. This refers to a shorter stay and meals are not included with the accommodation. Lodging is the provision of accommodation to travelers and those who are staying away from home for more than one night. We need lodging to sleep, rest, get shelter from harsh weather conditions or to store our luggage safely. If you prefer to try meals at different local places, then you should find lodging.

Sometimes, you see the term 'boarding and lodging' used in hotels. This refers to both accommodation and meals. Semantically, this usage is not correct; boarding refers to both meals and accommodation, and there is no need to use the term 'lodging'.

Terms like Lodging and board, bed and board (UK), room and board (US), fooding and lodging (Indian English) also refer to both accommodation and meals.

Difference Between Boarding and Lodging

The main difference between boarding and lodging is that boarding refers to the provision of both accommodation and meals while lodging refers to the provision of accommodation. The duration of the stay is another difference between these two types of accommodations; boarding refers to a longer stay while lodging refers to a shorter stay. In addition, boarding is a facility more used by students whereas lodging is more used by tourists, and those who are staying away from home for a short while.

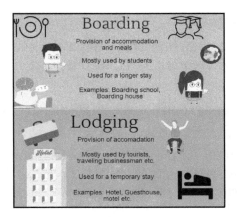

Lodging Facilities

Lodging is rental of a room or rooms for a temporary place to stay or live. Sales tax must be charged on lodging and related services furnished for a period of less than 30 days. Sales tax must also be charged on lodging furnished for periods of 30 days or more if there is no enforceable lease agreement with the customer that requires the lessor and lessee to give prior notice of their intention to terminate.

Taxable related services. Following are examples of other items or services sold by lodging facilities that are subject to sales tax: Admissions to recreational areas and fees for use of recreational facilities: Includes campgrounds, golf courses, mini golf courses, picnic grounds, playgrounds, tennis courts, health clubs, swimming beaches and pools. See Fact Sheet 123, Recreational Areas, Resorts and Campgrounds, for more information.

Admissions to recreational areas and fees for use of recreational facilities: Includes campgrounds, golf courses, mini golf courses, picnic grounds, playgrounds, tennis courts, health clubs, swimming beaches and pools. See Fact Sheet 123, Recreational Areas, Resorts and Campgrounds, for more information.

- Cable TV and in-room movie charges.
- Copies, including coin-operated machine receipts.
- Cot and crib rental charges.
- Fax charges.

- Food and liquor sales from an in-room courtesy bar.

- Jukebox, pool table and electronic game receipts.

- Laundry services: Charges to guests for laundry or dry cleaning services are taxable. Note: Charges for the use of self-service coin-operated laundries and dry cleaning facilities are not taxable.

- Parking fees, including valet parking, and charges for car washing.

- Popcorn prepared by the vendor.

- Rental of equipment such as audio-visual equipment, computers, public address systems, tables, chairs, flowers and decorations, if billed separately from nontaxable meeting room charges.

- Rental of game, athletic and recreational equipment, and boats, paddle boats, canoes, and pontoons.

- Telephone: Charges to guests for the actual cost of telephone calls they make are not taxable if the charge is separately stated on the guest's bill because the actual charge from the phone company to the hotel includes the sales tax. Charges to guests by hotels and other lodging establishments for access charges (charges for making telephone service available to the guest) are taxable. For example, if a hotel charges 50 cents per local call, it is an access charge and is taxable the phone company doesn't charge that amount for local calls, but the hotel charges this fee for access to the telephone service.

- Telephone call accounting systems: Many hotels use "call accounting systems" to track and determine the amount to charge guests for long distance telephone calls. Using these systems, hotel personnel don't know how much the actual telephone service costs until they receive their next bill from the telephone company. In this situation, the hotel must charge sales tax on the total amount billed to their guests for long distance telephone service. The hotel must also continue to pay sales tax to the telephone company for all telephone services. However, the hotel is allowed to make an adjustment to the taxable amount reported on the sales tax return by subtracting the amount they are billed by the telephone company for the actual costs of their guests' long distance calls made. This practice is only permitted when the lodging establishment can distinguish between telephone calls billed to guests and their own administrative costs for telephone service.

Nontaxable sales and services

The following are examples of related services sold by lodging facilities that are not subject to sales tax:

- Coat check.

- Meeting room or banquet hall rental.

- Messenger service.

- Rented space: Lodging facilities often enter into "management agreements" to provide space for a restaurant, barbershop, car rental booth or other vendor to operate. However, sales tax is due on that portion of the lease or rental attributable to use of the equipment, phones, furniture, parking spaces, etc.

Other Sales and Charges

Gift shop sales: Most gift shop sales are taxable. However, the taxability of food, clothing, and health products depends on the item sold.

Newspapers and tabloids are not taxable. Magazines or periodicals sold over the counter or through vending machines are taxable.

Gift certificates: Sales of gift certificates are not taxable. A gift certificate is treated the same as cash. When a gift certificate is redeemed, charge sales tax on any taxable amount and use the gift certificate as payment.

Cancellation vs. "no show" charges for lodging accommodations. Cancellation charges are not taxable— since the room was cancelled, no sale occurred and no sales tax is due. "No show" charges are taxable—since the room was held for the customer, a sale was made even though the customer didn't show up.

Damage charges. Charges for damage to tangible items, such as equipment or boats, are taxable. Charges for damage to real property, such as a hotel room or building, are not taxable. If the charge is a combination of the above and the nontaxable portion is not separately stated, it is taxable.

Equipment sales. Sales of equipment or other items used in a business may be subject to sales tax.

Coupons. When customers use a coupon for a discount or free lodging, charge sales tax only on the amount the customer actually pays unless the facility will be reimbursed by a third party. Subtract the coupon amount from the total price of the room and then calculate the tax. If the lodging facility is reimbursed for the coupon by a third party, charge sales tax first, and then subtract the coupon amount.

Tips and service charges. Tips left voluntarily by a customer are not taxable. Tips voluntarily added by the customer to a credit card slip are also not taxable. However, when a tip or service charge is added to the bill by the seller, that amount is taxable. This is true even if the amount is separately stated or distributed directly to employees.

Vending machines, coin-operated devices, or self-service honor system. All sales of food, candy, gum, cigarettes, pop and other beverages sold through vending machines are taxable. Items sold through vending machines that are not taxable are clothing (swimsuits, pantyhose, etc.), feminine hygiene products, aspirin and other analgesics, postage stamps, and newspapers. Generally, the person responsible for removing money from the vending machine or other coin-operated device is responsible for reporting and paying the sales tax.

Types of Lodging Facilities

Hotels

Hotels are found in center - city, suburban, and airport locations. Guest stays can be overnight or long - term, as much as several weeks in length. These properties sometimes specialize in catering to particular interests, such as conventions or gambling. Casino hotels usually take a secondary role to the casino operation, where the emphasis is on profitable gaming operations.

Motels

Motels offer guests a limited range of services, which may include reservations, vending machines, swimming pools, and cable television. The size of these properties averages from 10 to 50 units. Motels are usually in suburban highway and airport locations. Guests typically stay overnight or a few days. Motels may be located near a free standing restaurant.

All - Suites

The all - suites concept, a new addition to the hotel industry, developed in the 1980s as a separate marketing concept, offers guests a wide range of services, which may include reservations, living room and separate bedroom, kitchenette, optional public dining room and room service, cable television, video cassette players and recorders, specialty shops, personal services valet and laundry, swimming pool, and ground transportation to and from an airport. The size of the operation can range from 50 to more than 100 units.

This type of property is usually found in center - city, suburban, and airport locations. The length of guest stay can be overnight, several days, or long - term. Although this type of hotel may seem new, many downtown, center - city hotels have offered this type of accommodation with in - room kitchenette and sitting rooms since the early 1900s. Now with *mass marketing*- advertising products and services through mass communications such as television, radio, and the Internet - this type of hotel is considered new.

Limited - Service Hotels

Limited - service hotels appeared on the hotel scene in the mid - 1980s. Hampton Inn and Marriott were among the first organizations to offer limited - service properties. The concept of limited service was developed for a specific segment of the market business and cost - conscious travelers. The range of accommodations and services may include reservations, minimal public dining and meeting facilities, cable television, personal computers, personal services (valet and laundry), and ground transportation to and from an airport.

The size of the property can range from 100 to more than 200 rooms. Limited - service hotels are found in center - city, suburban, and airport locations. They are usually located near restaurants for guest convenience. Guest stays can be overnight or long - term. These properties sometimes specialize in catering to the business traveler and offer special business technology centers.

Extended - Stay Hotels

In "Survey Results of the Extended Stay Lodging Industry," The Highland Group of Atlanta, Georgia, reports the following information, about this newest hotel product on the market which includes the 31 extended - stay brands as well as some independent hotels.

Extended - stay hotel room supply in the United States increased more than 50 percent in 1997 over 1996. There will be more economy - price than upscale extended stay rooms before the end of 1998. This is a significant reversal from prior years and indicates a change in the way extended - stay lodging is used by American travelers.

Projected extended - stay hotel supply will be more than half a million rooms through 2002. At this level, extended - stay hotel rooms will represent some 12 percent of total lodging inventory.

Assuming supply growth projections are fully realized through 2002, this represents a significant change from the current price distribution of extended - stay hotels and marks a change in the way Americans use extended - stay lodging. Use of extended - stay lodging will have expanded from the corporate expense - account market to encompass most demographic segments. Corporations are taking advantage of the availability of these facilities for training, relocation and temporary assignments at all levels.

At Hilton's Home wood Suites, the following room amenities are included: kingsize bed or two double beds in the bedroom and foldout sofa in the living room; two remote - controlled color televisions; fully equipped kitchen with a microwave, refrigerator with ice maker, coffeemaker, twin - burner stove, and kitchen utensils; a spacious, well - lit dining area; and ceiling fans and iron and ironing board. Additional hotel services include a business center, an exercise room, and a pool. This hotel concept also structures its room rates to attract the long - term guest.

Market Orientation

Market orientation in the hotel industry is categorized into two segments:

- Residential hotels, which provide guest accommodations for the long term; and

- Commercial hotels, which provide short - term accommodations for traveling guests.

Residential properties include hotels, all - suites, limited - service, and extended - stay properties. Services may include (but are not limited to) public dining, recreational facilities, social activities, and personal services. These hotels are usually located in center - city and suburban areas where other activities (shopping, arts and entertainment, business services, public transportation) are available to round out the living experience.

Commercial properties service the transient guest, whose stay is short in duration. Services include (but are not limited to) computerized reservation systems, public dining, banquet service, lounge and entertainment areas, personal services, and shuttle transportation to airports. They may be located almost anywhere.

It is essential to note the very gray areas in using these two types of categories. Commercial lodging establishment may have a certain percentage of permanent residents. Likewise, a residential hotel may have nightly rentals available. Owners and general managers need to exhibit a great deal of flexibility in meeting the needs of the available markets.

Sales Indicators

Sales indicators, including hotel occupancy and average daily rate, are another means for describing hotels. This information is necessary for business investors to estimate the profitability of a hotel.

There are four factors that measure a hotel's degree of financial success: occupancy percentage, average daily rate, yield percentage, and revenue per available room (RevPAR). Occupancy percentage is the number of rooms sold divided by the number of rooms available. Average daily rate (ADR) is the total room revenue divided by the number of rooms sold.

Yield percentage, the effectiveness of a hotel at selling its rooms at the highest rate available to the most profitable guest, reveals a facility's success in selling its room inventory on a daily basis. RevPAR is used to indicate the ability of each guestroom to produce a profit. Once the daily sales opportunity has presented itself, it cannot be repeated (excluding the opportunity to sell a room at a half - day rate).

Occupancy

Occupancy percentages measure the effectiveness of the marketing and sales department as well as the front office in its external and internal marketing efforts. Occupancy percentage is also used by investors to determine the potential gross income, which is the amount of sales a hotel might obtain at a given level of occupancy, average daily rate, and anticipated yield. However, it is also important not to assume that occupancy is standard each night. Variations occur on a daily basis and by season.

Average Daily Rate

The average daily rate (sometimes referred to as average room rate) is also used in projecting room revenues - the amount of room sales received - for a hotel. However, this figure also affects guests' expectations of their hotel experience. Guests expect higher room rates to correlate with higher levels of service: the hotel with a rate of $150 per night is expected to offer more services than a hotel in the same geographic area with arate of $55 per night. These expectations have been extensively capitalized upon by major hotel chains, by developing different properties to meet the expectations of various segments of the hotel market.

Yield Percentage

Yield percentage measures a hotel manager's efforts in achieving maximum occupancy at the highest room rate possible. Prior to the 1990s, hotel managers relied on occupancy and average daily rate as indicators of meeting financial goals. Yield percentage forces managers to think in more active terms.

RevPAR (Revenue per Available Room)

RevPAR is determined by dividing room revenue received for a specific day by the number of rooms available in the hotel for that day. The formulas for determining RevPAR are as follows:

$$\frac{\text{room revenue}}{\text{number of available rooms}}$$

or

$$\text{hotel occupancy} \times \text{average daily rate}$$

For example, RevPAR for a hotel that has $10,000 in room revenue for the night of September 15 with 200 rooms available would equal $50 ($10,000 / 200 = $50).

This same hotel on September 15 with 200 rooms, room revenue of $10,000, 125 rooms sold, an average daily rate of $80 ($10,000 / 125 = $80), and hotel occupancy of 62.5 percent (125 rooms sold / 200 rooms available X 100 = 62.5 percent) would still produce the same RevPAR (.625 X $80 = $50).

RevPAR is used in hotels to determine the amount of dollars each hotel room produces for the overall financial success of the hotel. The profit from the sale of a hotel room is much greater than that from a similar food and beverage sale. However, the food and beverage aspect of the hotel industry is essential in attracting some categories of guests who want conference services.

Homestay

All around the world, from cities to off the beaten path locations, homestays are a type of accommodation that defines the phrase a 'home away from home'. In a homestay you book to stay with a local in their home. They are your 'host' during your stay.

Staying in a homestay you not only get to visit a destination, you get to really live it too. You see how the locals live their lives – something that is almost impossible to do when staying in other types of accommodation. What make homestays different to other types of accommodation are the hosts. No matter where you're staying, be it the Australian Outback or the metropolis of London, you'll never be in a homestay on your own. Your host will be there during your stay, to welcome you and make it as enjoyable as possible.

Whether you're planning a short break for two or three nights or a round-the-world trip, a homestay is ideal. If you're relocating to another country or city, a homestay is the perfect place to stay for a couple of months while you get to know your new location, meet the local people and look for more permanent accommodation.

The Homestay Student

Living in a homestay requires cooperation that involves some personal sacrifices. A homestay student is more like a family member, rather than a guest. As a result, homestay owners may have certain expectations from the student, such as:

- Participating in family activities.
- Cleaning one's room and bathroom.
- Keeping reasonable hours.
- Communicating with the family about one's schedule.
- Occasionally helping with minor household chores.
- Not inviting guests without the family's permission.

Not every student is prepared to live in a homestay; however, with cooperation and respect, living in a homestay can become one of the most positive and memorable experiences in a student's life.

What kind of student is best suited to live in a homestay?

A student who:

- Is able to recognize that being in a homestay is a privilege.
- Is able to appreciate and enjoy different kinds of people and appreciate a family environment.
- Is willing to make an effort to communicate and cooperate with others.
- Will follow the rules and preference of the family.
- Is mature, stable, flexible, and good-natured.

Benefits of Staying in a Homestay

Meet Local People

When you stay in a homestay you experience something that you won't in other forms of accommodation, not only do you meet the local people you get to live with them too. It's a way to live a destination, not just visit it.

Value for Money

Homestays are great value for money. There are hosts in Dublin offering double rooms for less than €30 per night. Others in the heart of Manhattan that offer accommodation from €55 per night. And to those travelling to Australia's sunny Gold Coast, you can book a double room from only €34 per night. For those looking for longer term accommodation many of the hosts offer great weekly and monthly discounts.

Moving to a New City

Moving to a new destination is both daunting and exciting. On arrival, you're in unfamiliar surroundings, and it takes time to get used to the place. Stay in a homestay and straight away you'll have met some local people, in their home, who will quickly help you to feel more comfortable, secure and generally at ease in your new destination.

Share a Meal

All the hosts are suggested to include a complimentary light breakfast in the per room price (some homestays can provide other meals too by prior arrangement). The best thing about this is that you'll share a meal with your hosts and learn more about the destination and local culture first-hand from them. And if you time is right, you could even share a Christmas dinner or any other festive procession together.

Perfect for Solo Travellers

Travelling on your own can be an extremely liberating experience, and some would argue it's the best way to travel. While there's no doubt it's a great way to see the world, there's always something comforting about staying with somebody who knows a destination well when you arrive. In a homestay, you'll meet interesting people, share stories and experiences and get to know the destination through the eyes of the locals.

Improve your Language Skills

If you're on the road and you're trying to pick up the language along the way, you need to be speaking it everywhere you go. What better way to do this than staying in a local's house when you travel? Or if you're a student attending a language school in another country, stay in a homestay, and you'll get to speak the language every day with your host family.

See Beyond the Tourist Trail

You can't go to Barcelona without visiting La Sagrada Familia or visit Sydney and not get your picture taken at the Opera House. They're part of the experience. But wouldn't it be great to see parts of a destination that only the locals know about? Stay in a homestay, and the hosts will be able to tell you about those hidden secrets like Howth Castle in Dublin.

Learn Local Cultures and Customs

You can read a lot about a destination's cultures and customs before arriving, but the only way to really get to know them is by experiencing them first-hand. Stay in a homestay, and your host will share with you an insight into local life that other forms of accommodation simply can't offer.

A Real 'Home Away from Home'

The phrase 'home away from home' is one that is used all too loosely by different accommodations around the world. While they may offer a homely atmosphere, they're not really homes. Homestays, on the other hand, are just that. Stay in a homestay, and you really will be staying in a home away from home.

Memories you'll Never Forget

Most people have stayed in plenty of hostel or hotel rooms and you wouldn't remember one room or receptionist from another on your trips. Not so a homestay. Your hosts a real, genuine people and by getting to know them and their world, you'll make memories you couldn't get from any other kind of accommodation.

Bed and Breakfast

Bed & Breakfast accommodations, also called B&Bs, can broadly be defined as independent small properties offering overnight lodging and breakfast in a home-like setting. Unlike the "sameness" in a motel or hotel, B&Bs are unique properties, making a singular definition challenging. Many are family-owned and run by individual innkeeper/owners. Often they are renovated old homes, many were once stately residences, a great number are in extraordinary locations, and each is distinctly individual. Many are in quiet residential neighborhoods, in small towns, or off the beaten path but they can also be found in large cities and in popular destination areas. By their nature, bed & breakfasts generally have fewer guest rooms and are more intimate than traditional hotels, motels, lodges, and resorts. Variety reigns, from one B&B to another as well as in an individual B&B itself. Each guest room or suite is usually unlike any other - in size, configuration, decor, and individual characteristics. Historic old buildings which are converted into bed and breakfast properties often will preserve the character of the past while discretely incorporating modern comforts and technology, like individual controls for heat/air, spacious rooms, private baths, large flat screen TVs, and sitting areas. Overall, a bed and breakfast is commonly designed to create an atmosphere of romance, comfort, relaxation, and charm - aiming for an extraordinary and memorable guest experience.

As with any lodging category, bed & breakfasts vary in their level of quality, so this description is a generalization a bed & breakfast which is far more than mere sleeping accommodations and a morning meal. B&B hosts strive to make guests feel at home, while spoiling them with extravagance beyond their normal day-to-day lives. Attention is friendly and personal, usually with flexibility to cater to guests' individual needs. Breakfasts are a major focal point, most often included in the room rate, and are typically non-traditional, gourmet, and prepared from scratch. Featured entrees for breakfast often change daily, and many B&Bs offer signature items, such as stuffed french toast, berry-laden pancakes, and egg-centric creations, accented with specialties like Inn-baked pastries, made-to-order fruit smoothies, freshly baked breads. There are chefs who add fresh harvests from their own gardens, others who incorporate regional specialties into the menu, and some who highlight locally-sourced ingredients. Breakfast is an event.

Extensive "free" guest amenities are often included in the overnight room rate. Offerings such as whirlpool tubs in the guest rooms, comfortable (often luxurious) bedding, decadent sweets, and plush robes are frequently included. Often the rooms and suites are furnished with lovely antiques, while some mix in period reproductions in order to satisfy modern desires like king-sized beds and flat screen televisions. Some have in-room gas-log or electric fireplaces to add ambience. Each property is unique in what is "included" in the room rate, and added value comes with features like complimentary use of bicycles, WiFi, free parking, made-to-order specialty coffees, afternoon refreshments, a swimming pool, and freshly baked cookies. A selection of "add-ons," such as massages, champagne and strawberries, gourmet picnic lunches, breakfast delivered to the guest room, complimentary tickets to local attractions, and other treats are commonly offered to enhance the guests' stay.

Another aspect of a Bed and Breakfast which makes it a preferred lodging choice for many people is the social interaction with the hosts and with fellow guests. Communal breakfast tables, all-day coffee service, and comfortable common areas of the property - such as living rooms, garden seating, poolside chairs, and porches - invite conversation. Activities like evening socials and nightly desserts facilitate casual mingling. Tips on area activities, good dining options, nearby landmarks, and local favorites are often shared, and lasting friendships are formed. On the other hand, opportunities for quiet, soothing "alone-time" are also provided at most bed & breakfasts, and romance takes high priority in the B&B experience.

What to Expect at a Bed and Breakfast

While some countries have specific regulations about what establishments can and can't consider themselves bed-and-breakfasts, there aren't any hard and fast rules in the United States.

In general, American bed-and-breakfasts are significantly smaller than hotels or inns, have owners who live on-site, and limited front desk and check-in hours. Some have shared bathroom facilities, especially in older buildings, but newer ones have rooms with en-suite baths.

All bed-and-breakfasts provide at least one meal to guests, served either in the guest's room or a shared dining room. This is usually a meal the hosts have prepared themselves, and as the name implies, it is nearly always breakfast. For the most part, the hosts also clean the rooms, maintain the property, and provide concierge services like booking tours of local attractions.

Bed-and-breakfasts vs. Home Sharing

With the rise of home-sharing sites like Airbnb, it can be difficult to differentiate between a bed-and-breakfast and a less formal arrangement. Most reputable bed-and-breakfasts are recognized by an organization like the American Automobile Association, trade organizations like the Professional Association of Innkeepers International, or the Association of Independent Hospitality Professionals.

In addition to converted private residences, some establishments are considered bed-and-breakfast inns. The same concept of "room and breakfast" applies. The major difference is that an inn has more rooms available than the usual one to four found in a private home. Inns often provide meals in addition to breakfast, as well as other services not always provided in a private home.

These two terms are used in the industry to distinguish the difference between a stay in a private home and an inn. But remember, no two homes or inns are alike. They vary even within the same geographic area.

Why Stay at a Bed-and-breakfast

Travelers usually are attracted to a particular area by recreational, cultural or historic sites or need to go there for business. Business travelers, especially women, will sometimes seek out bed-and-breakfast accommodations as an alternative to the typical lodge, motel, or hotel facility available in an area.

Sometimes this is for cost reasons or to provide a little peace and quiet on an otherwise hectic trip. Most of the time rates are lower than hotels and inns. Regular bed-and-breakfast visitors consider the low-key environment a big plus.

In the past, a bed-and-breakfast wasn't necessarily the reason a traveler would visit a given area, but as these establishments grew in popularity and improved marketing efforts, some of the most special ones have become attractions themselves.

Some Things that Guests should Tell hosts in Advance

Many B&Bs offer services and amenities specially tailored to the needs of individual guests. But because policies can vary from inn to inn, it's crucial to communicate your needs and expectations before your stay.

Tell your hosts about any dietary restrictions, food allergies, room preferences, and special requests you might have. If you have physical limitations, ask if your room is handicap-accessible. When traveling with kids, make sure your B&B is child-friendly. You may want to disclose your arrival and departure times too, especially at smaller properties where innkeepers personally welcome arriving guests.

Are you celebrating? Many innkeepers will happily help you plan something fun for an anniversary or birthday, as long as you inform them in advance. An Innkeeper's property's policy on special occasions: "For every celebratory getaway, we offer complimentary upgrades. For anniversaries, we do a split of sparkling wine and chocolates. For birthdays, we do a 6-oz. jar of Maine blueberry jam. For other special getaways, we'll offer sparkling wine or nonalcoholic wine."

Eating Breakfast with other Guests

A home-cooked breakfast shared with fellow travelers is a much-loved perk of the B&B experience. It may seem like breakfast is a must—after all, it's usually included in the price of your stay—but the reality is a lot more flexible. If you want to try a local restaurant, or if you'd like to skip breakfast and sleep until noon (a wonderful idea), go for it. It's your vacation, and innkeepers understand that.

If you're staying at a large property with a full-service restaurant, you probably don't need to announce that you'll be skipping breakfast. But at a smaller inn with limited seating and a small staff, it's a good idea to communicate your breakfast plans ahead of time. Check your B&B's website or contact the innkeepers if you're not entirely sure what to do.

Having Breakfast in your Room or Breakfast to Go

It depends on the property, but many B&B owners are happy to accommodate guests who'd like to grab breakfast and go. For example, at Snow Goose Bed and Breakfast in Keene Valley, New York, the innkeepers are happy to pack a healthy to-go breakfast for guests hoping to hike the Adirondacks trail routes the morning. Not all inns and B&Bs offer takeaway breakfast, of course, so get in touch with your innkeepers first.

Some B&Bs offer in-room dining, others don't. At B&Bs outfitted with antiques and period furniture, owners may prefer to keep food out of the rooms.

Running Late for Check-in

Flights get delayed. Traffic jams happen. Busses break down. Innkeepers are well aware of the uncertainties of travel. It's okay if you're late for check-in, but the important thing is to touch base with your hosts when there's a change in plans.

Before you leave, make sure you have the contact information for your B&B. Save your hosts' phone number and email address on your phone and keep a hard copy of these details in your carry-on bag (just in case your phone battery dies).

Bringing Pets

Each B&B has its own rules about pets. Some are perfect for them, while others are strictly humans-only. If you're traveling with a four-footed companion or two, ask your inn about its pet policy before you book.

Spilling Something in the Room

Accidents happen. Litchfield says, "We never shame or blame a guest. Be up front and honest so that it can be immediately cleaned. Especially if it is red wine, the sooner the better."

Advice for Conversation Topics Around the Breakfast Table

According to Eric Huenneke, owner of Prospect Place in Cambridge, Massachusetts, "Part of the adventure with breakfast conversation is to see what happens with the combination of guests." Have fun getting to know your fellow travelers—you never know what you might learn. A few of the innkeepers we talked to advised staying away from religion and politics as early-morning conversation topics with strangers.

A bit of breakfast hobnobbing is a great opportunity to discover more about your destination, too. We recommend using the morning meal as a means for gleaning travel advice. Ask guests what they've seen and done in the area, and share your own experiences. You could gain valuable first-hand guidance on the best way to explore your destination.

Asking Hosts for Trip-planning Advice

One of the best B&B benefits is the personalized travel advice on offer from extremely knowledgeable innkeepers. Few people know their home base better than B&B owners, and they can provide an insider's know-how combined with years of experience helping travelers explore their surroundings.

Benefits of Staying in a Bed and Breakfast

You will Often Pay Less than a Hotel

A research came up with a revealing infographic that compared average prices of hotels and B&Bs in major cities. In New York City, the average hotel charges $217 for a night, while a B&B comes in at around $169. That's almost $50 less a night.

Forget your Continental Breakfast - at B&Bs, you can Get a Homemade Breakfast

That delicious-looking pastry is the "famous" pecan sticky bun at Wickwood Inn in Saugatuck, Mich. The buns are part of their Champagne Brunch, which also includes apple bread pudding, vegetable frittatas and "Sugar And Spice Popovers." We're pretty sure you don't get anything even close to that at your hotel's sad continental breakfast.

Most Amenities are Free and Much Better at B&Bs

How many times have you wished your hotel would at least offer free wi-fi? Seriously, even Starbucks has that. Well, chances are, if you stay in a B&B, not only will you have free wi-fi, but complimentary parking and concierge services, too. Plus, while a hotel concierge might lazily direct you to a kiosk littered with impersonalized (and likely outdated) tourist pamphlets, many B&B owners are seasoned locals with a wealth of knowledge about the locale. Since these people were most likely born and bred in the town, you know they will happily tip you off to the best restaurants and things to do.

They are Great Place to Pull off a "Staycation" in your own Town

A room at The Black Dolphin Inn.

Perhaps you have lived in New Smyrna, Fla. your whole life, but you have never once gone fishing. And maybe you really need to take a quick vacation but don't want to spend the money on plane tickets and hotel accommodations. Well, you could quickly book a room at The Black Dolphin Inn and sign up for the "Mosquito Lagoon Blackwater Fishing Package." It includes a day of fishing with a local guide in the backwater flats and waters of the Indian River. Oh, and a six-pack of locally crafted beer comes as a bonus.

A B&B can Make you Feel Like you have Transported to a Completely Different Country

Not all American B&Bs embrace a "quaint Americana" theme. Take The Inn of Five Graces in Santa Fe, N.M.: The 24-suite inn is filled with Afghan and Tibetan crafts and artifacts. Their attention to detail really makes for a uniquely warm, lush getaway without leaving the States.

The Finer Details of B&B Rooms Go Beyond Pretty Decor and Focus on Comfort

At the Blue Lantern Inn in Dana Point, Calif., each of their 29 rooms includes a fireplace to keep you warm and make you feel more at home. Each room also provides a fridge with soda and an in-room Keurig coffee machine. And unlike most hotels, these drinks are complimentary, so no outrageous mini-bar charges.

You can Sleep on the Same Bed that a Number of U.S. Presidents did

The Rosemont Manor in Berryville, Va. is a 60-acre property that was previously the estate of late Virginia governor and U.S. Senator Harry F. Byrd, Sr. Many notable U.S. presidents have stayed at the inn, including Roosevelt, Eisenhower, Kennedy, Johnson and Nixon.

You can have your own Professionally Trained Chef Cook a Personalized Meal Just for you

The chef above is David Smythe, the man who would cook your breakfast for you if you stayed at Barclay Heights Bed and Breakfast at Smythe House in Saugerties, N.Y. He is not only a graduate of the Culinary Institute of America, but also a professor at the reputable culinary school. He could whip you up something nice, like this beautiful farm egg frittata:

If your Sleeping Experience is Uncomfortable, you can Fine-tune it at this B&B

At Stone Hill Inn in Stowe, Vt., if you are not feeling your bed's pillows, you can find the perfect one when you choose one from the inn's "pillow library."

Finally, at a B&B, you will Get the Care and Attention you Truly Deserve

The service at a B&B goes way beyond just providing you with comfortable lodging for your vacation. The main difference between a bed and breakfast and a hotel is that the owners of a B&B see their patrons as guests, while hotels may see their patrons as customers. Many B&B owners will go out of their way to make sure their home adheres to many levels of comfort. For example, they may have made sure to open their establishment away from loud freeways or roads, and they may allow guests to bring their pets if they want to. In fact, some B&B owners are willing to rent out their whole inn to a group for a weekend so they can have a fun get-together.

Guest House

The lines of distinction between a hotel industry and the guest house market are blurring. They both are based on a same principal to provide a temporary adobe to a person. The working of a hotel and that of a guest house are also pretty same. They both are meant for people who come to a city on short stay or a substantial longer stay either for leisure purposes or business. But there is a huge difference between the management, services and the expenditure that is incurred on either.

Every now and then, a person has to make a decision while visiting another city, to either choose a hotel or a guest house. Over the years the requirements of general population has been shifting towards a homely environment that truly feels like a home. Although hotels have been stating the facilities that ensure that you feel like living in home away from home, the reality is that each and every hotel room feels exactly the same no matter which part of the globe you are in.

A guest house is basically a house that has all the services and facilities comparable to a star hotel. As the name suggests it is like living as a guest in a house of another person. Along with the owner of the house, it also has the staff to take care of all your needs. Stribling hospitality has a well trained staff that does not let you miss the luxuries that come along with the services of a star hotel. There is also a common living room that is incorporated in the guest house where the guest can sit and socialize with other people. They tend to be cozier and one has the opportunity to get accustomed to the culture and locality.

One of the most important things that distinguish a hotel from a guest house is the overall ambiance. Each and every hotel room tend to be exactly the same and a person sometimes feel like trapped inside a room. A guest house has a feeling of spaciousness as the person feels like living in a big house rather than a single room. With services like kitchen, a living room or washing and drying facilities a person feels like living in a home away from home.

The biggest factor that makes a guest house always a best bet for a person who is on a longer stay to a city is the expenditure. The guest houses of Stribling Hospitality often tend to be cheaper as compared to comparative hotels. So if a person is able to get a homely environment, along with the services of a hotel at a price point that is very lucrative, then the logic says to go for a guest houses.

Types of Guest Houses

Now Guest Houses are not only a cheaper substitute of hotels, but are also an emerging segment with multiple branches. Presently there are many categories of Guest Houses like Corporate, Beach and Budget guest houses. Most of the Metropolitan cities are an ideal hub for Corporate Guest Houses. These properties consist of 8-10 rooms within a budget of 100-150$. They are mostly accommodated by corporates looking for a 10-15 days stay on their business trip. One can find good Beach Guest Houses along the ocean shore. Beach Houses have become a good substitute of expensive resorts and are a perfect blend of affordability & elegance. Budget Guest houses are living upto their name. They provide budget friendly accommodations. One can easily get a 10-20$ room in this category with basic amenities.

Boarding House

In a boarding house, a tenant rents a room, rather than the whole house. They share facilities such as the kitchen and bathroom with the other tenants. A boarding house is occupied, or intended to be occupied, by at least six tenants at any time.

Boarding House Tenancies are Different to Standard Tenancies

Boarding house tenancies and standard tenancies share a lot of the same requirements under the Residential Tenancies Act. However, some things apply only to boarding houses, such as the landlord being able to make house rules. A boarding house tenancy is intended to last 28 days or more.

The other difference between a boarding house tenancy and a standard tenancy agreement is that you can't have a fixed term tenancy in a boarding house.

Landlords need to ensure they comply with their local council requirements before establishing a boarding house, including obtaining the necessary resource consents. You may need to make changes to the property to meet these requirements. You can find out more about these requirements and establishing a boarding house by contacting your local council.

Boarding House Tenancy Agreement

A boarding house tenancy agreement must contain the same information as a standard tenancy agreement, plus:

- Whether the tenancy is intended to last for 28 days or more.

- One or more telephone numbers for the landlord.

- The room number that the agreement is for.

- Whether the room is shared by other tenants – and the maximum number of other tenants who may occupy the room.

- Whether the tenancy is a joint tenancy – and the names of the other people who will occupy the room.

- The services (if any) to be provided by the landlord.

- The name and contact address (including a phone number) of the boarding house manager (if other than the landlord).

- A description of the fire evacuation procedures.

Boarding House Landlords can Make House Rules

The landlord of a boarding house is allowed to make house rules. These set out how the boarding house can be used and enjoyed, and what services will be provided. The landlord can change the rules at any time, but must give each tenant at least seven days' written notice of the new rules.

The landlord must give the tenant a copy of the rules at the start of the tenancy, and make sure copies are displayed in the boarding house.

The house rules are not allowed to breach the Residential Tenancies Act or any other law (for example, the Human Rights Act or the Privacy Act). If a tenant believes a house rule breaches the law, they can apply to the Tenancy Tribunal. The Tribunal will decide whether the rule is allowed or not, or may tell the landlord to change the way the rule is applied.

Bond can be up to Four Weeks' Rent

A boarding house landlord can ask for a bond of up to the equivalent of four weeks' rent. They must give the tenant a receipt for bond straight away. The landlord must lodge the bond with Tenancy Services within 23 working days of receiving the money, unless the bond is the equivalent to one week's rent or less.

Rent is Paid Weekly or Fortnightly

Like a standard tenancy, rent for a boarding house tenancy is paid either weekly or fortnightly. A landlord is not allowed to ask for more than two weeks' rent in advance. If the landlord wants to increase the rent, they must give the tenant at least 28 days' notice in writing. The rent can't be increased within 180 days of the beginning of the tenancy or within 180 days of the last rent increase.

Landlords are Responsible for Repairs and Security

Repairs

A boarding house landlord must make sure the house is in a reasonable state of repair. It must comply with all requirements for buildings, including health and safety, under any enactment that applies. This includes supplying basic necessities such as cooking facilities, drinkable water and bathroom facilities (connected to an adequate means of heating water).

Tenants must notify the landlord as soon as possible if they discover any damage or anything that needs repairing. Tenants must not intentionally or carelessly cause any damage, or allow anyone else to do so. Tenants must not interfere with, or render inoperative, any means of escape from fire.

Security

A boarding house landlord must provide and maintain sufficient locks to ensure the house and all rooms are reasonably secure. They must also make sure tenants have access to their room and toilet and bathroom facilities at all times.

Before changing any lock or similar device, the landlord must tell every tenant who will be affected.

Tenants must not alter, add to or remove any lock or similar device.

Landlords and Tenants are Responsible for Cleanliness

The landlord must make sure the facilities (such as the kitchen, bathroom, garden and garage) are in a reasonable state of cleanliness.

Tenants must keep their rooms reasonably clean and tidy, and in a condition that does not create a health or safety hazard.

When the Landlord can Enter the Boarding House

The landlord is allowed to enter the boarding house at any time. However, they should have a valid reason for entering or they might interfere with tenants' quiet enjoyment (which they're not allowed to do).

A boarding house landlord may enter a boarding room without notice:

- If a tenant of the room agrees at, or immediately before, the time of entry,
- If the landlord reasonably believes there's an emergency, or serious risk to life or property,
- To provide services that the landlord and tenant have agreed to, as long as entry meets the conditions of the agreement or house rules,
- In accordance with an order from the Tenancy Tribunal.

A boarding house landlord may enter a boarding room after giving 24 hours' notice to the tenants of the room:

- To inspect the room, if no inspection has been made within the last four weeks.

- To inspect the room, if the landlord believes the tenant has abandoned the room or breached the Residential Tenancies Act (the Act) in another way.

- To show the room to a possible tenant or buyer.

- To fulfill their obligations under the Act.

- To inspect work the landlord required the tenant to carry out, or the tenant agreed to carry out.

- To show the room to a registered valuer, real estate agent, or building inspector preparing a report.

When entering a boarding room, the boarding house landlord must:

- Not interfere with tenants' property, unless it's necessary to achieve the purpose of entry.

- Do so in a reasonable manner.

- Not use or threaten to use unauthorized force.

- Not stay in the room longer than necessary to achieve the purpose of entry.

It is an unlawful act for a landlord to breach any of the points above.

Ending a Boarding House Tenancy

How much Notice Tenants and Landlords must Give

A boarding house tenant can end their tenancy with 48 hours' notice. Even though this notice doesn't have to be in writing, it's a good idea for tenants to put it in writing and keep a copy for themselves.

A boarding house landlord can end the tenancy as follows.

Immediately if the tenant has:

- Caused, or threatened to cause, serious damage to the boarding house.

- Endangered, or threatened to endanger, people or property.

- Caused, or threatened to cause, serious disruption to other tenants.

With 48 hours' written notice if:

- The tenant fails to pay overdue rent within 10 days of receiving a notice to do so.

- The tenant has used, or allowed the boarding house to be used, for an illegal purpose.

- The rent is overdue and the landlord considers the tenant has abandoned the room (after inspecting the room and, if possible, making contact with the tenant's contact person).

With 28 days' written notice in any other case.

What the Tenant must do at the End of their Tenancy

At the end of the tenancy, the tenant must:

- Leave the boarding house.

- Remove all their private property.

- Leave their room in a reasonably clean and tidy condition, and remove all rubbish.

- Return to the landlord all keys, security or pass cards, and other such devices provided by the landlord.

- Leave behind all chattels (such as furniture) provided by the landlord for tenants to use.

If a Tenant Abandons the Boarding House

If a tenant has overdue rent, and if the landlord believes the tenant has abandoned the boarding house, the landlord:

- May put a notice on the door of the tenant's room advising the tenant that the landlord will enter the room 24 hours later to confirm whether or not the tenant has abandoned the tenancy.

- Must make all reasonable efforts to contact the contact person (if any) identified in the tenant's tenancy agreement.

The landlord must not enter the room until at least 24 hours after putting the notice on the door.

Once the landlord has inspected the room and believes the tenancy has been abandoned, they must give the tenant a further 48 hours' notice that the tenancy will be ended. This notice must be placed on the door of the room and include the time and date that the tenancy will end.

It is an unlawful act for a tenant to abandon the tenancy without reasonable excuse.

If a Tenant Dies

A boarding house tenancy ends 48 hours after the death of a sole tenant under the tenancy.

Quiet Enjoyment Living in a Boarding House

If you live in a boarding house, the landlord and other tenants can't interfere with your quiet enjoyment of the premises. You can't interfere with other tenants quiet enjoyment either.

References

- What-is-bed-breakfast: stfrancisinn.com, Retrieved 11, July 2020

- 10-benefits-of-staying-in-a-homestay: homestay.com, Retrieved 24, April 2020

- Bed-and-breakfast-vacation_n_5072556: huffingtonpost.in Retrieved 27, June 2020

- Things-you-need-to-know-about-staying-in-casino-hotels: mappingmegan.com, Retrieved 19, July 2020

- What-is-a-homestay: tripping.com, Retrieved 14, May 2020

- Guest-houses: mghworld.net, Retrieved 14, May 2020

- Towel-animals-from-carnival-and-others-4062015: tripsavvy.com, Retrieved 11, May 2020

- Difference-between-boarding-and-lodging: pediaa.com, Retrieved 21, June 2020

- What-is-a-serviced-apartment: forenom.com, Retrieved 11, April 2020

- Airport-hotel-1895486: tripsavvy.com, Retrieved 25, March 2020

- What-is-eco-hotel: drinkteatravel.com, Retrieved 11, June 2020

- Connecting-suites-suites-different-rooms: suiteness.com, Retrieved 13, April 2020

- Vacation-rentals-vs-timeshares: tripping.com, Retrieved 29, June 2020

Role of Technology in Tourism

Technology is being increasingly used for various purposes within the tourism industry. A few of these are global distribution system, mobile ticketing, online hotel reservations, passenger service system and passenger information system. The topics elaborated in this chapter will help in gaining a better perspective about these applications of technology in tourism.

Travel Tech – technology that is used and developed within the travel and tourism industry – is revolutionising the way in which we travel.

There is no doubt that technology plays an important role in tourism and travel. Most of us are now used to booking our airline reservations on line, dealing with telephone trees and other cost saving devices. These technological advances have allowed corporations to save on manpower while at the same time empowering customers to make their own decisions. On the other side of the equation, travelers use more technology then ever before and often the tourism industry has taken advantage of this desire (need) to stay in touch with its clientele. Most of us are now used to being almost harassed with on-line surveys or computer driven telephone calls.

Technology then has become a mixed bag for the tourism industry. It creates a great deal of conveniences while at the same time has been used as a way to increase revenues and to lessen customer service. The world of technology has made air travel safe and abundant but has also brought about the need to go through long security lines and daily hassles. Certainly, some parts of the industry have begun to use technology prudently. When used ethically, technology can be a great help in increasing our communication and security.

Travel Websites and Apps

There is a plethora of online travel sites and apps, which can be used for many different purposes:

Research: Individual vendor websites, third-party booking sites, and online travel publications provide information, reviews, and price comparisons for travel products, including transportation, accommodation, excursions and car rental. Travelers who prefer to not work with a travel agent can easily complete necessary research and select the vendors with the best prices.

Booking: Both travel agents and consumers alike can book travel online, without ever having to speak to a vendor representative.

Travel updates: Travelers can now check in regarding their flight status via a website or a mobile app. In addition, many airlines now provide updated flight information via text or automated calls. In addition, family and friends can also use online systems to track the arrival of their guests.

Loyalty points: Many airlines and hotels offer loyalty point programs. Apps and websites allow loyalty point program members to check their status and redeem points as they wish.

Boarding passes: Travelers have been able to check-in to their flights online and to print boarding passes from their computer some time now. These days, however, travelers can simply add a boarding pass to their mobile phone wallet and skip the printing process.

Tour Systems

New technology allows individuals on group or self-guided tours to get the information they need as they view historical landmarks, architecture and artifacts:

Self-guided tours: Travelers can download an app to their smartphones, which provides expert commentary as they move through a museum exhibit, attraction or neighborhood.

Group tours: During a conventional group tour, guides sometimes struggle to make themselves heard. As a result, members of the group get jostled about, as others close in, so that they can hear what the guide has to say. New technology now allows a guide to wear a microphone and transmitter. The guide's words are broadcasted to members of the tour who are wearing earpieces tuned into the transmitter. This not only ensures that everyone can hear the guide, but also allows tour members to move around freely while taking in what the guide has to say.

Smartphone Communication Apps

When things go wrong while traveling, it's essential to to be able to communicate with people who can help, such as customer service representatives and travel agents. Some travel agents use apps to make themselves available to travelers who may need to reschedule a missed flight or book a new hotel. In addition, some resorts are also using smartphone apps, which enable guests to bring problems to the attention of management, so that they can be sorted out right away.

Allotment

Allotments (in the tourism industry) are used to designate a certain block of pre-negotiated hotel rooms which have been bought out and held by a travel organiser with a huge buying power like a wholesaler, OTA, tour operator or hotel consolidator. An allotment can be purchased for a specific period of time such as a whole season, part of a season or for any single dates and then sold to travel partners and final customers around the globe. A couple of days prior to hotel check-in any unsold rooms may be released back to the supplier if such an agreement exists between the two parties. Tour operators obtain discounts, through allotment or commitment contracts, primarily depend on the firm size and the bargaining power exercised and can vary from 10-50% according to the period of the year, the destination, the quantity and quality of services contracted upon.

Negotiating Allotments

Allotments can be negotiated between a tour operator and a travel service supplier such as airline company/hotel chain, or between two travel organizers such as a tour operator and a retail travel agent. Either way the buyer needs to prove a consistent level of business, because allotments are hardly granted without any previous sales history.

Rooms or seats that have not been contracted between the travel company and the product supplier are handled as 'on-request', where each booking of an airline seat or hotel room needs to be confirmed with the supplier before being confirmed with the client.

The Allotment or Allocation Contract

The amount of the contracted rooms/seats to be specified in the allotment contract is a result of the estimated, during the negotiation, volume of sales to be realized by the tour operator. Tour operators book a certain number of rooms in hotels or seats on carriers and have the right to use them by a given date, also known as a release date, that usually is some days prior to tourist's arrival (hotels)/departure(carriers). The allotment contract reduces the risk of any unsold products by the supplier and grants relative price advantage to the travel organizer helping him to stay competitive on the market by offering extra discounts.

Tour operators obtain discounts, through allotment or commitment contracts, primarily depend on the firm size and the bargaining power exercised; they can vary from 10% to 50% according to the period of the year, the destination, the quantity and quality of services contracted upon. Some big tour operators are able to obtain up to 70% of discount.

Global Distribution System

Global distribution systems (GDSs) are computerized, centralized services that provide travel-related transactions. They cover everything from airline tickets to car rentals to hotel rooms and more.

Global distribution systems were originally usually set up for use by the airlines but were later extended to travel agents. Today, global distribution systems allow users to purchase tickets from multiple different providers or airlines.

Global distribution systems are also the back end of most Internet-based travel services.

However, different global distribution systems still service a limited number of airlines. For example, Sabre is used by American Airlines, PARS by USAir, TravelSky by Air China, Worldspan by Delta, etc. Other major global distribution systems include: Galileo, TravelSky, and Worldspan. Global Distribution Systems are also sometimes called Computer Reservation Systems (CSRs).

GDS is a computerized web service that provides pricing, real time availability, centralized data display with reservation functionality to the global travel industry in a very unified process. The four main GDS providers in the travel industry are Amadeus, Sabre, Galilio and Worldspan helping travel agents growing volume of travel transactions.

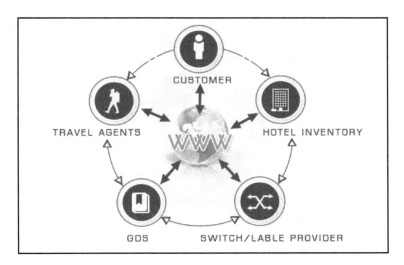

It was revealed that the GDS is and will remain as the most important channel of distribution for airlines, hotels and car rental companies alike. However, Internet also allows the GDS companies, label providers and even the traditional travel agents to host websites directly which access to their connections and provide the services previously offered by offline travel agents.

Example of a Booking Facilitation done by an Airline GDS

A mirror image of the passenger name record (PNR) in the airline reservations system is maintained in the GDS system. If a passenger books an itinerary containing air segments of multiple airlines through a travel agency, the passenger name record in the GDS system would hold information on their entire itinerary, each airline they fly on would only have a portion of the itinerary that is relevant to them. This would contain flight segments on their own services and inbound and onward connecting flights (known as info segments) of other airlines in the itinerary. e.g. if a passenger books a journey from Amsterdam to London on KLM, London to New York on British Airways, New York to Frankfurt on Lufthansa through a travel agent and if the travel agent is connected to Amadeus GDS. The PNR in the Amadeus GDS would contain the full itinerary, the PNR in KLM would show the Amsterdam to London segment along with British Airways flight as an onward info segment. Likewise the PNR in the Lufthansa system would show the New York to Frankfurt segment with the British Airways flight as an arrival information segment. The PNR in British Airways system would show all three segments. One as a live segment and the other two as arrival and onward info segments.

Some GDS systems (primarily Amadeus CRS and SABRE) also have a dual use capability for hosting multiple computer reservations system, in such situations functionally the computer reservations system and the GDS partition of the system behave as if they were separate systems.

Future of GDS Systems and Companies

GDS in the travel industry originated from a traditional legacy business model that existed to inter-operate between airline vendors and travel agents. During the early days of computerized reservations systems flight ticket reservations were not possible without a GDS. As time progressed, many airline vendors (including budget and mainstream operators) have now adopted a strategy of 'direct selling' to their wholesale and retail customers (passengers). They invested heavily in their own reservations and direct-distribution channels and partner systems. This helps to minimize direct dependency on GDS systems to meet sales and revenue targets and allows for a more dynamic response to market needs. These technology advancements in this space facilitate an easier way to cross-sell to partner airlines and via travel agents, eliminating the dependency on a dedicated global GDS federating between systems. Also, multiple price comparison websites eliminate the need of dedicated GDS for point-in-time prices and inventory for both travel agents and end-customers. Hence some experts argue that these changes in business models may lead to complete phasing out of GDS in the Airline space by the year 2020.

Lufthansa Group announced in June 2015 that it was imposing an additional charge of €16 when booking through an external Global Distribution System rather than their own systems. They stated their choice was based upon that the costs of using external systems was several times higher than their own. Several other airlines including Air France–KLM and Emirates also stated that they are following the development.

However, hotels and car rental industry continue to benefit from GDS, especially last-minute inventory disposal using GDS to bring additional operational revenue. GDS here is useful to facilitate global reach using existing network and low marginal costs when compared to online air travel bookings. Some GDS companies are also in the process of investing and establishing significant offshore capability in a move to reduce costs and improve their profit margins to serve their customer directly accommodating changing business models.

Benefits of Global Distribution Systems

- The Use of Global distribution system shows a rise across corporate and leisure travelers.

- GDS is highly effective in alluring the international travelers. This is the reason why using of GDS among the travel agents is growing exponentially every year.

- OTAs have greatly improved the travel shopping experience and convenience for consumers and have increased pricing transparency.

- GDSs enable the retail travel agency and OTA business models.

- The GDSs enable the travel agents to make their travel services available to consumers globally where they might not otherwise be able to achieve efficient worldwide market penetration through direct marketing efforts.

- Booking through Global distribution system is most preferable for corporate travel agents as a suitable reservation process for holidays, air, hotel and rental cars.

- Travel agents can get global platform for their business with strong market penetration.

- Global distribution system is the base to enter into corporate clients across the world.

- GDS is the ability to update the status of inventory in real time. Due to its real-time status update capability managers can view rates change and can easily alter price points or make special offers. Agents can view all the changes instantly and will be able to suggest the new updates and offers to clients without any interruption to make the deal.

- Its a wise decision to invest in a GDS. The system places your holiday booking services and inventories in front of huge clients without affecting your marketing budget.

- The unique selling point of GDS is that it Can provide best rates to your guests, which no other systems can provide. Your gusts can find packages that include a hotel stay, air travel and car rental.

The Future of Global Distribution Systems

There's no doubt that global distribution systems will play an important part in the travel landscape for many years to come, but their traditional role is changing and being challenged by all the changes taking place in the travel industry. Two important considerations impacting the role of global distribution systems are the growth of online travel websites that offer price comparisons and the increased push from airline and other travel service providers to push consumers to make bookings directly via their websites. For example, to recoup additional money, over the past few years many airlines have pushed travelers to purchasing tickets directly from the airline websites. Some airlines are even imposing additional fees for tickets booked through a global distribution system, rather than the airline's website.

Mobile Ticketing

Mobile ticketing is a process involving the purchase of a ticket through mobile phone. An m-ticket does not need to be printed. Instead, it is a ticket that you can directly download to your smartphone.

Example

Imagine you are going to board for a flight, the only thing you need to do is to present your smartphone to the stewardess. She will scan it and you will be able to board.

A mobile ticket offers multiple opportunities. It allows consumers to order, pay for, obtain and validate tickets wherever they are and whenever they want by using their smartphones.

Besides, mobile tickets offer more advantages than traditional ones : better commodity for users, less queuing at the entrance of a theater, concert or event. And costs will also drop because of the reduced printing and diffusion costs. Furthermore, it will be impossible to lose your ticket.

Consumers now gain time because they have the possibility to buy and use their tickets whenever they want and wherever they are thanks to their smartphones.

M-tickets are only the beginning of a more digitalized way of living. Indeed, smartphones are becoming real digital wallet and retailers cannot wait anymore before exploiting this major opportunity.

The M-ticket is also eco-friendlier, compared to the E-ticket it doesn't need to be printed, paper consumption will thus decrease, making it even better for our planet.

Applications

- Airline check-in
- Airline ticketing
- Tourist Attraction Ticketing
- Zoo Ticketing
- Museum Ticketing
- Cinema ticketing
- Railway & Bus ticketing
- Concert/Event ticketing
- Consumer voucher distribution
- Mass transit
- Trade shows

Usage

Mobile Purchase

The International Air Transport Association (IATA) 2007 announced a global standard that paves the way for global mobile phone check-in using two-dimensional (2D) bar codes. The industry has set a deadline of the end of 2010 to implement 100% bar coded boarding passes (BCBP). Upon full implementation, BCBP is said to be able to save the industry over US $500 million annually.

Mobile tickets can be purchased in a variety of ways including online, via text messaging or over the phone from a voice call, WAP page, or a secure mobile application. For repeated purchases such as daily train tickets, mobile applications or text messaging can be used. The drawbacks to text message purchasing is that either the vendor loses 40% of their revenue to the mobile operator, or any credit card purchase has to be achieved through a web page as the SMS has no security suitable for credit card entry, and very few ticket choices can be easily remembered and entered by SMS.

SMS Purchase

There are two distinct forms of SMS purchases: so-called 'premium SMS' purchases charged to the mobile operator bill; and SMS purchases charged to a payment card. Mobile ticket purchases are primarily user-initiated messages whereby a keyword is sent to a short code service number (e.g. GV for a single adult ticket in Gothenburg, Sweden or GN as a night-tariff ticket). A return message is sent containing the mobile ticket as either an MMS message, a URL leading to a 2D barcode, or as plain text with the ticket information.

With premium SMS the price of the ticket can be added to the users mobile phone bill or debited from their pre-paid service using SMS billing. The main business limitation is that when premium SMS is used for billing, by default around 20-40% of the transaction value is retained by the mobile operator and sms aggregator. Normally, this would not be viable for low margin tickets, however, in many cases much more favourable commercial terms have been negotiated e.g. between the public transport organisations and mobile operators. Payments charged to payment cards require an initial registration to associate the user's mobile phone number to their credit card, but have a far more favorable fee structure for service providers.

Online Purchase

Online purchase is still an option for mobile tickets, allowing the user to set up an account and choosing payment options etc.

Delivery

Delivery of tickets to mobile phones can be done in a variety of ways:

- Text messaging (SMS) - visual inspection or OCR.

- Text messaging with WAP Push - visual inspection or OCR.

- Picture messaging (SMS, EMS, WAP Push and MMS) - usually uses a barcode.

- Dedicated Mobile application - which can store and render barcodes delivered via SMS, GPRS, Bluetooth, IRDA or RFID. Barcodes rendered on the device by a dedicated application have the advantage of being full screen without clutter, meaning faster and more successful scanning. A dedicated mobile application can also help the user to organise and sort their tickets better than when an SMS or MMS inbox is full of similar tickets, which is especially useful for transport tickets.

- Device RFID - This is the method proposed under the Near Field Communication (NFC) specification but only used by the Osaifu-Keitai payment system in Japan.

Southend United Football Club is currently the only team in the UK to have a mobile ticketing facility offered to fans.

Very few phones outside Japan have RFID/NFC tags and so this method of delivery is largely unsupported. Picture messaging is supported by almost all phones and is generally the delivery method of choice. It usually requires the sender to know the phone model in advance so that the picture is rendered at the correct resolution. Text-only messaging is supported by all mobile phones and is the simplest method of delivery.

Redemption

Visually validated mobile tickets are validated without connection to a back office system. Other forms of mobile ticket systems contact a server that is able to verify the ticket and record that it has been used.

New systems that make use of encryption of the data inside the barcode enable off-line scanning and validation, which is especially important if users are purchasing tickets immediately prior to use, and the portable venue or on-vehicle scanning devices cannot always have a connection to the live ticket database. (Many transport ticketing systems, such as the London Oyster card travel system and the M-PhaTic system of the Swedish state railways SJ are designed so that scanners can operate as disconnected islands when connectivity to central systems is lost).

The benefits of mobile ticketing are:

1) The Ticket is already in Users' Pockets

Access to the transport service when and where users need it. No more excuses about finding the right ticket: fare evasion is fought, providing at the same time occasional users with the opportunity to travel easily.

2) The Days of Paper are Numbered

Digital solutions, if designed and realized carefully, prevent the forgery of travel tickets which is typical of paper tickets: at the same time they improve traceability and control by dedicated field personnel.

3) It Makes the Math Work

Clearing operations and usage statistics are accurate to the ticket and not based on hypotheses or corrective factors of statistical origin: in this way all the data related to ticketing is punctual, complete and available also in real-time.

4) The Power of Control

With the data available it is possible to have a complete and precise control of the sales operations. In this way it is possible not only to size and optimize services, but also to run tests to explore new proposals, from routes to tariffs, and have immediate and objective feedbacks from the ridership.

5) Objective: Dematerialization

Dematerialization yields to economic benefits and also helps the environment: it avoids producing plastic cards and paper tickets that in many cases soon become garbage. All resources that can be used to offer a better service.

6) More Close to Users

The smartphone is a powerful two-way communication channel with its users: listening to feedbacks or providing accurate and up-to-date information can make the difference. It is also possible to communicate in other languages to allow tourists to move easily in an unknown territory.

7) More Efficient Ticket Offices

Mobile ticketing decreases the pressure at the ticket office, which can therefore provide with a better service; this benefits all users, with the reduction of the waiting time in line.

8) Money Flows

Less cash circulating both in the ticket offices with staff and in the automatic ticket machines (which must be emptied or give the change). Better tracking of money flows. Possibility of accepting payments in multiple currencies to facilitate access to transport for tourists.

9) Users' Smartphones

Purchase, maintenance and connectivity of devices for mobile ticketing are responsibility of users, unlike what happens for any physical installation for sales (eg: automatic ticket machine).

10) A Look into the Future

Unlike other transport technologies, mobile ticketing presents very short times and low costs of implementation, if not almost zero. All software components do not suffer from the typical obsolescence of hardware devices and can be easily updated to benefit from the technologies available in the future.

Check-in

Check-in is a Procedure by which an airline or hotel formally registers the arrival of a passenger for a flight or a guest for a stay.

Airport Check-in

Checking in for a flight is the process whereby a person announces their arrival at the airport. The check-in process at airports enables passengers to confirm they will be on the respective flight, obtain a boarding pass, possibly select their seat (if hasn't happened already or allowed by airline), and check in luggage onto a plane, if desired.

Boarding Pass

A boarding pass is a document provided by an airline during check-in, giving a passenger permission to board the airplane for a particular flight. At a minimum, it identifies the passenger, the flight number, and the date and scheduled time for departure. Boarding Passes are always required to board a flight. Often times airlines accept paper or electronic boarding passes (on phone or tablet).

Three Ways to Check-In

1. In-person at a staffed check-in counter at airport

    Checking-in in-person allows you to check in your baggage, if checking luggage, at the same time as checking in for your flight.

    Items needed for check-in counter check-in:

    -   Passport (when traveling internationally),

    -   Paper ticket (less and less common),

    -   or a confirmation number—usually sent via email if ticket is purchased online or through a travel agency,

    -   or printed itinerary with a confirmation number.

2. In-person at airport using a self check-in kiosk

    At this time passengers can select a seat (if hasn't happened already or allowed by airline), enter number of bags to be checked (if desired), and print boarding passes. Passengers will then need to submit luggage to staffed counter or checked luggage stations. Airline staff will need to check your passport either at time of check in or at gate.

    Items needed for kiosk check-in:

    -   Confirmation number (usually sent via email if ticket is purchased online or through a travel agency),

- or the credit card used for payment of the ticket,

- and or a passport. Passport required when traveling internationally.

3. Check-in online before arriving to airport

   Passengers can check in online starting 24 hours (usually) before departure. Passengers will need to submit luggage to staffed counter or checked luggage stations if checking luggage.

   Benefits of online check-in:

   - Avoid potential check-in lines at airport,

   - Print boarding pass at home (can also wait or reprint at self-service kiosk at the airport),

   - Select seat assignment(s) before others (if applicable),

   - Choose to get updates of possible changes to departure times leading up to flight.

Check-in and Boarding Timelines

Check-in deadlines

- Many airlines have a deadline for passengers to check-in before each flight. Check-in deadlines are usually between 60 to 30 minutes before boarding, and you are often not able to check in after those times (meaning you cannot go on your flight).

- Check-in deadlines allows airlines to to load luggage onto the plane, offer potential unclaimed seats to stand-by passengers, and to finalize documentation for take-off.

Boarding deadlines

- Boarding times are usually between 30 minutes to an hour before scheduled take-off.

- Your boarding pass will list the time the flight will start boarding.

- Flights tend to board in shifts—they might call by rows or by groups. Your boarding pass will indicate your row or group.

- Timeline considerations for boarding: be sure to take into account the time it takes to get through the check-in line, to pass security and then to walk or ride (tram, bus) from the check-in area to your boarding area (your terminal and gate—listed on your boarding pass). Getting through the airport steps can take several hours at some airports or during busy travel times of the year.

- On international flights, you will need to account for more time to clear immigration and customs.

- For international travel, a good rule is to arrive at the airport 3 hours prior to departure and 2 hours for domestic travel. International flights often start boarding 45 minutes to 1 hour prior to the departure time.

- Most airlines will list their specific check-in policies and timelines.

Hotel Check-in

At hotels or similar establishments, guests are usually required to check in (also called register or sign-in), which involves providing or confirming the guests' personal information and providing a signature. The laws of some countries require guests to sign a register (or a registration card) and some also require the provision of identification documents, such as a passport or drivers licence, which the hotel can copy and retain for its records. Usually, only one guest per room is required to register. Sometimes, the register may need to be provided to a government agency, such as members of the police, sometimes with a court warrant or similar authority.

The establishment may require guests to provide a credit card guarantee to cover potential costs such as room service or mini-bar for the duration of the stay, and to enable an express check-out at the end of the stay. At the end of the check-in, the reception staff will provide guests with a room key.

Check in times vary but this can range from 12pm until about 3pm depending on the establishment's rules and regulations. Late check-ins can be arranged through the hotel as long as the guests book this in advance and arrange all the necessary details. Hotels usually specify a check-in time after which they expect guests to check-in. If a guest wants to occupy a hotel room before the hotel's check-in time, some hotels charges for an additional day or treat it as a previous day's stay (as compared to occupying the hotel room after the check-in time). Most hotels, however, allow a grace time (typically 30–60 minutes) on request by a guest, without any additional charge, if a guest wishes to take the room before the check-in time. Some hotels also have a latest check-in time, often 6pm-8pm, after which they may give a room to someone else if the room is not pre-paid or the guest does not phone in to indicate a time of arrival. Some hotels have a deadline for checking-in because the reception may close for the night. For the most cost-effective usage of hotel room occupancy, a guest should try to reach at about hotel's check-in time and leave or hand over the hotel room at about the hotel's check-out time, but it may not be always practical because the guest's arrival and departure time of flights or car trips may not align with the hotel check-in and check-out time and for other reasons.

Online Hotel Reservations

Online hotel reservation is becoming a very popular method for booking hotel rooms. Travellers can book hotel rooms from home using online security to protect their privacy and financial information and using several online travel agents to compare prices and facilities at different hotels. The benefit of using global distribution channels is that they provide a single database from which all reservation sources draw immediate room availability and room rates.

Earlier travellers contacted hotels directly or used a travel agency to make a room reservation. Nowadays, a traveller can make reservation on hotel websites that give them pictures and virtual tours to make their choices. Room tariffs are shown on the websites along with deals and discounts. Non-franchise hotels require a "booking engine" application to be attached to their website to permit persons to make online reservations. Travel agents too have access to these websites and may even confirm room reservations directly. There are also websites that specialize in searches for the best deals. Hotels have the challenge of maintaining accurate room inventories and rates.

Large hotel chains typically have direct connection to the airline global distribution systems (GDS) (Sabre, Galileo, Amadeus and Worldspan) that in turn provides hotel information directly to the hundreds of travel agents who subscribe to these systems. Individual hotels and small hotel chains may not afford the cost of subscription to the GDSs and rely on other companies to provide the connection.

Several large online travel sites are in effect travel agencies. Hotels send their information "downstream" to travel agent websites and give commission to those travel agents who made reservations from travellers who connected to their website.

Hotels use several of the distribution channels to ensure full occupancy. In such cases, individual agreements and tariff structures are negotiated with each distribution channel. Nowadays, it has become imperative for hotels to integrate with all supply channels so that their guests are able to make accurate online bookings.

Connections to Air Travel

Large hotel chains typically have direct connections to the airline national distribution systems (GDS) (Sabre, Galileo, Amadeus, and Worldspan). These in turn provide hotel information directly to the hundreds of thousands of travel agents that align themselves with one of these systems. Individual hotels and small hotel chains often cannot afford the expense of these direct connections and turn to other companies to provide the connections.

Large-scale Travel Sites

Several large online travel sites are, in effect, travel agencies. These sites send the hotels' information and rates downstream to literally thousands of online travel sites, most of which act as travel agents. They can then receive commission payments from the hotels for any business booked on their websites.

Individual Hotel Websites

An increasing number of hotels are building their own websites to allow them to market their hotels directly to consumers. Non-franchise chain hotels require a "booking engine" application to be attached to their website to permit people to book rooms in real time. One advantage of booking with the hotel directly is the use of the hotel's full cancellation policy as well as not needing a deposit in most situations.

The online booking engine applications are supported by Content management system(CMS).

Database Systems

To improve the likelihood of filling rooms, hotels tend to use several of the above systems. The content on many hotel reservation systems is becoming increasingly similar as more hotels sign up to all the sites. Companies thus have to either rely on specially negotiated rates with the hotels and hotel chains or trust in the influence of search engine rankings to draw in customers.

Passenger Service System

The PSS usually comprises of the Central Reservation System (CRS), in other words booked inventory, an airline inventory system (free inventory) and a departure control system (DCS). It is basically the technology an airline needs:

- The CRS is the system that allows an airline to sell their inventory (seats). It contains information on schedules and fares as well as a database of reservations (or passenger name records) and of issued tickets.

- The airline inventory system may or may not be integrated with the CRS. The system contains all the airline's flights and the available seats. The main function of the inventory system is to define how many seats are available on a particular flight by opening or closing an individual booking class in accordance with rules defined by the airline.

- The departure control system is the system used by airlines and airports to check in a passenger. The DCS is connected to the reservation system, enabling it to check who has a valid reservation on a flight. The DCS is used to enter information required by customs or border security agencies and to issue the boarding document. In addition, the DCS may also be used to dispatch cargo and to optimize aircraft weight and balance.

Major Systems

Name	Description	Vendor
ACCELaero	Comprehensive PSS	Information Systems Associates FZE
AeroCRS	Comprehensive PSS	Enoya-one LTD
AirCore®	PSS	Unisys
Altéa	Comprehensive PSS	Amadeus IT Group
ameliaRES	Comprehensive PSS	InteliSys Aviation Inc.
ARCO	PSS	Alitalia
Astral	PSS	Aer Lingus
Avantik	Full PSS	
AVOS	Full PSS	Proavos
Crane PAX	Full-fledged PSS	Hitit Computer Services
Delta AIR	Full-fledged PSS	Delta Air Lines, Inc.
Horizon	PSS	SITA
Agilaire / Shares (former EDS/HP Shares)	PSS	DXC Technology
iFly Res	PSS	IBS Software Services
KIU SYSTEM SOLUTIONS	PSS	KIU
Mercator (MARS)	PSS	Mercator

Navitaire	Comprehensive PSS	Navitaire
QUICK	Passenger Retailing System	TravelSky Technology Ltd.
Radixx	Comprehensive PSS	
RESIBER	PSS	Iberia
SabreSonic Customer Sales & Service	Comprehensive PSS	Sabre Airline Solutions
Sell-More-Seats	Comprehensive PSS	WorldTicket
SkyVantage Airline Solutions	Comprehensive PSS	SkyVantage Airline Management System
Takeflite Solutions	Comprehensive PSS	Takeflite
Travelport Meridian(TM)	PSS	Travelport
Zenith	PSS	Travel Technology Interactive

Central Reservation System

A central reservation system (CRS) is a computerised system used to store and retrieve information and conduct transactions related to travel. Originally designed and operated by airlines, they were later extended to travel agents and hotels.

Most hotel chains have their own central reservation system to coordinate reservations globally. This is convenient to a traveller who has a 'one stop shop' for reservations of hotels in the chain anywhere in the world. Most franchisees that adopt the name of a branded chain have the benefit of filling their rooms from these reservation systems. The chain may tie up with referral hotels in destinations where they do not have their own hotel. The attempt by the hotel chain is to be represented in the most popular destination so as to capture the tourist market.

A central reservation system (CRS) is a computerised system used to store and retrieve information and conduct transactions related to travel. Originally designed and operated by airlines, they were later extended to travel agents and hotels. Most hotel chains have their own central reservation system to coordinate reservations globally. This is convenient to a traveller who has a 'one stop shop' for reservations of hotels in the chain anywhere in the world. Most franchisees that adopt the name of a branded chain have the benefit of filling their rooms from these reservation systems. The chain may tie up with referral hotels in destinations where they do not have their own hotel. The attempt by the hotel chain is to be represented in the most popular destination so as to capture the tourist market.

Airline Reservation System

Airline reservation systems originated in the mid-1950s as relatively unsophisticated internal systems to help with tasks such as seat assignments, maintenance scheduling, and aircraft loading. Modern airline reservation systems are multi-faceted, full-service systems that assist with a variety of airline management tasks and service customer needs from the time of initial reservation through completion of the flight.

Expanding Reservations Services

Following deregulation of the airline industry in 1978, the major computerized reservation systems such as Sabre and Apollo began listing airline reservations for all competing major carriers as well as for their host airlines. This networked a large number of travel agents with the major airlines and yielded a very profitable per ticket booking fee for the host airline.

Accusations of favoritism toward the host airline, based on the order in which available flights were listed on terminal screens, surfaced early in the 1980s. Since studies reveal that 90 percent of flights are booked from the first reservation screen, a favorable position can dramatically affect ticket sales. The U.S. Department of Transportation investigated this allegation and issued a ruling to prohibit favoritism toward the host airline by requiring that flight information be presented in a neutral order. Because of the prohibitive cost of developing their own computerized reservation systems, the airlines ultimately agreed to pay the per ticket booking fee to the major computerized reservations providers, and a code-sharing scheme was developed to help alleviate the screen order bias. Sabre, one of the most widely recognized information systems ever developed, was spun off as a private company by AMR Corporation in 2000.

Full-service Travel Management

Computerized reservation systems have grown in sophistication and are able to offer customer services such as electronic tickets, wireless database access, hotel room reservations, rental car reservations, frequent flyer program mileage, and provision for special meal requests. The systems also provide airline management assistance by addressing financial, administrative, and staffing issues. These include crew management, flight operations, planning and scheduling airplane maintenance, loading aircraft to maintain balance, baggage tracking, decision support for control of overbooking, discount seat allocations, and yield management programs that dynamically adjust the number of special fare seats based on the number of reservations.

Enhancements are made to computerized reservation systems with the understanding that interruptions in service are not acceptable. To be successful, a reservation system must be reliable with a very low failure rate. Hardware and software redundancy for immediate backup in the event of a failure is an absolute necessity.

Impact of the Internet

In the mid-1990s an increasing number of consumers began purchasing airline tickets and other travel needs online. To meet rising customer interest in booking online air travel reservations, computerized reservation systems have evolved into convenient, user-friendly systems that are available via the Internet twenty-four hours per day. The long-established computerized reservation systems are experiencing a gradual technology migration away from traditional mainframe -based systems and large databases in favor of client server systems with effective web-based interfaces. Search results that previously required an individual to interpret complex codes are now presented in straightforward, easy to understand notations.

In 1996 Sabre launched Travelocity.com, the first of the major comprehensive Internet travel sites. Travelocity.com and other systems, such as Expedia.com, allow consumers to gather information about flights using search criteria such as airline, lowest price, shortest flight, and departure and arrival times. Many airlines offer their own online ticket purchasing services. Also joining in the quest for online reservations is an airline collaborative called Orbitz.com, sponsored by American, United, Delta, Northwest, and Continental Airlines. Many online systems also allow for selection of hotels, rental cars, and other travel necessities.

The wealth of customer data collected by these systems is used to target marketing and incentive programs that appeal to specific consumer interests. Internet-based systems offer many of the capabilities of the traditional computerized reservation systems, but in a customer-friendly format that is easy to use and understand.

Airline reservation systems incorporate airline schedules, fare tariffs, passenger reservations and ticket records. An airline's direct distribution works within their own reservation system, as well as pushing out information to the GDS. The second type of direct distribution channel are consumers who use the internet or mobile applications to make their own reservations. Travel agencies and other indirect distribution channels access the same GDS as those accessed by the airline reservation systems, and all messaging is transmitted by a standardized messaging system that functions on two types of messaging that transmit on SITA's high level network (HLN). These messaging types are called Type A [usually EDIFACT format] for real time interactive communication and Type B [TTY] for informational and booking type of messages. Message construction standards set by IATA and ICAO, are global, and apply to more than air transportation. Since airline reservation systems are business critical applications, and they are functionally quite complex, the operation of an in-house airline reservation system is relatively expensive.

Prior to deregulation, airlines owned their own reservation systems with travel agents subscribing to them. Today, the GDS are run by independent companies with airlines and travel agencies being major subscribers.

As of February 2009, there are only four major GDS providers in the market: Amadeus, Travelport (which operates the Apollo, Worldspan and Galileo systems), Sabre and Shares. There is one major Regional GDS, Abacus, serving the Asian market and a number of regional players serving single countries, including Travelsky (China), Infini and Axess (both Japan) and Topas (South Korea). Of these, Infini is hosted within the Sabre complex, Axess is in the process of moving into a partition within the Worldspan complex, and Topas agencies will be migrating into Amadeus.

Reservation systems may host "ticket-less" airlines and "hybrid" airlines that use e-ticketing in addition to ticket-less to accommodate code-shares and interlines.

In addition to these "standardized" GDS, some airlines have proprietary versions which they use to run their flight operations. A few examples are Delta's OSS and Deltamatic systems and EDS SHARES. SITA Reservations remains the largest neutral multi-host airline reservations system, with over 100 airlines currently managing inventory.

Inventory Management

In the airline industry, available seats are commonly referred to as inventory. The inventory of an airline is generally classified into service classes (e.g. first, business or economy class) and up to 26 booking classes, for which different prices and booking conditions apply. Inventory data is imported and maintained through a schedule distribution system over standardized interfaces. One of the core functions of inventory management is inventory control. Inventory control steers how many seats are available in the different booking classes, by opening and closing individual booking classes for sale. In combination with the fares and booking conditions stored in the Fare Quote System, the price for each sold seat is determined. In most cases, inventory control has a real time interface to an airline's Yield management system to support a permanent optimization of the offered booking classes in response to changes in demand or pricing strategies of a competitor.

Availability Display and Reservation (PNR)

Users access an airline's inventory through an availability display. It contains all offered flights for a particular city-pair with their available seats in the different booking classes. This display contains flights which are operated by the airline itself as well as code share flights which are operated in co-operation with another airline. If the city pair is not one on which the airline offers service, it may display a connection using its own flights or display the flights of other airlines. The availability of seats of other airlines is updated through standard industry interfaces. Depending on the type of co-operation, it supports access to the last seat (last seat availability) in real-time. Reservations for individual passengers or groups are stored in a so-called passenger name record (PNR). Among other data, the PNR contains personal information such as name, contact information or special services requests (SSRs) e.g. for a vegetarian meal, as well as the flights (segments) and issued tickets. Some reservation systems also allow to store customer data in profiles to avoid data re-entry each time a new reservation is made for a known passenger. In addition, most systems have interfaces to CRM systems or customer loyalty applications (aka frequent traveler systems). Before a flight departs, the so-called passenger name list (PNL) is handed over to the departure control system that is used to check-in passengers and baggage. Reservation data such as the number of booked passengers and special service requests is also transferred to flight operations systems, crew management and catering systems. Once a flight has departed, the reservation system is updated with a list of the checked-in passengers (e.g. passengers who had a reservation but did not check in (no shows) and passengers who checked in, but did not have a reservation (go shows)). Finally, data needed for revenue accounting and reporting is handed over to administrative systems.

Fare Quote and Ticketing

Fare Basis	Airline	Booking Class	Trip Type	Fare	Cabin	Effective Date	Expiration Date	Min / Max Stay	Adv Purchase Req
TA14A0SP	DL	T	One-Way	189.00(USD)	E		02/16/11		14
TA03A0SG	DL	T	One-Way	209.00(USD)	E		02/28/11		03
UA10A0UY	DL	U	One-Way	236.00(USD)	E				10
LA10A0VY	DL	L	One-Way	251.00(USD)	E				10
LA07A0NY	DL	L	One-Way	286.00(USD)	E				07
KA07A0UY	DL	K	One-Way	326.00(USD)	E				07
QA03A0NP	DL	Q	One-Way	396.00(USD)	E				03
HA00A0NY	DL	H	One-Way	466.00(USD)	E				
UC14A0NJ	DL	U	Round-Trip	482.00(USD)	E			V / 30	14
HA00A0UY	DL	H	One-Way	616.00(USD)	E				
MA00A0RY	DL	M	One-Way	694.00(USD)	E				
MA00UPNY	DL		One-Way	1076.00(USD)	B				
BA00UPRQ	DL		One-Way	1348.00(USD)	B				
Y0	DL	Y	One-Way	1435.00(USD)	E				
YUP	DL		One-Way	1527.00(USD)	B				
F0	DL	F	One-Way	1826.00(USD)	F				
Y	DL	Y	One-Way	1889.00(USD)	E				
C	DL	C	One-Way	2213.00(USD)	B				
F	DL	F	One-Way	2766.00(USD)	F				

List of fares for travel on Delta Air Lines from San Francisco, CA to Boston, MA. Applicable booking classes, as well as specific restrictions such as minimum stay and advance purchase can be seen.

The Fares data store contains fare tariffs, rule sets, routing maps, class of service tables, and some tax information that construct the price – "the fare". Rules like booking conditions (e.g. minimum stay, advance purchase, etc.) are tailored differently between different city pairs or zones, and assigned a class of service corresponding to its appropriate inventory bucket. Inventory control can also be manipulated manually through the availability feeds, dynamically controlling how many seats are offered for a particular price by opening and closing particular classes.

The compiled set of fare conditions is called a fare basis code. There are two systems set up for the interchange of fares data — ATPCO and SITA, plus some system to system direct connects. This system distributes the fare tariffs and rule sets to all GDSs and other subscribers. Every airline employs staff who code air fare rules in accordance with yield management intent. There are also revenue managers who watch fares as they are filed into the public tariffs and make competitive recommendations. Inventory control is typically manipulated from here, using availability feeds to open and close classes of service.

The role of the ticketing complex is to issue and store electronic ticket records and the very small number of paper tickets that are still issued. Miscellaneous charges order (MCO) is still a paper document; IATA has working groups defining the replacement document the electronic multipurpose document (EMD) as at 2010. The electronic ticket information is stored in a database containing the data that historically was printed on a paper ticket including items such as the ticket number, the fare and tax components of the ticket price or exchange rate information. In the past, airlines issued paper tickets; since 2008, IATA has been supporting a resolution to move to 100% electronic ticketing. So far, the industry has not been able to comply due to various technological and international limitations. The industry is at 98% electronic ticket issuance today, although electronic processing for MCOs was not available in time for the IATA mandate.

Description of Major Systems

Name	Description	Vendor
AirCore	Unisys AirCore is a passenger services suite of modular, open-platform, web applications that replace core legacy systems to lay the foundation for the passenger-centric services era. A Cloud Based offering - it includes new suite of advanced transportation solutions that allow airlines to optimize their sales and customer service capabilities across all aspects of the passenger journey.	Unisys
AirKiosk	Professional Airlines Reservations system, which can be downloaded and operated on the local airline's server(s), includes CRM, Accounting, Loyalty Program, IBE with CMS and Check-in. Also offering the quickest implementation of the Industry links, with IATA compliant ET, IET, Interactive Sell, Dynamic Scheduling, and TTY messaging.	Sutra, Inc.
ameliaRES	PSS, DCS, Reservation Management, Codeshare, Interline and re-al-time inventory control system for airlines of all sizes and business models.	InteliSys Aviation Systems
Avantik	Full PSS allowing any type of airline to manage its passenger flow from booking all the way through to boarding and aircraft weight & balance. Avantik caters for diversified distribution channels (offline, its own internet booking engine, 3rd party API, online travel agents, global distribution system, travel agents, tour operators & charters etc.).	
ACCELaero	PSS, reservations, departure control, inventory and e-commerce platform.	Information Systems Associates FZE
Radixx International	Radixx is a hybrid travel distribution and PSS designed to enable airlines to increase revenue and profitability by expanding distribution to sell through any channel whether ticketed or ticketless.	
QUICK	QUICK is a hybrid system composed of features derived from a Passenger Service Solution (PSS) and e-commerce tools, hence referred to as a Passenger Retailing System. QUICK is based on the principles of NDC and ONE Order and puts the customer in the center of attention.	TravelSky Technologies Ltd.
Crane PAX	Crane PAX is a web based airline reservations and ticketing system. With inventory control, fares, pricing and ticketing, advance reservation, Internet Booking Engine, seat selection and sales distribution functions it manages the whole airline operations cycle up to the point of departure.	Hitit Computer Services
Travel Technology Interactive Solutions	Integrated Airline Management System and global distribution system (GDS).	Travel Technology Interactive
iFlyRes	Next generation airline passenger services platform.	IBS Software Services
Navitaire New Skies Integrated Customer Centric Passenger Service System	Integrated reservations, departure control, inventory system and e-commerce platform.	Navitaire

SabreSonic Customer Sales & Service	Integrated reservations, departure control, inventory system and e-commerce platform.	Sabre Airline Solutions
SITA Horizon Customer Sales & Service	Integrated reservations, departure control, inventory system and e-commerce platform.	SITA
Skyline	Reservations, Ticketing, Charter Management, Statistical Analysis, Sales Reconciliation, Cargo Management, Flight Operations, Revenue Accounting, Online Booking	Skyline Aviation Software Ltd.
SkyVantage	Integrated reservations, departure control, inventory system and e-commerce platform.	SkyVantage Airline Software
Altéa Res	Integrated Airline Reservation System and global distribution system (GDS).	Amadeus IT Group
KIU	A computer reservations system (CRS) and global distribution system (GDS).	KIU System
RESIBER	A Passenger Service System (PSS).	Iberia
Videcom VRS	Videcom Reservations System, GDS,IET,Codeshare for regional and international airlines.	Videcom international
Takeflite Solutions Limited	Integrated reservations, departure control, inventory system and e-commerce ERP platform.	Takeflite Solutions Limited
AeroCRS	AeroCRS is a cloud based reservation system which include GDS & OTA's connectivity, CRM, DCS, Frequent flyer program, reporting center and BI, inventory management, IBE and more.	Enoya-one

Benefits of Flight Reservation System for Passengers

In addition to airline travel agencies, the highly useful system prove quite beneficial for the passengers as they get the required flight details within less time by simply sitting at your home or office without waiting in the long queue. The customer can search the details about any flight to reserve the ticket after knowing the exact schedule or cancel the reservation based on the details. They can check the availability of flights with different timing on particular day or date that helps to make the reservation, cancellation or modification. Even the regular passenger gets information about the great offers or discounts provided by the airline agency.

The complete fight details get displayed such as Airline Logo, Arrival Airport Details, Airline Name, Departure Time, Arrival Airport Details, Travel Time, Arrival Terminal and Time, Fare Rules, Seat Map, Departure Terminal, Sorting option on Airline Name and etc.

In short, we can say that Flight Reservation System is the most useful software that is specifically designed with integrated GDS to offer easier and convenient booking procedure to both passengers and airline companies.

Passenger Information System

The Passenger Information System, PIS, is the operating tool responsible for providing, at any time, visual and audio information to passengers at stations and transfer facilities, both automatically or programmed manually.

It includes information management on routes and their display via different display elements deployed at passenger platforms. These devices may be of different types:

- Screens

- Indicators at platforms

- Indicator panels in general

The layout of all information to be displayed may be adapted to the needs of different clients and languages. Furthermore, the same visual and audio means can be used to display corporate or commercial information at passenger platforms.

In turn, all information displayed in visual format may have an associated audio accompaniment issued over the PA Systems, and it is possible to limit this emission to specific station areas, a series of stations or throughout a complete line of stations.

The system allows for the management of operating plans to permanently control valid routes. These operating plans may be generated through the system itself, or imported from external operation assistance systems (OAS).

The emission of these events may be manual or automated, based on the information provided by the route control and monitoring systems.

References

- "What are allotments?" (PDF). Tourismnt.com.au. Archived (PDF) from the original on 21 July 2008. Retrieved 17, August 2020

- Computing, News wires white papers and books, airline-reservations: encyclopedia.com, Retrieved 22, March 2020

- Technology used hospitality tourism-31033: smallbusiness.chron.com, Retrieved 05, April 2020

- Broll, W.; Ohlenburg, J.; Lindt, I.; Herbst, I.; Braun, A. K. (2006). "Meeting technology challenges of pervasive augmented reality games". Proceedings of 5th ACM SIGCOMM workshop on Network and system support for games - NetGames '06. p. 28. doi:10.1145/1230040.1230097. ISBN 1595935894

- Tidbits, Tourism in a world of technology: tourismandmore.com, Retrieved 25, February 2020

- Richmond, Riva (September 10, 2010). "Three Best Ways to Use Location-Based Social Media". The Wall Street Journal. Dow Jones & Company, Inc. Retrieved 30, August 2020

Permissions

Index

CPSIA information can be obtained
at www.ICGtesting.com
Printed in the USA
BVHW061959260822
645617BV00004B/196